THE FALL OF A SPARROW

A Concept of Special Divine Action

THE FALL OF A SPARROW

A Concept of Special Divine Action

VERNON WHITE

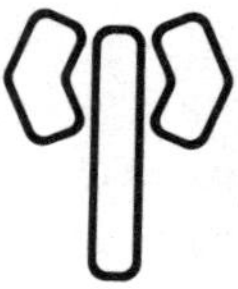

Exeter
The Paternoster Press

AUSTRALIA
Bookhouse Australia Ltd.,
P.O. Box 115, Flemington Markets,
N.S.W. 2129.

SOUTH AFRICA
Oxford University Press,
P.O. Box 1141, Cape Town.

The lines quoted on p.9 are reprinted by permission of
Faber & Faber Ltd. from T.S. Eliot, *Selected Poems*,
London 1961.

British Library Cataloguing in Publication Data

White, Vernon
     The fall of a sparrow : a concept of special divine action.
     1. God 2. Philosophical theology
     I. Title
     211'.01   BT102

ISBN 0-85364-415-2

Typeset by Busby's Typesetting & Design, Exeter, Devon
and Printed in Great Britain for The Paternoster Press,
Paternoster House, 3 Mount Radford Crescent, Exeter, Devon
by A. Wheaton & Co Ltd, Exeter.

Contents

To Joy

Preface

Like most books which have grown from a thesis this is a specialized and sometimes technical discussion. It deals quite specifically with the concept of special divine action from the standpoint of contemporary English philosophical theology. The issues are primarily theological and are treated at times with the tools of analytical philosophy. As such it is intended as a contribution to academic debate.

On the other hand, I have also tried to set the discussion in a wider context of general experience and biblical teaching. This, I hope, gives it more integrity, for the issues it deals with have arisen for me as much from experience and biblical revelation as from the narrower confines of academic debate. I hope too this may make it more accessible to the non-specialist reader.

As for the issues at stake, I have no doubt whatsoever that they matter desperately, both within and without the academic community. They happen to be specially topical at the time of writing, but I suspect they will always matter. How can God be said to act personally, specially, and with sovereignty? A definitive answer can no more be captured than we can snare the lightning which struck York Minster to test it for a divine spark. But we will surely keep straining to know and to believe as much as we can and should.

In the face of an apparently disintegrating world Morris West wrote in one of his novels: 'I found myself drawn with poignant yearning, back to the beliefs of my childhood: a personal God to whom not even the fallen bird was unimportant . . . And then I knew that I had reasoned Him out of my universe and that he was forever beyond my appeal.' This is just one small attempt to help faith reason him back in: a God of the details of life, a God of the sparrows.

CHAPTER ONE

The Riddles of Experience

Amongst the many and varied temptations which afflict us there is one which is peculiarly ancient and basic: the tendency to self-dramatization. It is the tendency to think of ourselves against the background of our life's experiences rather as a spectator would watch a performance of himself on stage. We watch carefully what fate or providence throws at us to experience, encounter or suffer, then imagine what kind of part we like to think we are playing in response. Probably we see ourselves strutting on the stage with great character, for it is relatively easy to portray our failures as tragedy, our cowardice and dishonesty as force of circumstance. In any case we are always the leading actor, always at the centre of the stage. It is a tendency basic to all self-consciousness, and that means it begins with earliest childhood experiences. It then becomes particularly acute in the painful and extreme self-awareness of adolescence. But I doubt if it ever leaves us: indeed, T. S. Eliot would have it most pathetically portrayed in the experience of an old man:

> . . . Gull against the wind, in the windy straits
> Of Belle Isle, or running on the Horn.
> White feathers in the snow, the Gulf claims,
> And an old man driven by the Trades
> To a sleepy corner.[1]

This is a grandiose, sentimental, and sterile reverie—the way an old man would like to see himself against the background of his experiences. It is dismissed scathingly by Eliot in the conclusion of the poem as 'thoughts of a dry brain in a dry season', and there are all sorts of good reasons why we might agree with Eliot's assessment. It is indeed a *temptation*—to introversion, to egocentricity, to life in a fantasy world. Perhaps most seriously it implies a merely aesthetic response to life (which paints ourselves in the best possible light, to satisfy our taste) rather than a moral one (which faces up to what is real and admits responsibility).[2]

However, like most temptations it will not go away simply because we have named it. It is, precisely, ancient, basic and persistent. And as such, regardless of how well or badly we cope with it, it betrays one of the most fundamental features in the structure of human experience, and an enduring riddle at the heart of it. The structure is the polarity and interplay between the individual and his ever-changing environment. I am me, irreducibly me, and I am not the world, but I am also affected by the world and related to the world, so that what the world throws at me, and how I react to it, makes a difference to me. The riddle arises immediately out of that interplay: what meaning do we give to it? More precisely, where does the meaning lie? Is it to be found only in our reaction to the events of the world, in how nobly (or shamefully) we 'strut and fret our hour upon the stage'? Or does it also lie in the events themselves: is there some meaning and purpose actually designed for us in the rush of reality that we encounter? In short, should we wake up to a day asking only how we should cope with it—or should we also be asking what purposes the day has in store for us? Do the morning chores (and surprises) arrive by mere chance—or by design? That is the stark form of the riddle. Its subtleties range themselves readily between the alternatives. If the day has no designs for me, might it still serve some broader purpose for the world? Is the merely chance event I have to deal with actually the consequence of a far bigger design for others? Or if there is some specific purpose, even for me, does it lie in all the events of the day—or only some, with the rest consigned only to chance, or that bigger design?

Just to put these questions on paper reminds us how inseparable the temptation is from the riddle. Already the questions sound egocentric. Yet they are not necessarily so, and they are insistent. Above all they remain in the form of a riddle because experience suggests answers on both sides. On the one hand we undoubtedly do experience events as if they bear meaning for us. Consider for a start the force of childhood experience: so many of our earliest childhood perceptions were of a world charged with meaning in its smallest detail. The riddle then was more a game: to see which wave would reach the sandcastle first; which cloud would best turn into the shape of an animal. It is not as though we would now defend that particular world of meaning which we constructed as children as being a true one; but our childhood sense that the sea and the sky and the people around us were all specifically designed for us and our good pleasure, that *general* sense, is still to be reckoned with. It may betray precisely this deep down datum of experience we are dealing with. We might be experiencing some kind of broken reflection of a true meaning from things outside us, not simply projecting a childish meaning at them.

Even growing up, we can recall a quest for omens: as the adolescent who counts the buses on the way to school to see how well he previously guessed the number, then takes the result to heart: it bodes well (or badly) for the result of his soccer match that day. Older still, and we played more serious games with our first important decisions. Does the coincidence of meeting the same girl on the same bus mean that we are *intended* to meet? And is the newspaper left on the park bench with the job advertisement *meant* for me? Even in adulthood it persists, in spite of ourselves, in one way or another. Often it operates in retrospect: we can hardly resist reconstructing the past according to a pattern of meaning. Is there not still a strong temptation to trace the course of 'fortuitous' events which have brought us to the place where we now stand? 'If only the cat hadn't run out at that precise moment I would never have met the girl who told me about the exhibition where I tripped over a trestle and so met you', and so on. The poor cat has unwittingly set in motion a chain of events culminating in some disaster or good fortune, and in the very construction of such a tale there lurks the hint of design: was this meant to happen? Of course, of any particular instance, and of any particular interpretation, we might well say we are only playing a game (or indulging in idle superstition). If pressed we are very likely to admit the absurdity of it. But still we have betrayed a general context in which we expect meaning from events. The very form of the stories we tell ourselves has let this other cat out of the bag: our experience is such that we *do* toy with ideas of meaning; the notion persists.

Such a notion is also betrayed in the language we use when we begin consciously to interpret the meaning of events. In this respect there is no more revealing a place than a hospital ward. With extraordinary frequency the telling phrase slips out (bravely enough), 'these things are sent to try us', or, more generally, 'it's all for the best'; or else much talk of punishment and reward. Of course a lot else is also said, in and out of hospital, which flatly contradicts all this—and that is why we are talking in riddles— yet the fact remains that this side of the riddle persists: 'these things are *sent*'.

The notion is even more persistent within a specifically religious context. Admittedly the experience of meaning in events does not depend directly on explicit or conscious religious belief, for it is more pervasive and fundamental than that (though that is not to deny some kind of relationship at an unconscious level, or a more basic ontological relationship in fact, regardless of any connections in human knowing). But there is no doubt that where events are deliberately and consciously interpreted according to religious belief the experience of meaning can be sharpened and deepened. In Christian theism, for instance, a God even remotely like the personal 'Father of our Lord Jesus Christ', personally interested in the welfare of individuals, who is also the almighty creator and orderer of all things, such a God as that 'must' be dealing with us purposively through the events of our lives. The principle of belief is given classic expression by St Augustine: God's power is 'just and perfect in its rule even to the last item of creation'.[3] Then by this principle of belief his own experience is interpreted accordingly: he looks back over his own erring past and perceives God at work to bring him back, both in the internal ordering of his desires and in the external ordering of events like the favourable winds which steered him away from Carthage and Manichean ideas towards Rome and the true faith. It all seems to fit very nicely, in retrospect.

Nor are more contemporary instances lacking. The world of evangelical literature in particular is full of the same kind of testimony, be it Hudson Taylor's experiences in China in the nineteenth century,[4] or David Wilkerson's in twentieth-century Harlem.[5] They all reflect the *prima facie* power of a religious dimension in the ordinary experience of meaning, and they are only the spectacular instances of countless more commonplace claims from religious believers the world over ('If the traffic hadn't been so unusually thick I would have caught the plane which crashed: thank *God!*').

Yet of course there is the force of the other, darker, side of experience as well. There is the entirely contrary case that experience can provide, both in its own terms and in criticism of its rival; it can so easily suggest there is no meaning from events. Sartre was not innovating or inventing when he expressed the view[6] that authentic meaning is only to be found in the self and the self's struggles, and in nothing else. He reflects a strain of universal experience derived from the intransigence of things. Crops do not, for the most part, grow themselves and present themselves on a plate. Rain, sun and wind do not accommodate themselves precisely to every farmer's need—and even when they do the sailor may suffer for it, and *vice versa*. The things and events which present themselves to us take on meaning only in so far as they can be pressed into service. Meaning is projected onto them by our efforts; only as 'instruments' do they have any significance, and that significance in no sense derives from themselves or anything directing them.

Another way of putting it is simply to observe the basic independence of the world outside me. It proceeds under some logic of its own without due regard to my every whim and fancy, nor even to my basic needs (and this is as painfully true of other people as of the natural order). To the pre-scientific mind this independence may or may not be vested in the divine whim and fancy; it may be dictated by mere chance. To the scientifically conditioned mind it is usually sufficient to vest both its independence and direction in self-explanatory 'laws of nature' (and, possibly, of human behaviour). But either way it is a common and basic perception that things have a 'life of their own'. It was fun to pull the cat's tail, and we were tempted to think that the cat and its tail were put there just for our pleasure, like the waves of the sea and the clouds in the sky. But when pussy walks out on us, then we have to acknowledge an independence in things, an indifference to us, which provides a rival account of why we then 'met the girl who told us about the exhibition' and so on.

Furthermore, this other side of experience weighs more heavily still when its rival is pressed for some reasonable interpretation of the meaning alleged. Just because it is a basic experience of life that our normal diet of reality is *not* obviously aimed purposively at us, then the claim that it is begs a mocking and searing series of questions. *What* purpose could it possibly have? How can a rainfall which has merely followed its own laws of precipitation and gravitation be designed for you and your cabbage patch? Is it not rather a coincidence—merely your good fortune? And what about the other man's cricket match, washed out by the same rain? Is it supposed to be for him too? More seriously, what then about the earthquake and tornado? Or if some things are designed but some are not, then why? Does the designer—whoever he or it may be—only operate part-time? Or has he become so baffled by the complexity of his design that he simply cannot 'get it all together'? The same series of questions can seem even more searching when appeal is made to religious belief. Christian theism in particular takes away with one hand the support it seemed to give with the other. After all, if this supposed designer is actually the good and almighty God of Christian faith then his selection and ordering of events for us can seem damningly incomprehensible. The winds he is supposed to have made favourable for Augustine can hardly have suited travellers in the opposite direction; the traffic which saved one traveller from an air disaster was not sufficient to save the others. Favourable events for some and not others should not be arbitrary if he is really good; nor constrained by the complexity of things if he is really almighty; nor even determined by our state of soul, since the fortunate Augustine was supposed to have been rebelling in sin at the time. So why are they favourable for some and not others? In short, once the ancient sense of providential meaning is backed by a Christian God it crumbles into the credibility gap of an equally ancient conundrum: why does a good and almighty God allow so much evil? Who so callously and arbitrarily selective, this God of power and love? Most telling of all, why does the believer always have to retreat when pressed to give specific examples of what the meaning of events might be? He tends to resort to the merely general assertion (that there is still some meaning somewhere, even if he is not sure what where!), and so becomes vacuous. Thus, ironically, he has become quite meaningless himself even as he defends the notion of meaning. So would it not make more sense to abandon such a claim, which is neither verifiable, falsifiable nor specifiable?[7]

All these questions—and more—will emerge later and for closer consideration. Some of theology's proposed solutions will also be reviewed. But for the moment I am content simply to draw attention to the obvious force of the questions. They really can seem damning. They tax a sense of meaning, even more a belief in a divinely backed providence, with a sickening and cumulative force that can hardly be overestimated. They have afflicted some to the extent of robbing them of all faith in God (the case of Michael Goulder is a recent example);[8] they afflicted even the great saints who have kept the faith; they run through the experience of biblical writers too, especially the psalmists and Job; and they climax, I believe, in the Gethsemane experience of Jesus himself. That is the other side of the riddle.

Yet there is an irony here, almost a perversity: for it is the very force of these questions which also underlines the persistence of the notion they seem to challenge. The ancient basic sense of meaning persists nonetheless. The riddle remains—precisely a riddle. What possible reasons can account for its survival? It is clearly worth returning to the first side of the riddle—the sense of meaning from events 'nonetheless'—to dig deeper. To do this seriously is to uncover some of its more powerful resources: these are 'constituents' of our sense of meaning which can lay claim to being as basic a feature of human experience as anything else considered so far, and as such they might well shed light on its survival. They arise out of the combination of two other notions: a sense of ultimate (and benevolent) order, and a sense of the unique importance of the individual.

The sense of order is picked out by Peter Berger as one of the most fundamental data of human experience (which for him also signals the transcendent). He characterizes it in the words of a mother reassuring a frightened child: 'Don't be afraid—everything is in order, everything is all right.'[9] It does not matter for the moment that all evidence is to the contrary, nor that we are all prone to wishful thinking (especially to silence a wailing infant!), for common language still betrays the deepest sense of things. Something similar is also described by F.W. Dillistone in this passage about the experience of catharsis in tragedy:

> There is . . . the recognition of a transcendent *orderliness*, however mysterious and inscrutable, which governs the universe . . . Beyond the horror and disaster there are glimpses of transcendent glory. Through this recognition the almost unbearable strain which comes from looking steadily at the sufferings of humanity, begins to be resolved into a feeling that the universe is not an anarchy of uncontrolled forces but an infinitely mysterious movement towards the goal of ultimate harmony.[10]

Of course, ultimate order of itself gives no assurance that the order of events is taking every individual into account. Things may be governed to a far more general end. But Berger's reassuring mother clearly implies something different when she says '*everything* is all right': she implies that things are all right specifically for you and me. And this also suggests a powerful link with that other datum of experience, the unique importance of the individual. This notion of individual significance may in fact be an even deeper resource of human experience. It is betrayed in a hundred-thousand daily thoughts, words and gestures. It is the presupposition of almost every action and reaction, from birth to death. The very temptation with which we began and the kind of experience it presupposes imply it: there is not just differentiation between the individual and the world, there is special value and significance in the relationship just because the individual is unique.

A poem found among the possessions of an old lady after her death in a Dundee hospital speaks movingly of this. It begins:

> What do you see, nurses, what do you see?
> Are you thinking when you are looking at me—
> 'A crabbit old woman, not very wise,
> Uncertain of habit, with far away eyes
> Who dribbles her food and makes no reply'?

It continues as a review of her life, memories of all that is unique to *her* experiences of relating to the world:

> I'll tell you who I am as I sit here, so still;
> As I do at your bidding, as I eat at your will,
> I'm a small child of ten with a father and mother,
> Brothers and sisters who love one another.
> A young girl of sixteen with wings on her feet,
> Dreaming that soon a lover she'll meet.

It ends:

> So open your eyes, nurses, open and see
> Not a crabbit old woman, look closer—see Me.

Given prosaic, discursive analysis by a professional philosopher the same basic experience sounds like this:

> . . . the unique individual and his unique actions and experiences and relations to other individuals can never be fully rationalized. And it appears to be just this irrational realm of unique individuality which makes human relations important. Most people would feel, for example, that what makes their lives worth living would largely be destroyed if they themselves, and their lives, were in no sense unique but in all and every respect typical of a class of people, so that they repeated exactly all the actions and experiences of all other men who belong to this class.[11]

Again, taken by itself, this experience does not fulfil all requirements: it does not necessarily require that every event is designed to feed this individual and his unique significance. It could be precisely the opposite, whereby he gains his significance in his own actions and reactions towards an otherwise meaningless world. But taken in conjunction with the other sense, the world's ultimate order, then the experience does seem loaded: if there is ultimate order and purpose in all things, and if each individual is a matter of unique importance, then where else is that order 'aimed' but at individuals? This neither presents itself (nor succeeds) as a form of deductive or inductive proof. But it does offer itself as an analysis of the alchemy of experience to shed light on the *persistence* of providential meaning. It does indeed seem that our deepest instincts are aroused in this matter.

Furthermore, this analysis does not just make the general point that our experience of meaning 'resonates' with these other basic constituent experiences. There is also the specific fact that these constituent resources seem to arise characteristically out of tragedy, out of the very experience which is supposed to contradict our sense of meaning. This means that the sense of meaning is being supported at the point where it seemed to be weakest. It should also be pointed out that these constituent experiences of order and individual significance find natural support in religious belief, such as the Christian belief about the createdness of the world by a rational God, and ourselves in his image. Indeed, they may already *be* religious experiences in the sense that they are coloured and conditioned at some unconscious level by some specifically religious concern.

Yet of course it also has to be said that even all this will not count decisively to explain and justify that sense of meaning. These wider, constituent 'resources' are themselves ambivalent. They too can be stated in the form of a riddle, a double-sided coin. So although one mother may betray a deep sense of order even in the troubles of her child, someone else (equally immersed in tragedy) may sense the opposite, like the narrator of Joseph Conrad's *Lord Jim*, who describes his feelings about the story of a girl's mother who had 'died weeping':

> "The tears fell from her eyes—and then she died," concluded the girl in an imperturbable monotone, which more than anything else, more than the white statuesque immobility of her person, more than mere words could do, troubled my mind profoundly with the passive, irremediable horror of the scene. It had the power to drive me out of my conception of existence, out of that shelter each of us makes for himself to creep under in moments of danger, as a tortoise withdraws within its shell. For a moment I had a view of a world that seemed to wear a vast and dismal aspect of disorder, while, in truth, thanks to our unwearied efforts, it is as sunny an arrangement of small conveniences as the mind of man can conceive.[12]

Here the sense of order (reality arranged 'for our convenience') is turned on its head: it is perceived to be merely the construct of the mind, and we are back with the view that it is mere projection. The really fundamental experience is grasped instead as chaos and disorder.

Again, this other side of experience (this other interpretation) finds backing as much in criticism of its rival as in itself. For every catharsis which produces 'a feeling that the universe is not an anarchy of uncontrolled forces but an infinitely mysterious movement towards the goal of ultimate harmony' there is also the terse protest of Ivan Karamazov: 'Why should they (innocent tortured children) . . . be used as dung for someone's future harmony?'.[13] That is to say, whatever ultimate purpose there may or may not be in the world's events, they seem to bypass some individuals. Worse, some individuals are randomly sacrificed to them. As a matter of observable fact there seems no accommodation whatsoever to some individuals, so if there is an ultimate order it does *not* relate to the uniqueness of the individual. This naturally makes Karamazov's protest all the more bitter against any divine author of this order of things. And if there is no author and orderer to blame we are simply back with the basic perception of the world's independence: whatever impersonal order it has proceeds without regard to individual concerns. That is an equally fundamental datum of experience. The significance and uniqueness of the individual is *not* an uncontested experience, as Marxist practice (if not theory) reveals.[14] We have to admit therefore that the riddle remains woven through every layer and constituent of our experience. If the wider resonances of meaning account for the persisting sense of providence, they do so only as enigmatically as the sense of providence itself.

But *still* the sense that events are ordered to give meaning persists. It is a great survivor. Is there any way we can determine the truth of it? Alas, persistence itself is no necessary measure of truth, and even if it was we would be in no better position to deal with it just because both sides of the riddle persist. What then of some of the other possible reasons for it, already hinted? For instance, could it simply be that the temptation with which we began is too strong? Egocentricity, it may be said, demands we find a meaning for ourselves against all odds, and that alone accounts for it. It is certainly possible, but then this would not necessarily account for the full sense of meaning from events, for it implies only that general structure of polarity in which the meaning might be vested solely in our reaction to events. Or could it simply be the residual power of those childhood experiences, conceived as mere wishful projection of meaning, haunting us nostalgically? Again, it certainly could be, but we also have to say that no such projection could ever be convincingly falsified or verified. Or could it be that it is always parasitical on specifically religious backing—conscious or unconscious—so that the rival experience of meaninglessness (and its critical questions) is always opposing much wider, deeper, more complex resources than appear at first sight? Put another way, are there demands of faith and revelation which, for some people, override even the gravest difficulties? Again, we can only say it is possible.

The trouble is, even if all—or any—of these reasons were compelling in themselves they only count as reasons why, as a matter of psychological fact, an experience persists. They do not and cannot arbitrate decisively on the truth of the interpretation. And here surfaces the problem which has been lurking throughout this long preamble. We are always dealing with a tantalizing mixture of experience, interpretation and belief, culled from a variety of sources. It is now commonplace, and rightly so, to admit that we can never get a 'pure', 'basic' experience: it is already laden with interpretation according to inherited belief systems. Nor can we get at a world beyond our interpreted experience to test it. So of course we cannot simply find the truth of things by checking off our experience against a world objectively considered. There is no access to such a world and such a test. Instead we are always testing our experience within the context of a system of belief and interpretation, whether acknowledged or not. The tests which are appropriate here are a mixture of the intuitive (what 'fits the pattern', 'rings a bell') and rational (what contributes to the system's internal coherence and comprehensiveness),[15] though of course these criteria themselves are likewise related to a wider system—however loose—of belief, value and interpretation.

Thus it goes without saying that the concerns of this book, the discussion of whether we may expect meaning from events, is bound to be subject to these same strictures. It is an attempt to determine the truth of the notion that events are ordered with meaning for us within a certain, acknowledged, context of belief, namely Christian theism. This is a very specific context. It means the form of the question at stake is, specifically, whether and how we can conceive the Christian God acting in events for us, for within the context of Christian theism all meaning derives ultimately from God and his action. This basic question must also include questions about the scope of that action: does he act in all events, or only some? Naturally, within this context, the criteria for considering the question must include those 'demands of faith and revelation' already referred to.

It is also important to remember that just because of the inescapable interplay with wider contexts of thought, experience and belief, these additional criteria of faith and revelation do not and cannot stand alone as self-sufficient and self-interpreting. They are not a clear-cut key to unlock the riddles of experience and easily 'override the gravest difficulties'. Admittedly, some Christian theology handles the concept of revelation like that, as a magic wand which can be waved at any obdurate fact or experience to make it go away without further thought. But this will not do. Faith and revelation cannot be isolated from a wider context of thought and belief nor from the whole range of human experience. Without for one moment reducing them to merely human constructs, without denying their *sui generis* quality, they still arise within and relate to human thought and experience (otherwise, of course, we could neither talk nor even think of them at all, let alone 'handle' them). It is a relationship of two movements, whereby revelation has both to be received or recognized in our experience, and has to interpret that experience to us. These two movements must involve the whole range of human experience if the Christian claim is to a revelation of finality and universality: there is no question that the demands of revelation could simply ignore one area of human experience. More will have to be said in the next chapter on the concept of revelation and the kind of appeal being made to it, but this much should at least explain why the preceding pages have been dealing with the *riddles* of providence: the depth and breadth of both sides of experience are the context in which the revelation of Christian faith and belief is to be received, and which it purports to interpret.

The structure of what follows now falls naturally into place. The *prima facie* demands of biblical faith and revelation (with respect to God's action in the world) will be briefly laid out. Following that there is a consideration of some contemporary theology in its attempt to handle these demands in relation to experience, especially the experience of so-called 'modern', 'scientific' man. My belief is that these attempts compromise the demands of revelation, and fail to interpret adequately the full range of these riddles of experience, so that an alternative account if required. With some fear and trembling the rest of the book seeks to expound just such an account and its coherence within the wider scheme of Christian belief. Throughout all this the form of the basic question remains the same: how can and should we conceive God acting in specific events for us—and with what scope—in all or only some?

There need be no secret from the beginning about what will soon become plain, that the positive thesis of this book portrays a God who can and must be conceived as acting through all events, specifically, for us. That is to say, we cannot ignore the 'fortuitous' breeze and the portentous dropped remark. In my own experience I tried for a while, but still, persistently, they pluck at my sleeve. Nor, indeed, as I have insisted, can we ignore the apparent indifference of a world which also seems cruel and random: yet within the deep mysteries and demands of the Christian story I believe we can trace glimpses of a divine action which does encompass both sides of the riddle. How this can be conceived and expounded is the chief aim of this book.

But let it also be clear from the beginning how modest a task this is. For it is first and foremost a discussion of the bare conceivability that God has meaning for us in the events around us, with few pretensions to show what that meaning could be in any particular instance: to seriously attempt the latter would be the task of a prophet, as well as a theologian, and I am not a prophet.

CHAPTER TWO

The Demands of Revelation

'What does it mean to say that "God is"? What or who "is" God? If we want to answer this question legitimately and thoughtfully we cannot for a moment turn our thoughts anywhere else than to God's act in His revelation.' So says Barth,[1] and he surely has a point: to be thinking and talking about God at all already assumes a certain kind of God, namely one who has given himself in a revealing action. True, we can conceive of merely inert objects, undiscovered, indifferent, making no claim upon us: it is possible to think and talk of a tenth planet or cluster of asteriods circling the sun in benign anonymity. But as such they would have no meaning for us. Only if they acted upon us in some determinate way (like moving the tides, or landing in the back garden, or simply providing that equilibrium of forces which keeps our planet in place) would they have meaning of their own. Only then would they mean something more than the mere imaginative extrapolation from our experiences of other planets. So with God, who exists for us in his determinate action towards us, and has a meaning of his own for us in that action. It is in his action towards us that we assert that he is not just an imaginative extrapolation from other experiences. Furthermore, as Christians we assert that God's most significant point of action on us was in Jesus Christ, the historical man who lived and died and rose in the context of Jewish religion. God is supremely revealed acting there, and so there, as Barth would have it, we must 'turn our thoughts'.

These of course are the assertions and assumptions which determine that context of Christian theism in which we are operating. They are not necessary truths of mathematical and logical certainty, nor are they strictly deducible from experience. They are the bare bones of the demands of revelation which constitute a 'given' in a chosen context. In that sense the fact that this book began with the riddles of experience does not imply a certain kind of theological method whereby experience always comes first to set the agenda of theology. Far from it: theologically there is this priority about the given demands of revelation. The action and meaning of God in Christ is the first and greatest presupposition.

However, all that was said before still stands. Even this bare fact of revelation is grasped from within our experience, even as it also transforms and interprets it. So experientially and epistemologically there is always an unbreakable circle of revelation and experience, and we can never jump in at any one point to disentangle one from the other and claim its priority in pristine purity. This is particularly evident when we begin to ask more precise questions about the form and content of this revelation as it relates to the nature and scope of divine activity, as we must now do. For simply to have identified these assertions and assumptions is by no means to have settled the matter: they are not so easy to handle, and remain the subject of many and varied unsolved theological debates.

For a start, *where* precisely is the 'there'—the location of God's revelation to which we should 'turn our thoughts'? The 'life, death and resurrection of Jesus Christ, as witnessed by the New Testament and grasped against the background of the Old Testament'? In short, the canon of the New Testament and Old Testament scriptures? Is this the place where we should be looking? We should certainly start there, and few Christians would deny that, even if the limits have to be re-drawn later, one way or another. But then we must also ask *what* is 'there'? It is still an unresolved question within the church whether and in what sense the Bible is the revelation of God, and in what sense a human witness to it. Above all, how then do we 'turn our thoughts' upon it? How can we possibly understand and interpret such complex phenomena as 'recorded events' with any integrity? We undoubtedly select, colour and distort the revelation through our own subjectivity, according to our own concerns and conditions. If Barth wants us to answer any question about God 'legitimately and thoughtfully' he must not just point us to the right place: he must also equip us with the very mind of God with which to think about it. Otherwise we are in danger of asserting with conviction only the fact of revelation, eschewing all knowledge of its content and actual, specific demands. It is a tall order—to provide ourselves with the sure and certain mind of God—and of course it can never be perfectly done.

Nonetheless there is no reason why these difficulties should completely incapacitate us, as long as we are aware of them. The content and demands of revelation would be wholly relativized, wholly opaque and meaningless to us, only if there was *nothing* common to human perception of things from one time and place to another, and if God had absolutely no interest in enabling our perception. Neither of these kinds of total scepticism—historical or theological—can be sustained, in spite of recent attempts.[2] What it does require is caution in the way the demands are presented. Because they are not self-interpreting, because they are susceptible to all kinds of interpretation in the very moment they are grasped, we need to begin with as circumspect a presentation as possible.

Naturally we cannot delve here into the full range and history of biblical hermeneutics. Suffice it to say that I do see value in a kind of 'phenomenological' presentation of biblical material, not so very different, at least to begin with, from the aims of the biblical theology movement. By this I do not just mean a *prima facie* reading of the Bible which brackets off awkward questions of metaphysical truth; I also mean a certain comprehensiveness: there should be a consideration of all the major themes of biblical faith which might have a bearing on the particular matter in question.

The advantages of such an approach are clear. In the first instance the dangers of arbitrary (or prejudiced) selection are reduced—though not eliminated. Furthermore, to the extent that some interpretative technique is being employed (consciously or unconsciously) then comprehensiveness at least ensures that its adequacy in illuminating one area is subject to being tested in another area. So in the case of Bultmann's technique of demythologizing, its success in illuminating (for example) the activity of God in loving judgement of human individuals has to be set alongside its comparative failure to illuminate the meaning of God as sovereign creator of all things. Only if the latter theme has been included at the outset does it pose the critical question. This does not of itself prejudge the technique, but it stretches and tests it out of the 'given' resources of the whole text. There is therefore some measure of objectivity to this approach.

By 'phenomenological' I also mean an attempt to present the material which is as faithful as possible to the original meaning and intentions of the authors, implying at least some kind of historical approach. This does not mean that knowledge of the writer's original meaning and intention is in every instance an end in itself.

In fact it is neither sufficient nor even necessary as a condition of doctrinal truth. After all, it is impossible to discover in many cases, and even when possible we are not bound in every instance to accept that meaning (how could we when even authors within the Bible do not treat each other like that, quite apart from the exigencies of our different cultural standpoint?).[3] But it does mean that any overall intention which emerges consistently in major themes must count seriously as a given resource. To depart significantly from that would indeed be questionable as an interpretation. For instance, it may be legitimate to reject the view that the drought and rainfall of Elijah's time were brought about by a kind of direct divine interference in which all normal sequences in the natural order were overridden, even though that may have been part of the original meaning (if we assume at least a quasi-scientific view of 'normal natural sequence' in the mind of the writers). But to go on to deny any sense of God's sovereign control through the workings of the natural world would be to take leave of a major overall intention of the biblical writers: this would be checked precisely by the initial insistence on comprehensiveness and 'overall' faithfulness to the original meaning—a 'phenomenological' approach. It is something like this: I may come across individual members of a government discussing intervention in certain areas of the economy, but if I have also allowed myself a truly comprehensive survey of government policy I may also have discovered consistently intended principles and enacted policies of non-interference (of a certain kind). This drives me to re-examine the kind of intervention mentioned before, and it may well emerge that the individual government spokesman did not himself fully grasp the true meaning of his own part in the overall policy. (Always assuming, for sake of the analogy, that we can count on a certain consistency and pattern in government policy!)

It can hardly be stressed enough that this kind of biblical survey is neither the beginning nor the end of revelation. What emerges 'phenomenologically' will still have engaged already with the unconscious colouring of our particular experience, reason, metaphysical assumptions, moral sensibilities etc. And these must also *consciously* engage with it, afterwards, if the demands of revelation are to be truly grasped in our own time and situation, something the biblical theology movement largely failed to do.[4] But it is still an important and crucial way to *get going*. Thus what follows in this chapter is an attempt to produce just such a survey: a brief but wide-ranging consideration of those major themes of biblical faith which are most relevant to the nature of God's activity towards us.

God as personal agent

Take the biblical witness as God's revelation of himself in any sense
and you cannot fail to be struck by its consistent witness to a
personal God whose identity is to be found primarily in his actions.
This is not just true in the sophisticated sense indicated above in
Barth's doctrine, that any concept of revelation is already the
doctrine of a certain kind of God who acts to reveal himself to us. It
is also true in the more straightforward sense of being the explicit
and implicit teaching of the biblical material in both form and
content. Its form, as narrative, assumes precisely a God who can
and does act like the character of a story, or like the author of the
story, or indeed like both. For just because so much of the material
of the Bible takes the form of a story, a sequence of events which
are ordered towards an end, then we already find the meaning of
God determined (in part) by that context. R.H. King comments:

> The model of personal agency is the dominant biblical model for
> God . . . This model gives biblical literature its characteristic tone
> and shape. It is, for instance, one reason why narrative figures so
> prominently in this literature. If God is identified by what he does, it
> is important to keep alive the memory of his actions . . . Without
> renouncing this tradition altogether, we have difficulty seeing how
> we could avoid assigning a prominent role to personal agency.[5]

Certainly narrative is by no means the only biblical form, as we
have been properly warned,[6] but there is no doubt that it
dominates. This is not just a quantitative statement, but a
judgement about its major concerns even where the form is not
narrative. So where the form is shaped by the didactic, the
hortatory or the epistolary, the concerns still relate back to the
narrative. In Paul's great exposition of the meaning of the gospel in
his epistle to the Romans, for example, he frequently trembles
tantalizingly at the edge of Old Testament and gospel narrative in
order to justify and explain that meaning:

> We hold that a man is justified by faith apart from works of law . . .
> *what then shall we say about Abraham?* . . . He did not weaken in
> faith when he considered his own body, which was as good as dead
> because he was about a hundred years old, or when he considered
> the barrenness of Sarah's womb . . . There is therefore now no
> condemnation for those who are in Christ Jesus . . . For God has
> done what the law, weakened by the flesh, could not do: *sending his*
> *own Son in the likeness of sinful flesh* and for sin, he condemned sin
> in the flesh, in order that the just requirement of the law might be

fulfilled in us . . . if Christ is in you, although your bodies are dead because of sin, your spirits are alive because of righteousness. If the Spirit of him who raised Jesus from the dead dwells in you, he who *raised Christ Jesus from the dead* will give life to your mortal bodies also through his Spirit which dwells in you.[7]

The essence of the gospel faith even for Paul the great theologian, teacher and preacher, still lies in the form of a story and he makes it explicit in the great summary statement of 1 Corinthians:

Now I would remind you, brethren, in what terms I preached to you the gospel . . . that Christ died for our sins in accordance with the scriptures, that he was buried, that he was raised on the third day in accordance with the scriptures, and that he appeared to Cephas, then to the twelve. Then he appeared to more than five hundred brethren at one time . . . Then he appeared to James, then to all the apostles. Last of all . . . he appeared to me.[8]

Because of this narrative form it seems impossible to grasp the meaning of God apart from the business of story-telling; that is, a personal involvement in events ordered towards some end or goal.

The content of much of the biblical material clearly supports this inference from its form. The Old Testament context which Christians inherit witnesses overwhelmingly to a personal God who wills, thinks, speaks and acts in clear analogy to ourselves. Indeed, at times the language is barely analogical; it seems virtually univocal: God is referred to in shameless anthropomorphisms—God has ears[9] and eyes,[10] he walks,[11] laughs,[12] pants and groans.[13] And although these stark anthropomorphisms were dropped or softened in later parts of the Old Testament, and certainly in its Greek translation (presumably because of hellenistic influence),[14] the personal analogy itself remained paramount. It is a crucial presupposition of so many of the powerful images of God's relationship with his people, from the basic notion of covenant relationship,[15] to the more intimate images of family relationship, of parent and child, husband and wife.[16] It is implied not only in the whole range of emotions attributed to God[17] but, more tellingly, in their unpredictability in action. For it is a peculiar mark of the personal with its complex interaction of mind, will, instinct, emotion etc. that action flows *inscrutably* out of this complexity. Westermann makes this interesting comment specifically about God's compassion:

In its talk about God, the Old Testament contains a very peculiar feature which makes God's actions at a certain point appear very human. As opposed to other contexts, which emphasize the holiness

of God in contrast to man, here a human emotion is attributed to
God: the emotion of compassion. The Hebrew word for this, *rhm* (or
its plural), actually means "mother's womb"; or the compassion of
the father for his child (Ps. 103) can become the image of this divine
compassion. It is very often connected with an "inconsequence of
God", i.e., this divine compassion frequently occurs where a totally
different reaction of God would be appropriate. This is why this
divine compassion appears so human.[18]

And he proceeds to give examples; the expulsion of Adam from
Eden when God makes clothes for the man and woman, and of the
mercy of God after the destruction of Israel's state, kingship and
temple. God's personhood is in the very life and breath of Old
Testament religion.

More specifically, God's personal identity is defined by his
actions. This is a normal way in which we identify a person,
arguably the only way, certainly a crucial way—and central to the
Old Testament way of identifying God. Thus Exodus 20:2 ('I am
the Lord your God, *who brought you out of the land of Egypt, out
of the house of bondage'*) denotes a God who is revealed and
identified in terms of his personal action. This test is no casual or
arbitrary selection but may be taken as the broadest and most basic
affirmation of the distinctive identity of God in the pages of the Old
Testament'.[19] We see it again in the wake of catastrophe and exile,
when Israel once again had to be summoned to recognize God: he
reveals himself over against all other claimants as the one who has
acted and will act—in giving birth to Israel, in nurturing, saving
and judging them.[20]

The New Testament addresses this general context with even
more specifically personal language about God. As Father of Jesus
he is identified immediately in terms of personal relationship. The
anthropomorphic tendency is still present in allusions to 'the finger
of God'[21] or to his 'swearing oaths'.[22] He is frequently defined by
his relationship to personal life (for he is the God of living men),[23]
by his capacity to give personal life,[24] and by his own aliveness.[25]
He is in the fullest sense of the term, the living God.

More crucially, the unique presence of God in the person of Jesus
is the boldest possible statement of God's own personhood.
Whatever metaphysical interpretation is given (or withheld)
concerning the claims of the fourth Gospel and Colossians they still
have to imply a strong analogy of personhood in the being of God.
For the man Jesus to be 'one' with the Father, or for the 'fullness of
God' to dwell in the man Jesus, in any sense, demands this. One
might also add to Westermann's comment from the Old Testament
its New Testament corollary: the God of grace on the pages of the

New Testament acts as 'inconsequentially' (and therefore as 'personally') as the God of compassion in the Old Testament. He is not an impersonal dispenser of proportional justice but the whimsical owner of the vineyard who pays to the last labourer the same wage as the first;[26] who will have mercy on those whom he wills to have mercy;[27] whose decision can only be rooted ultimately in the opaqueness of his personal will.

Again, the identification of this personal God (the Father of our Lord Jesus Christ) is primarily in his action. In the synoptic gospels this action is particularly associated with the kingdom, a dynamic concept best understood as the rule of God enacted in the person of Jesus Christ. In pauline literature the God and Father of our Lord Jesus Christ is one who has 'blessed us in Christ . . . destined us in love to be his sons through Jesus Christ, according to the purpose of his will . . .' and who demonstrated 'the immeasurable greatness of his power . . . when he raised him [Jesus] from the dead', and so on.[28] To the Greeks at Athens Paul identifies God as the one who acts in creation, in giving life and ordering it, in judgement, and in the resurrection of Christ.[29] The author of the epistle to the Hebrews likewise defines God in terms of his act of creation, speech and resurrection.[30] Thus form and content together bear powerful witness to God as personal agent.

But are there also rival models of God in the biblical material? Some images are impersonal. In the Old Testament God is associated with fire[31] and light,[32] for example. However even these images are referred to in a primarily personal context. The light is like a garment, and it surrounds the likeness of a human form. Fire is actually the locus of a personal 'voice', the place of words. 'Wind' or 'Spirit' too could just bear impersonal meaning, were it not for the evidently personal context.[33] Perhaps more significant is the strand of thinking which, as we have already noted, opposed the anthropomorphic tendencies of much of the Old Testament. This opposition—characteristic of the priestly tradition of Old Testament literature—derived essentially from a concern with the unapproachable holiness and otherness of God. Taken to extremes it had two effects: it emphasized the static and abstract separateness of God from the affairs of this world, over against his dynamic and concrete involvement against hostile powers proclaimed so insistently by the prophets; and it invited the use of mediating concepts between God and the world and abstract terms by which to designate God himself. However this extreme did not gain a dominating foothold in the Old Testament itself (as we have it), but rather in the Targums and the Septuagint version.[34]

The New Testament does occasionally refer to God with

impersonal images such as light[35] and love,[36] and fire.[37] But again the context is overwhelmingly personal: the 'light' is of the Father, and is something in which we walk in personal fellowship; the love of God is manifest in that he 'sent his only Son into the world'; the 'consuming fire' echoes the Old Testament scenario—it is the place where God speaks. 'Spirit' is again used by New Testament writers, and has recently been favoured as a dominant model (or 'co-ordinating concept'—which is not quite the same thing).[38] However its primitive and impersonal meaning as wind or breath is as unlikely to be primary in its New Testament Greek context as it is in its Old Testament Hebrew context: 'God is Spirit' (in John 4:24) most probably means that he is not material, not a localized individual—but still worshipped as a Father—and Geoffrey Lampe's comment serves well for both Testaments: '. . . the Spirit is God in his outreach towards men, interacting with their created spirits and integrating their thoughts and emotions and wills with his own'.[39] Nor does the New Testament insistence on the holiness and transcendence of God, through such expressions as the 'majesty on high' of Hebrews or the 'Almighty' one 'seated upon the throne' of Revelation, imply a static or impersonal deity: rather it indicates the place where intercession is made and adoration offered, the power-base of God's personal action in the world.

Purposive activity

For any action to be truly personal it has to be purposive—this is actually a defining characteristic of action as distinct from mere event, as we shall see.[40] Accordingly, biblical faith consistently recognizes the fact of purposiveness ('intentionality') in God's activity, even where it is not always clear about what the purpose might be.

Generally speaking it is a presupposition of the whole history of Israel that some purpose of God is being worked out through this one nation. Deutero-Isaiah then extends the notion of God's purposive action to encompass the course of the world's history.[41] It also provides the most explicit summary statement of the general fact of divine purposiveness as integral to the very identity of God:

> I am God, and there is none like me,
> declaring the end from the beginning
> and from ancient times things not yet done,
> saying, 'My counsel shall stand,
> and I will accomplish all my purpose . . .'
> I have spoken, and I will bring it to pass;
> I have purposed, and I will do it.[42]

The fact of purpose is also made to reach right back into the act of creation. The very structure of the world exhibits teleology; animals are made for man (and man for gardening!). The yahwist account is clear enough in this respect, and Eichrodt deems the priestly account in Genesis 1 to be even more revealing:

> [The priestly writer] achieves an impressive presentation of the purposeful arrangement of the cosmic structure. Moreover, he exhibits the inner necessity of this structure by ascribing each particular work of creation to God's word, and by allowing the older ideas of making and shaping by God's hand to recede right into the background. This word of creation, however, does not imply simply ease and effortlessness, but also systematic thought and self-conscious will, which remain fundamentally distinct from all unconscious generation or quasi-instinctive emanation.[43]

Further, these purposes of creation cannot be separated off simply as past event: creation is continued, precisely as *purposeful solicitude*.[44] So Deutero-Isaiah's powerful testimony to the purposes of God takes its place within a wider tradition of the continuing working out of divine purpose through nature[45] and history:[46] it is not just that a purposeful creation requires sustaining, as Greek thought suggested; its purposes are 'in constant need of divine positive activity'.[47] Purposiveness is also implied by the foreknowledge of God, made explicit in Daniel's visions and often implied elsewhere, whether or not we understand the plan as being actually determined in advance.

Purposiveness in the New Testament is enhanced and rooted primarily in the person of Jesus Christ. Jesus moves through the pages of the gospels on a divine mission. The Son of Man came to fulfil purposes: to serve and give his life as a ransom;[48] to seek and save that which is lost;[49] he came that we might have life and have it abundantly.[50] He moves always under the pressure of purpose, the unremitting demand to 'fulfil all righteousness',[51] to 'preach good news to the poor',[52] and then to 'set his face to go to Jerusalem'.[53] None of these things is purely arbitrary, contingent or spontaneous; they are expressions of the inner necessity of the divine intentions:[54] the Son of Man 'must' (*dei*) go to Jerusalem and suffer many things.

But while rooted in Jesus, the purposive action of God is proclaimed more widely too. One of the central themes of the Acts of the Apostles is to show how the guiding hand of God directs and purposes the spread of the Christian gospel through a whole range of things—through the activities of Peter, Paul, the early church, and through natural and historical circumstances of various kinds.[55] God's purpose for Christians is clearly stated in the *locus classicus* of Romans 8:28-29 ('We know that in everything God works for good with those who love him, who are called according to his purpose'), but more widely still (and more daringly) in the following chapters, Romans 9-11, which declare an all-inclusive purpose of God for Jews and Gentiles, believers and unbelievers. Even those who find themselves hard of heart, 'against' the purposes of God, do so in order to contribute to a still wider intention of God's judgement and mercy.[56] Indeed the pauline literature refers explicitly to the divine purpose with a persistence that makes it into a central motif. It is the fact of divine purpose which lends to a whole range of characteristic ideas their proper perspective: foreknowledge, foreordination, 'preparing beforehand', 'counsel of his will' all cluster round the concept of purpose. It is at least arguable (as H. Ridderbos claims) that the central thesis of Romans 9-11 is to show the fact of God's (gracious) *purpose* in the history of unbelieving Jews, rather than to establish a particular doctrine of predestination.[57] For however we are supposed to understand foreknowledge and predestination in relation to human freedom, it must always imply a divine plan—no matter how effectively or how dictatorially it is worked out.

The New Testament also enhances the purposive element in creation—and continuing creation—in the same Christocentric way. Nearly all New Testament references to creation express divine purposiveness, and this even extends to the 'futility' of creation, 'for the creation was subjected to futility, not of its own will but by the will of him who subjected it'.[58] No trace of mere contingency here, even in these aspects of creation which (like human sin in Romans 9-11) seem to fall outside or against the divine purpose. Rather, all things which were made through Christ exist *for* him, and are reconciled by him.[59]

Thus it is almost impossible to find any significant strand of biblical faith which denies God's purposiveness in any aspect of existence. There is perhaps a tendency in the Old Testament wisdom tradition to celebrate and expound the glories and complexities of the natural world in its own terms, in a quasi scientific style, without explicit reference to divine purpose in it. But the wider context of the creator God's purposes is always there, even when their content is quite mysterious. This is also true of Paul's appeal to mystery in the New Testament. In context it can never mean mere arbitrariness or randomness; it is simply an acknowledgement of divine opaqueness, and the limitation of human discernment: it is still the mystery of his *will*. As with Deutero-Isaiah, God's ways are not our ways, but they are still his *ways*, leading somewhere according to his purposes.

God's Universal Activity

It is already apparent that the scope of God's activity is broad. The idea of 'continuing creation', for instance, establishes the broadest possible base across time and space for the divine action. If creation is an assertion of distinctively divine activity ('for where were you when I laid the foundations of the earth?'),[60] and concerns all that is ('I am the Lord who made all things, who stretched out the heavens alone, and spread out the earth'),[61] then it is significant that both the Old Testament and the New Testament use the category of creation for present and future events as well as past:[62] all that is now and all that will be is equally the field of God's activity, as much as all that was. This is a particularly important insight to emerge from a faith (in the Old Testament) which is dominated by the special activity of God in relation to Israel. Yet it is widely affirmed as a legitimate interpretation of the developing traditions. J. Goldingay comments:

> The OT sees Yahweh as present and active in the regularities of nature as well as in the once-for-all events of history, in the blessing of everyday life as well as in salvation from periodic crises, in an overall lordship over the cosmos as well as in particular historical events, in the lives of all men as well as in the history of Israel.[63]

Even where the particular and special electing activity of God (*re* Israel) is being stressed, it is often done with at least some acknowledgement of the existence of other nations,[64] and at best with an awareness of some mediating role towards them.[65] There is an explicit prophetic insistence on Yahweh's activity towards other nations, even before the exile,[66] which then develops significantly under the special pressures and constraints of that period.[67] Nor is this consciousness peculiar to the prophetic tradition: the meaning of the cult is also developed to accommodate a less localized conception of God's presence and activity (in space and time). As R. E. Clements says, a 'theologization of the cult took place', so that new or expanded concepts such as 'spirit' came to portray God's activity independent of the symbols of the cult, even to the 'uttermost parts of the earth'. He also speculates that this was probably very important in sustaining faith in the post-exilic age of the diaspora where there was no access to an established cult.[68]

The whole realm of nature is also the field of God's activity: this is not only true in the particular instances of saving activity (when he causes it to rain for Elijah, or causes the wind to blow back the Sea of Reeds), but also in a more generalized sense. Thus the 'fruit of the ground' referred to in the important historical credo of Deuteronomy 26 is a direct benefit of the saving God;[69] likewise the 'seedtime and harvest' which 'shall not cease'[70] whether or not its divine provenance is known and acknowledged (for 'she did not know that it was I who gave her the grain, the wine, and the oil').[71] Clearly there is 'blessing' from God through universal features of experience, the powers of fertility, growth, life and death. He also acts, therefore, in relation to a great variety of human endeavour in economy and agriculture, as well as in culture, politics and social life.[72] More generally still, the creator-redeemer God works out his purposes 'from the beginning' through the whole range of natural order, creating the wind,[73] decreeing the weather[74] ordering the oceans,[75] even directing the paths of the animals,[76] and giving them their food and drink.[77] None of this implies any pantheistic or animistic identification of Yahweh with the powers of nature, unlike some other Near Eastern religions of the time;[78] but it does imply their instrumentality in the working out of his purposes.

It is important to emphasize the immanent nature of this transcendent God's activity. He really is operative within the events of the world in which Israel lived, both historical and natural. This is even true during the difficult period from the eighth to the sixth centuries in which the events of the world might justifiably have seemed senseless, as Zimmerli points out:

> The great prophets were commissioned to *prevent* Israel from fleeing into such a retreat [of hidden inner faith] . . . and to make her encounter her God in the midst of the storms of that world. Isaiah sees Assyria as the instrument of God's angry judgement. Jeremiah dares to describe Nebuchadnezzar as 'the servant of Yahweh'. And Deutero-Isaiah . . . addresses . . . Cyrus with the title of the anointed one, the Messiah of Yahweh.[79]

Thus we can confidently assert a real and pervasive sense of universalism: *all* events of both natural and historical worlds are embraced in some way within the divine activity. The whole of the created order, sun, moon and stars, is to return praise to the God who created and commands them.[80] To be sure, the precise nature of that relationship between all events and the divine intention is not easy to determine, and is not so clearly expressed in the biblical material. That is a question to which we shall be returning in much more depth in later chapters.

The New Testament takes this universalism on board without demur—indeed it takes it further. In Romans 9-11 the history of the Gentiles as well as the Jews is most insistently placed under the providential ordering of God. And while the history of the church certainly begins from the particularity of Christ and his first followers in Judea and Samaria, it is only in order to move out 'to the end of the earth'.[81] All history is caught up in the purposes of God, not just in anticipation of the apocalyptic denouement, but from beginning to end through all time and space. In the pauline picture the plan for the 'fullness of time' to unite 'all things in heaven . . . and earth' is achieved through the Christ by whom all things were created, and in whom they hold together and are reconciled.[82] Here the logic of universalism is once again rooted in the doctrine of continuing creation, though unlike the Old Testament, of course, it is referred entirely to Christ. This thought is by no means unique to Paul: the same notion is found in Johannine material where the 'Word' functions as 'the personal principle of creation which impregnates the world and the course of history'.[83] Not, let it be said, that Christ is merely 'fitted in' to the Old Testament scheme of 'continuing creation'. Far from it. Redemption in Christ was no doubt grasped within the context or universal and continuing creation-redemption, but it also carried within itself a logic of universal significance which expanded and clarified that context into which it was born. Thus L. Scheffczyk comments:

> The association of Creation and redemption in Christ . . . must be chiefly attributed to the total and universal validity of the event that is Christ . . . Redemption could be universal only if it were derived from the same source as Creation . . . But Christ's position as the mediator of redemption was not deduced from his role in Creation, rather the reverse; the divine plan of salvation was grasped [. . . and worked back.][85]

As in the Old Testament, it is not just in the realm of history that this wide-ranging divine activity takes place: in the healing and nature miracles of the gospels Jesus is re-ordering the very structure of creation in nature as well as history, arguably in line with the primeval ordering of chaos which never entirely disappeared from Judaism and its cult.[85] He also seems to assume God's care for birds and flowers[86] and his activity in sun and rain.[87] Paul assumes God's control of the seasons in his Lystra address,[88] and more generally finds the whole realm of creation groaning in hope for its salvation.[89] Nor does the New Testament confine all talk of God's activity to the great saving events. Just because of his great pre-occupation with the particular events of Christ it is all the more notable that Paul also teaches God's cooperation for good in *all* things for Christians, and a general providence of revelation and judgement for all men through natural and historical reality.[90] Characteristically more concrete, Jesus himself urges us to pray for daily bread, a petition almost certainly based on his Father's providential care in daily living (especially in the wider context of Matthew 6). It does indeed seem that the activity of God is 'all in all'. There is no time or space where he is excluded, no kinds of men or society or natural phenomena which are not caught up in some way within the pervasive, perpetual and purposive motion of God.

God's special activity

God's universal activity, however, is neither the whole story nor the primary story of the biblical material. That story is of God's special activity, first in relation to Israel, then in Christ, and thereafter in relation to the church.

Although God's activity is not found exclusively in particular events relating to a particular people, that is where it is found pre-eminently. This is probably true in historical as well as theological terms. That is to say, the earliest strands of Old Testament tradition bear witness more exclusively to Yahweh as God of Israel than do later strands. Yet even after the exile experience the particular concern for Israel, or at least its righteous remnant, is never lost, and this at a time when Yahweh's wider purposes for all mankind were being canvassed more and more. Gray comments on Deutero-Isaiah, 'Nor does the author confine himself to general statements of the sovereignty of God in Creation and history. The general is particularized in the deliverance of Israel, the main theme of Deutero-Isaiah', noting how chapter 41:8ff. ('But you, Israel, my servant, Jacob whom I have chosen . . . whom I took from the ends of the earth . . . fear not, for I am with you') follows immediately from Yahweh's dealings with all the peoples, and how the victory of Cyrus, delivering Israel in chapters 41:25-29 and 42:5-9, follows the matter of the idols.[91] Thus it can be fairly stated that the God who defines himself in Exodus as the God who performs the particular action of bringing Israel out of the land of Egypt (Ex. 20:2) never compromises or denies that particularity or specialness throughout the whole of the Old Testament, even where the scope of his activity is broadened far beyond the bounds of Israel. It is noteworthy that whether an Old Testament theology is sys-tematized around a central motif like 'covenant' (Eichrodt), or whether (with von Rad and others) the Old Testament is the story of divine acts in history which have to be grasped within their particular historical circumstances, the particularity and specialness of God's activity is presupposed. The covenant is a particular relationship with a particular group of people, and the acts of God in history are (by the definition of an act) discrete, selected, and particular.

Much the same can be said of the New Testament. New Testament theology might well be co-ordinated around the concept of the kingdom in the synoptic gospels, or (more comprehensively) around the concept of salvation, or it can be conceived as a theology of history, or else (more like von Rad's treatment of the Old Testament) it can be considered historically, as the revelation of God given and grasped in a variety of historical circumstances.[92] Yet all these options imply the particularity of God's action. In preaching the kingdom, Jesus preached its reality in himself, a particularizing *par excellence* of God's presence and activity.[93] Likewise, the concept of a righteous remnant has been whittled away to just one person; and the concept of election, as Barth in particular is at pains to point out, though initially applied to Israel (the many), is only properly fulfilled and understood in the New Testament doctrine of the election of the one man, and then of the church through him. Thus the activity of God in reconciling and saving all things is to be achieved in the one person of Jesus Christ—who lived and died 'for our sins in accordance with the scriptures . . . was buried . . . was raised on the third day' and so on. These discrete acts of Jesus Christ are then 'embodied' in some sense in the acts of God through the apostles' activity and through the church's continuing mission in the world.

However it is important to distinguish the sense in which God's activity is special. Clearly there is a special significance in the divine activity found in particular events surrounding Israel, the man Jesus and the church: *but what kind of significance?*

The dominant New Testament pattern is that the activity of God primarily in the event of Christ and derivatively in the church is specially significant as a constitutive means to a wider end. That is, the purposes of God for the whole world are specially accomplished in and through particular events, like an edifice is built on some crucial cornerstone, or a play depends on some key, pivotal action. Thus Jesus came to declare and constitute the kingdom for an ever widening group of people—his disciples, the lost sheep of the house of Israel, then even for the Gentiles— a movement which Luke-Acts makes especially explicit in both form and content.[94] So too the fourth gospel portrays the 'true light that enlightens every man' as made particular ('became flesh') in order to draw all men to himself.[95] The pauline literature likewise sets forth Christ as the particular basis for that 'plan for the fullness of time, to unite all things'.[96] And the epistle to the Hebrews demands that we conceive the 'once for all' sacrifice, constituted in the particular time and place of Christ, as the bearing away of 'the sins of many'.[97]

The pattern of limited means serving wider ends is less dominant in the Old Testament, but certainly incipient, and occasionally marked. The chosenness of the particular man Abraham is for the blessing of others;[98] the chosenness of Israel will bring prosperity to the world,[99] and it will serve as a focus for the pilgrimage of other nations to reverence Yahweh;[100] and most radically it will become in the 'servant songs' a means of serving the nations.[101]

This pattern is therefore a crucial model for relating the special significance of particular events to God's wider activity and universal purposes. Using the somewhat different category of 'self-limitation' C.F.D. Moule summarizes its manifestation in the New Testament thus:

> The New Testament . . . constantly represents God as content to achieve his purposes by self-limitation, by specialization, by selection, by contraction in order to expand . . . And the very climax of this purpose is the Incarnation itself . . . . No election or specialization could be more drastic: it is what has been called the 'scandal of particularity'. But it is in order to save the whole world that God thus limits himself . . . and the apparent self-limitation turns out to be, after all, precisely the universalizing of God's kingly rule. It is thus, and only thus, that God will ultimately be vindicated as himself the sum of all things, absolutely all-embracing (1 Cor. 15:28).[102]

Admittedly the precise means by which the particular event of Christ constitutes a universal redemptive action of God is not so clear (it belongs primarily to atonement theory), but the pattern itself is inescapable.

On the other hand it is not the only pattern. It should not be taken to mean that God's special activity in relation to particular events and groups is always as a means to a further end. It seems that in God's purposes particulars also constitute ends in themselves, as well as means. This is most easily grasped in the context of God's personhood and personal relationship with his people: personal action may justify itself in terms such as 'love' or 'compassion' without reference to any wider context. So, as we have seen, God acts to save in particular events 'inconsequentially'. He appears to elect a particular group 'arbitrarily', simply on the basis of his loving decision.[103] It becomes clearer still when the individual is represented as the object of God's action: God does not just act in relation to a particular group or person for the sake of general ends concerning the salvation of the world *qua* world, or group *qua* group, but for the sake of individuals. And this degree of specificity must highlight the fact that God finds and intends *ends* within the particular. It constitutes an 'attention to detail' which implies meaning and value in the part as well as the whole, especially when the 'detail' is the personal life of an individual.

In the Old Testament this is expressed especially in the psalms of lament, where God's compassion falls on individuals as well as the group,[104] and in the book of Job. In the New Testament God's care for individuals is assumed even down to the hairs of our head,[105] and is assured us in the reference to guardian angels.[106] It is the great presupposition of the 'Abba' relationship with God which Jesus invites his disciples to share. Still more tellingly it is acted out in the actual drama of Jesus' life: he proclaimed the fact of the kingdom in cosmic terms and with more than a trace of apocalyptic imagery, but still interpreted it through an implacable commitment to caring for the needs of individuals. Indeed the whole form and structure of the incarnation could be read off as a particularizing of God's concern for the individual, not just as a particular means for some general and universal end: Jesus addressing himself to (say) the widow at Nain is God stepping into one moment of history like the producer of a play stepping onto the stage at one moment of the plot, choosing just one obscure time and place to do it, a backwater of the Roman Empire, a small town within that, a crowd within the town, an unknown woman within the town, then proceeding to deal with her as if she was a person of unique importance. The most insignificant member of the cast, barely more than a mere member of the crowd scene, is actually worth the producer's unique attention. It is not surprising, therefore, that Paul's theological reflection likewise deemed the providential care of God to be directed not only towards the world, but towards a people, and not only towards a people, but towards individual believers, including, of course, himself.[107] For he too had been 'found out' by God in Christ.

So it is that we have to speak of the universal scope of divine activity in nature and history as specialized too, relating equally to particulars both as means and ends. The crucial issue which must now follow concerns the efficacy of that activity; whether and in what sense God actually achieves his purposes in every particular.

Sovereignty and efficacy

It would be hard to overestimate the Old Testament's concern with Yahweh's sovereignty and kingship. It reaches something of a climax (interestingly) out of the paradoxical experience of exile, and particularly in the writings of Deutero-Isaiah where God's sovereignty operates coterminously with his activity throughout the whole range of creation so that it becomes a defining characteristic, an identification, of his activity: he rules the heavens and all history with a 'peremptory, controlling will';[108] he will accomplish all his purposes . . . he has purposed and he will do it.[109]

The basis for such sweeping powers is found first in creation. As von Rad and others are quick to point out, this need not imply that the 'doctrine' of creation is a central subject of Old Testament faith, but it does undergird its covenant faith:[110] the God who made a covenant with Abraham and at Sinai is also the creator of the world, with all that that implies. So, beginning with the yahwist account of creation, we find a clear doctrine of the dependence and subordination of all things to the divine will. This is distinct from other Near Eastern religious ideas of creation which compromise divine sovereignty by depicting a struggle with chaos, or else the generation of things from divine beings.[111] Then in the priestly account this emphasis is even greater: all those powers of nature, which for Israel's neighbours were vested with mystery and power of their own, derive their being and significance entirely from God's will and command. Thus there is no particular mystery about the sun and moon: they are simply the instruments of God (the 'greater and lesser light').[112] Even the trace of craftsmanship present in the yahwist account—whereby God might be said to fashion men out of some pre-existent material—has disappeared for the sake of emphasizing God's absolute priority and control. It is often pointed out that the Hebrew word reserved for divine creation (*bara*) has no real analogy in human creating just because the divine act is not subject to the same limitations as human endeavour.

It is true that there is some residual idea of a divine struggle against chaos: the notion is not entirely excluded. For while the priestly account of creation rules it out (in any sense of ultimate metaphysical dualism) it occurs in some psalms as the conflict of Yahweh against the personified Rahab and Leviathan,[113] or against the hostile powers of water,[114] and in the apocalyptic passages of Isaiah in the context of a battle for the consummation of all things.[115] On the other hand these references rarely, if ever, establish a real dualism. Leviathan and Behemoth are tamed: they are no longer hostile forces over against God in any absolute sense; they are God's creatures.[116] Moreover, the chief import of these passages is to convey God's victory rather than the importance and status of his enemies. The hymns especially may be taken as a call to wonder and exult at the might of God, not as sober teaching about the nature of the opposition. Thus the apocalyptic strands of the Old Testament need not imply any contradiction with God's sovereignty; indeed they actually imply a celebration of that sovereignty *de facto*, by assuming it already and demonstrating it in action. This is especially true of the book of Daniel.

There is also a strong basis for asserting God's sovereignty in the continuing creative work of saving, judging and redeeming. From the very beginnings of Israel's religion, God is victoriously active on behalf of his people to save them from their enemies. The ancient poetry sings of the God who achieves his purposes most effectively by hurling the Egyptians into the sea;[117] he is also constantly and effectively active in flushing out the Canaanites to establish the promised land.[118] Likewise, the more sophisticated doctrine of judgement and redemption proclaimed by the prophets depends on the absolute power of God to execute his judgements and effect his redemption in the manner he determines, whether through the unwitting Assyrian,[119] or through the unwilling Jeremiah who is set 'over nations and over kingdoms, to pluck up and to break down, to destroy and to overthrow, to build and to plant'.[120] In the light of all this it is hardly surprising that the specific motif of kingship should be found (by some at least) to be so persuasive. Arguably the kingship theme which is so predominant in Deutero-Isaiah is no novelty but reaches well back to pre-exilic religion in an autumn festival, wherein, together with the celebration of the covenant, there is a 'cultic assurance of the effective kingship of God in historical conflicts of His people'.[121] It climaxes, as we have noted, after the exile in Deutero-Isaiah, and then persists in the prophetic eschatology of Joel and Zechariah.

The apocalyptic literature proclaims divine sovereignty in more general terms than the specific motif of kingship: it is the final and decisive revelation of the power of God. What is particularly significant (and a point to which we shall be returning) is the specific context in which this power is asserted, namely the context of the suffering of the righteous, the apparent contradiction in experience of the sovereignty being proclaimed. Gray comments:

> This is the problem which has continually emerged in the plaints of the Sufferer in the Psalms . . . occasioned the agony of the writer of

the Book of Job. In the eclipse of Israel under the great imperial powers after the fall of Jerusalem in 586 B.C. it was answered by prophets in the eschatological development of the traditional liturgical theme of the Reign of God as a glowing hope . . . In apocalyptic its solution is confidently proclaimed in the final denouement of the Reign of God which was on the point of realization.[122]

The New Testament understanding of how this realization of God's power takes place is complex. Future and universal consummation in apocalyptic style is not absent (witness the book of Revelation), but as we have seen before it is also being worked out through the apparent limitations of particularity—in Christ. The context in which sovereignty is revealed is also paradoxical, even more obviously than it was in the Old Testament: God's power and glory is grasped not just in spite of evidence to the contrary, but in and through that evidence; power made perfect through weakness,[123] glory in suffering.[124] Nonetheless, the fact of God's sovereignty is asserted no less than in the Old Testament: he can and does do what he wills, by whatever means, throughout the whole range of created reality. God is omnipotent,[125] omniscient,[126] and is acclaimed as Lord and sovereign. Jesus' Father in heaven[127] is preached in the early church as the 'sovereign Lord who made heaven and earth',[128] establishing this same link between sovereignty and creatorhood. Interestingly the gospels do not refer specifically to God's kingship as much as the important concept of kingdom might lead us to expect[129] (he is more often referred to as judge); but the implication is still obliquely present in references to the 'throne' of God,[130] and possibly the notion of a heavenly court.[131] In the epistle to the Hebrews his sovereignty is clearly referred to as the 'Majesty on High'. The book of Revelation makes frequent references to God the 'Almighty' which is the Septuagint equivalent of 'Lord of Hosts', the ruler of the heavenly court. Paul proclaims a God reigning over all.[132]

The effective exercise of this sovereignty is demonstrated in the realm of nature by Jesus' healing miracles, and in the stilling of the storm. It is taught, as well as demonstrated, in the realm of society, particularly in the parables of growth: the mustard seed, the leaven in the dough, the farmer with his crop, all express an irresistible process of the working of God's purpose. It is then demonstrated in the progress of church growth described in the Acts of the Apostles, and taught in more sophisticated fashion in Paul's doctrine of history laid out in Romans 9-11: God will achieve his purposes, even through rebellion and unbelief, for both Jew and Gentile.

This sovereignty also extends to the 'rulers and powers' which lie behind the events of this world: in the synoptic gospels the demons are subject to Jesus, and Satan is put to flight from the temptation narratives through to the resurrection; for Paul the rulers of this age and all the powers of heaven and earth are decisively conquered and reconciled even in their activity against him.[133] Once again the basis of this faith is found particularly in the doctrine of creation: these powers are created by him, sustained in him, and therefore subject to him. Paul does not resort to any kind of ultimate dualism.[134] Even the Johannine literature with its insistent contrasts of light and darkness, truth and falsehood, does not imply metaphysical dualism. The 'Word' precedes all things and is the creative principle of all things. Those who do not receive him are still 'his own people', made through him.[135] There is still some sense, therefore, in which he will draw all men to himself;[136] even the devil himself is able to be used in God's plan.[137] Thus while there is indeed bitter opposition and real antagonism between light and darkness, there is no original or final disjunction of a kind which leaves the darkness altogether beyond God's purposes and power.

It is notable that while the logic of God's universal power derives formally from his creating, it is only through the concrete work of the redeeming Christ that this is effectively realized and properly understood. In that sense the effective sovereignty of God is demonstrated and constituted primarily in Christ's work of re-creation. This does not just mean what we have already noted, that in the historical Jesus we see a particular example and demonstration of God's power working through apparent failure: it means that the living, dying and rising of Christ constitutes a 'mighty act' of God actually *effective* for the *whole* work of God in the world. This 'work that he was given to do', the 'hour which has come' and which constituted something 'finished', is interpreted by Paul as an accomplishment 'for our sins' which reconciles all things.[138] For Paul, Jesus' resurrection from the dead completes an act of God which is treated as a vital achievement for us all, a great reversal of Adam's sin.[139] The epistle to the Hebrews conveys a similar idea in the language of sacrifice.[140] A crucial point in all this is that it was always the will of God, 'from before all things'; the lamb was 'slain before the foundations of the world'; the plan was 'set forth' in Christ: in short, Jesus came, was 'sent', 'emerged' (however it is expressed) to achieve the momentous prior purposes of God—and he was successful. God's sovereignty is effective. To be sure, there are grave problems of intelligibility: it is difficult to understand how God's will for the world is actually constituted in the living, dying and rising of the particular historical Jesus, even supposing we can understand him to be God himself. This has led naturally to a demythologized account in which the 'achievement' is merely potential or demonstrative, not actual. But that is already to 'turn our thoughts upon it' more deliberately than we are yet intending. Such problems should not detract from the *prima facie* force of the notion revealed in our 'phenomenological' approach to the material. It remains a bold assertion of effective sovereignty.

One final aspect of God's power to act, already touched on more than once, calls for special attention. God acts effectively not least because he can act independently of, and prior to, the action and response of his creation. This is assumed in the manner of his creating as related in the Genesis account: the priority of the divine command means the creator does not surrender himself to what he has created.[141] He does not depend on it as a mind depends on the response of its body. We see the natural extension of this idea in what Clements has called the 'theologizing of the cult', already noted: God could not be conceived locally in time (festivals) or space (the temple) if this implied he was at Israel's beck and call. He is not summoned by his creatures, but freely summons them.[142] It also applies to the control of history in judgement and redemption: Yahweh is the 'first' in all matters of control and direction.[143] He does not require Israel's faith in order to act in the histories of the nations, indeed Israel may not even be involved at all in any direct way.[144] Thus Walter Zimmerli neatly characterizes the normal pattern of Yahweh's redemptive action in the five elements of need, call for help, hearing, saving and response of the saved (following Dt. 26:5-11); but then points out that only the first and fourth are invariable, which simply means that God does not depend on our call even though he may prefer to use it. What is true for specific redeeming acts is also true for everyday 'blessings': he will guarantee 'seedtime and harvest' as he pleases; Israel does not have to know who 'gave her the grain, the wine and the oil'.[145] Furthermore, when man's own summons or response is forthcoming, God is even prior to that in some sense. This is expressed in terms of his foreknowledge and predestination (as with Jeremiah and Job). It even has to be said that his will lies behind the unbelieving or rebellious response, so that the Old Testament sometimes appears to risk attributing evil to God rather than admit to dualism.[146]

The New Testament inherits and enhances all this and, as usual, roots it in Christ. The Jesus of the gospels exhibits this same kind of belief in relation to the kingdom; namely that 'the time of the coming of God's kingdom depends entirely on God's will and that the kingdom of God comes without any human contributing factor'.[147] A number of his parables taught much the same thing, emphasizing that the reign of God is effective in spite of, or independently of, paltry human effort.[148] This naturally entails the doctrine of grace, whereby God's favour is realized beyond all effort or deserts of man (in the parable of the vineyard labourers, for example). Thus Gray summarizes: 'The Biblical concept of the Kingdom of God is not a . . . programme which [we] may adequately fulfil by [our] organised efforts . . . rather the dynamic power of God as Sovereign'.[149] As we have already seen, Jesus also senses himself subject to the sense of predetermined divine necessity, likewise assuming the absolute priority of the divine action. It is a picture adopted again and again in the early church, and especially by Paul, as an exegesis both of divine sovereignty and of grace. Jesus is betrayed and crucified not primarily by men, but by 'the definite plan and foreknowledge of God'.[150] The whole act of redemption in Christ is not regarded as a spontaneous contingency plan, a reaction of God to the world's events, but as a plan decided upon 'before the foundation of the world' to be realized in 'the fullness of time'.[151] Thereby it is also the action of supreme grace in that Christ came and died for us 'while we were yet sinners', while we were 'dead' and 'powerless', not requiring our summons of faith.[152] What is true of Christ also becomes true of those in Christ, who are also called from the beginning to enter into blessings prepared before all things. Paul believes himself called like the Old Testament pattern of predetermined prophets.[153] Even more marked is Paul's development of the Old Testament understanding of creaturely resistance and rebellion: God is represented quite unequivocally as the author behind the rebellion, the 'hardener of men's hearts', for the sake of his wider purposes for all men.[154] Such priority of God's action is best characterized in personal terms as his *initiative*.

Of course, this does not tell the whole story of God's relationship with the world and human response, and we shall turn now to deal with another perspective on it. Nonetheless it is notable that Stauffer can devote a substantial New Testament Theology precisely to this theme of divine priority. He aptly summarizes:

> The fundamental datum of any theology of history, the primary fact to which the old biblical tradition always goes back, is not sin, nor even creation, but the absolute priority of God over the whole world and its history.[155]

God has 'the first and last word'.[156]

Apparent Frustrations and Limitations to Divine Activity

As indicated, it is also possible to read the Bible from a somewhat different perspective. Within certain frames of reference the Old Testament can be seen as a record of failure and frustration, not just of man's endeavour, but of God's. God's initiatives of creation, covenant, monarchy and the restoration disintegrate into the fall, into disobedience, and the dispersion.[157] There is a particularly dispiriting period recorded in the history of the book of the Judges, and von Rad reminds us that the prophets' perspective is equally blunt: they 'deny the efficacy of the old divine actions for their contemporaries' (and therefore declare new acts of salvation to come). Far from determining events independently of his creatures God is sometimes represented as changing his mind, 'repenting' of his purposes in reaction to his creatures.[158] At times this reads like an internal struggle ('How can I give you up, O Ephraim! How can I hand you over, O Israel . . . My heart recoils within me, my compassion grows warm and tender. I will not execute my fierce anger, I will not again destroy Ephraim').[159] And even if there is no failure (internally) of the divine nerve, there may still be an external struggle on hand. Success is not handed to God on a plate but has to be wrested out of intractable matter (a trace found faintly in the Yahwist account of creation), or against the sporadic resurgence of the powers of chaos who may still be marshalling their forces for a great showdown to come, either in history or at the end of it.[160] Thus Bultmann consigns the Old Testament to the entirely negative realm of *unheilgeschichte*, a kind of shadow side to the New Testament message that God's rule is not realized in history at all, for the new creation in Christ is to be located in the supra-historical reality of existential encounter. This could be taken not just as a failure of man's understanding of God's will and way but as God's own failure, which he then remedied in Christ.

Yet even the New Testament itself could be subject to the same strictures, if viewed within a similar frame of reference. Jesus' encounter with unbelief appears to leave him helpless,[161] and for the author of 2 Peter the kingdom he proclaimed does depend in some sense and in some measure on creaturely response.[162] Maurice Wiles reminds us that Jesus' sense of the power and presence of God must be set alongside a sense of the divine absence and even impotence on the cross.[163] The sense of ongoing struggle is also inherited, as if the New Testament merely continues the Old Testament scenario of a battle against the powers of chaos. For Jesus this is represented in his fight against demons and disease, the work of a devil still alive and kicking. Arguably this was not always easy, as in the case where the blind man seemed to need more than one treatment.[164] Often (though not always) it appeared to depend on faith.[165] More generally the New Testament is aware that a final consummation is still required beyond chaos and catastrophe, even though the new order is already present in some sense in Christ. Thus the Old Testament tendency to push victory beyond history is repeated in the New Testament. Or, to put it another way, if the sovereignty of God in the Old Testament seems to require at least the further perspective of the New, then the New requires something still further. This could well be seen to imply the continuing failure of God's 'first' creation.

However it is important to recall those hints already offered which show how all such apparent frustrations of the divine activity can be incorporated within the wider perspective of God's overall sovereignty, and with no real indication that the reverse could be true. Paul's theology of history in Romans 9-11 is most illuminating in this respect: the Old Testament is indeed a history of disobedience (in which the Jews of his day persisted) but this is no frustration of the divine will, rather the means by which he is able to show a greater grace and mercy.[166] Similarly the great 'failure' of the divine mission in Christ is actually the paradoxical means of victory in which the opposition is nailed to the cross.[167] Karl Barth delights to emphasize this paradox, especially in his treatment of Judas: the starkest betrayal, the worst conceivable sin, is actually the divinely appointed means for liberation and victory.[168] All that has been said before about the priority and predetermination of divine action thus encompasses such apparent frustrations and failures within the divine will. Likewise, the overwhelming rejection of ultimate dualism already noted reorientates the scenario of struggle against chaos within the wider perspective of a creator dealing with his creatures according to his foreknowledge and predetermination. As we saw, Behemoth and Leviathan are revealed as creatures and Satan himself is but an instrument in God's hands. In New Testament terms, therefore, the 'works of the devil' may also bring glory to God and provide opportunities of grace and growth;[169] the prince of this world has no ultimate power,[170] but all will be subject to God who is all in all.[171] As far as the significance and status of the old creation is concerned, the same pattern holds true: the perspective in which its destruction is emphasized can be incorporated into the larger perspective of its re-creation, not as the failure of God followed by a new beginning but as the pre-ordained means by which the final perfection is to be brought about. Thus this world is not wasted but transformed, as a seed dies into the glories of the flower which can

be produced in no other way.[172] And there is no indication
whatsoever that we should see it the opposite way round: there
seems no more satisfactory way of incorporating the perspective of
sovereignty into a wider perspective of failure.

Love and freedom

This kind of conclusion may well be generally acknowledged as
long as it is cast in such general terms. But as such it does not
sufficiently take account of some other assumptions and
consequences of the biblical material which also bear upon the
question of divine efficacy: there are, for instance, the important
assumptions of creaturely freedom, and the consequences of that
particular mode of divine activity which is non-coercive love. Do
not such love and freedom have the effect of limiting the divine
activity? Admittedly there is the danger here of straying too far
from the 'phenomenological' approach. After all, 'freedom' does
not arise as a straightforward issue from the biblical material, it
only emerges as such—and somewhat artificially at that—under
the scrutiny of a twentieth-century mind conditioned by western
philosophy. Yet the love of God most certainly *is* a biblical datum,
and is demonstrated in Christ in a way which makes it very hard to
abstract it from the question of freedom.

As regards freedom in the Old Testament, it is assumed rather
than stated, and is most clear in the yahwist account of man's
garden experience where the possibility of disobedience is established.[173] Thereon throughout the chequered history of the Old
Testament it may be assumed at every point where God addresses
himself to man as a sinning, responsible, thinking, covenant-
partner who may respond. Thus we are invited to come and reason
together, seek and call him, forsaking our evil ways[174]—or not, as
the case may be. On the other hand it is qualified at every point
where the divine priority is assumed and declared, as when
Pharaoh's response is 'hardened'[175] or when Jeremiah's prophetic
role is predetermined.[176] A paradox is undoubtedly set up. Yet
because the primary meaning of freedom related to the historical
bondage of slavery, and to a lesser extent the existential bondage of
sin, there is no way of reading off a direct philosophical analysis of
this paradox in terms of, say, final and efficient causality. Nor is
there much indication as to how far down the created order such
freedom extends. It is possible only to speculate that God's creation
of any reality which is not merely an emanation of himself implies
some kind of relative independence, and perhaps to find support in

the evident delight he finds in the things he has made, such as in Job chapters 38-41 where we do actually find a notion of freedom ('Who has let the wild ass go free? Who has loosed the bonds of the swift ass . . .?'),[177] though naturally we cannot establish a doctrine of divine and creaturely causality on this alone!

In the New Testament freedom is more insistently existential. The Son of Man has come to set us free—from self, sin, and the works of the devil, in our minds and bodies. The manner of his coming, with humility and persuasion rather than dictatorial power, also presupposes some prior vestige of freedom in us: he comes to engage with that, as well as to bring us a new kind of freedom. In pauline language we are set free by Christ from the 'bondage of sin' (and all creation with us),[178] that is, from a state in which we cannot do the things we want, but do the thing we do not want.[179] Yet even in our 'former state' it is assumed that we are able in some measure to respond (or not to respond) with concomitant responsibility.[180] Certainly when we are in Christ we are to be treated as susceptible to discipline, education and progressive revelation, rather than as automata to be coerced and imposed on by absolute divine fiat.[181] On the other hand, as in the Old Testament, all this is also significantly qualified when Paul echoes the theme of divine priority, even in our responsiveness: as Pharaoh's heart was hardened, so were the hearts of the Jews—[182] their failure to respond lay within God's will, as well as their own—and as Jeremiah was called before he knew how to respond, so too is the Christian.[183]

It is impossible to read off a clear doctrine of freedom from the complexity of this material, certainly not *prima facie*. Nor it is immediately obvious what this entails, if anything, for the concept of divine limitation. For instance, it is often claimed that human freedom is the primary reason why not all are saved in the end even though God wills all to be saved, but divine condemnation is not represented as occurring primarily because of human freedom but because God determines it. (This, incidentally, does not necessarily imply a doctrine of double predestination whereby God wills some for damnation from all eternity, and it still does not exclude *some* sense in which God wills them to perish consequent upon abused freedom: deciding on these sorts of option, however, requires the further steps of Ch. 5., a 'turning our thoughts upon the matter' to come.) Similarly, in less ultimate matters, there is no direct suggestion that Job's suffering, or Judas' sin, or the falling tower of Siloam, are due to a creaturely freedom which limits God's purposes: they are due to God's will for his greater glory, in one way or another. Again, these may not be mutually exclusive

explanations; here too we must resist the temptation to overreach
the limited brief of this chapter. Perhaps the most that can be fairly
said at this stage is that God's chosen method of working in the
world *involves* some sense of creaturely freedom; his will *includes*
an operation of our wills (and perhaps a causal operation of wild
asses and earthquakes!); but this should be stated without prejudicing the sense, if any, in which God's purposive activity is
limited or frustrated. Drawing on late Jewish sources, Stauffer
extends this principle even to the freedom of the cosmic powers,
and summarizes it eloquently:

> The order of God's creation is *a principio* an ordering of wills . . .
> God calls the light and tremulously it obeys. He calls the stars, and
> they answer: 'We are here' . . . The same considerations explain why
> angelic figures play so surprising a role in later Judaism and in the
> NT. The angels are symbols of God's voluntarist world order! . . .
> But the God of the NT is no magician's apprentice who is dominated
> in the end by the powers he once controlled . . . The Word of God,
> which brought creation's freedom into being, retains its authority
> over the liberated powers . . . The more self-willed the freedom of
> God's creation proves to be . . . so much more certain is God's pre-
> mundane plan put into operation . . . Such is the greatness of God.
> There is no limit to his love of freedom; and yet his omnipotence
> knows no bounds.[184]

Love, by contrast, is not left to implication but consistently
declared. In the Old Testament the loving relationship between
God and his people is expressed primarily in terms of the covenant
bond: the basis of the covenant is God's choice, his election, and
this is an act of love (*ahabh*). His faithful care once the covenant is
established is also an act of loving-kindness (*chesed*). The relationship is described in the language of love between father and son,
man and wife, lover and beloved.[185] Usually the wider context of
these metaphors is the history of Israel's unfaithfulness and God's
faithfulness to them—in mercy and judgement. So D.D. Williams
comments:

> The place to look for the meaning of love is in the history of a people
> who have been called into an intimate, personal relationship with
> God, and who have begun to learn the meaning of responsibility
> with God, and who have begun to learn the meaning of respon-
> sibility and consequences of irresponsibility in that relationship.[186]

The New Testament also bases the meaning of God's love in election and the covenant, but it is specifically the election of Jesus and

the new covenant through him. He is the beloved and the chosen (*agapetos*).[187] Then in him and his action the Father's love for the Son is also demonstrated towards the world.[188] Paul develops the specific character of this love as gracious and undeserved;[189] as self-giving to suffering and death;[190] and as unfathomable in its faithfulness and resources.[191] It is well known that such a character required the unique word *agape* to distinguish it from other kinds of loves. Elsewhere in the New Testament the theme is equally important: God is love, says the author of 1 John, and we know it because of the way it was 'manifest in Jesus'.

But the specific question which concerns us is the extent to which this love constitutes a limitation to the divine purposes—and again we need to be careful to limit ourselves as far as possible to direct statements or immediate implications. In the first instance it may certainly be said that God's loving activity involves suffering and struggle for God as well as man. The Old Testament provides only a tentative glimmer of such an idea, if at all: does God 'agonize with himself' over Israel;[192] is there something of God himself in the 'suffering servant' of Deutero-Isaiah?[193] But the New Testament is much bolder. Even assuming that what is predicated of the Son cannot *simply* be predicated of the Father (which is the main point of the old Patripassian controversy) such a proviso still allows the New Testament to speak of God in Christ reconciling the world to himself through the blood of the cross, and of the Word who was God becoming flesh, to live and serve, and give his life a ransom for many. It perfectly justifies Williams's statement that God deals with humanity 'through the divine self-giving and suffering . . . The character of the divine love is shown by Jesus' obedience, his acceptance of his vocation, and his giving of himself for all'.[194]

Yet of itself this does not necessarily answer the question of divine limitations. Certainly, to suffer *could* be construed as limiting, and much contemporary theology is very quick to posit God as significantly subject to the effect the world has on him. He then has to act in the light of an agenda the world has, at least in part, put to him. This all arises because of his character of love and the personal nature of the relationship he wishes to establish with us, which constrains him to respect these effects of the world. It rules out the coercive option which merely ignores the world's effects and sets its own agenda regardless. The concept of personal freedom is thus combined with the vulnerable nature of love, and the divine limitation deduced. Williams's full quotation illustrates this well, it actually reads: 'God *has* to deal with a humanity which can learn to love and be reached by love *only* through the divine self-giving and suffering.')[195] But divine suffering could also be viewed in a rather different perspective: it could be seen as an eternally willed means of dealing with his creatures which produces a greater glory and more perfect fulfilment of his purposes than any other option.[196] For Bonhoeffer, although 'the Bible directs man to God's powerlessness and suffering', it is 'only the suffering God [who] can help', and who actually 'wins power and space in the world by his weakness'. So far from constituting a fundamental limitation divine suffering and 'weakness' open up new possibilities.[197] Thus the two perspectives are not necessarily at odds with each other, and this illustrates once again the difficulty of deriving implications directly from the biblical material without already stepping in the deep end of wider interpretation.

If we do attempt to stick more closely to the Bible's immediate statements on (or around) the matter, perhaps the most that can be said is this: God is represented as reacting to the world's events, especially of sin and rebellion, and this is attributed specifically to his love (as well as his righteousness); on the other hand it is nowhere clearly stated that this constitutes a frustration of his purposes, except in the sense that his purpose then incorporates the event in the fulfilling of some other end. Thus Jesus in Matthew 23 weeps bitterly over Jerusalem because 'they would not', but then finds that very rebellion already foreseen and accommodated purposefully within the great scenario foretold in the next chapter. Maybe the nearest we get to an explicit view of divine 'frustration' is in the matter of timing: the kingdom may be delayed on account of our disobedience, or possibly hastened on account of our obedience—and patient love is the reason.[198] But here again there is no doubt about the final outcome, and it may in any case be inappropriate to speak of the frustrations of time in connection with the eternal God to whom 'a thousand years are but as a single day'. It must therefore be emphasized again that where the New Testament appeals to divine love, it appeals more to its possibilities than to its limitations: it bears, hopes, believes and endures all things, with a breadth, length, height and depth which is invincible and incomprehensible.[199]

Present and future fulfilment

The one other undercurrent of divine sovereignty which deserves special mention has now been identified. It is the question about the 'timing' of the divine purposes. There is a persistent tension between present reality, promise, and future fulfilment. God's purposes are achieved effectively, and in relation to particular events, but they often depend on a wider perspective for the truth of this to be established. The wider perspective is normally represented in terms of the future. God will act in the future to make sense of his activity in the present and past.

In the Old Testament this may be represented in individual stories of promise and fulfilment as with Abraham and Isaac; in stories of the nation's fortunes as with the experience of exile and restoration; and in the broad sweep of cosmic history, as with the vision of Isaiah 27 which envisages a positive consummation of things 'not far from the idea of an eschatological new creation, of creation as an event embracing not only the original establishment of the world and its continued governance but its ultimate perfection as well'.[200] We have already had occasion to note that the victory of God is sometimes pushed to the end—or beyond—of history: the point being emphasized here is that the foregoing events are not therefore made redundant; they are integral to the final and wider activity.

This becomes specially apparent in the New Testament. The kingdom proclaimed by and embodied in Jesus straddles present and future in a special kind of symbiosis. The reality of the kingdom is undoubtedly present,[201] yet depends for its reality on teaching about the future: God is future judge,[202] the present reality of whose forgiveness seems to require a future dimension.[203] In pauline theology the fulfilment of God's purposes and the fullness of God's being himself is likewise present in Christ, yet future in consummation. So there is a sense in which all things (past, present and future) are united and reconciled in Christ, yet this objective truth relates to our experience of space and time as a kind of 'dissociation' of reality. God's purposes are already achieved in Christ, yet we are still 'groaning' as we wait for the completion of God's purposes.[204] The epistle to the Hebrews, too, proclaims the 'once for all' effectiveness of the sacrifice of Christ, but also his continual intercession and second appearing in the light of which we still have to strive to enter the sabbath rest.[205] Says Schillebeeckx, 'the kingdom of God is here already, but the laughing with satisfaction, that still lies in the future'.[206]

Clearly much work of clarification is going to be necessary if this tension is to be properly understood, and this would take us a long way beyond the immediate biblical data. For our purposes the questions at stake are not so much about the Hebrew and Greek views of time—whether linear or cyclical or whatever—as about the anatomy of purposive action within any sequence of time. In what sense can one event within time be abstracted from other events and considered purposive in itself? Or do all events derive their

purposiveness only from a wider context of time—and of space?
(The question could be put to both cyclical and linear views.) How
can purposes be realized in any event that has already slipped away
into the past and depends on a future yet to come? The trouble is
that these questions are neither asked nor answered in this form
from within the biblical perspective. On the other hand it can and
should be said that the biblical doctrines of promise and fulfilment,
of cosmic re-creation and the 'cosmic' Christ who somehow
brought all things past, present and future into one place and time,
do set some kind of agenda, some kind of reference with which to
operate. They imply at the very least that a wider perspective is
always needed to understand God's purposes, and that God can
and does relate the whole of time to the part, as well as the part to
the whole. This much does seem clear. All philosophical exposition
of such notions must be dealt with later, with no pretensions that it
is directly 'biblical'.

Summary and prospect

Naturally there are other major themes of the Bible relating to
divine action in the world. But so far as possible we are trying to
limit the discussion to the fact and form of the divine activity,
rather than its content; to the bare conceivability of God's purposive activity towards us in the events of the world, rather than
the specific content of those purposes; and therefore to the fact that
there is meaning in events, rather than what that meaning might be.
As such it is precisely the personal, purposive 'form' of God's
activity, its scope and efficacy, that counts as most relevant. A
category such as 'love' has been considered only insofar as it relates
to efficacy, not because it defines the content of his purposes. Other
major categories of the divine purpose and character (such as
righteousness and holiness) have not been considered directly just
because they have less to do with the form, however important
they are for the content.

Of course this distinction between form and content cannot be
sustained absolutely. There will come a time when the conceivability of the bare fact of divine meaning and purposes will require
a credible account of what those purposes are—and that job will
not, I hope, be shirked when it becomes necessary. Nevertheless as
a working distinction it will serve well enough to begin with. What
it leaves us with are demands of relevation regarding the nature,
scope and efficacy of God's activity in the world which cannot be
ignored by any Christian theology dealing with the riddles with

which we began. God acts personally, universally, with priority and sovereign efficacy; he acts in relation to particular events in which he finds ends as well as means. Certainly, as we have already insisted, such demands are not self-interpreting: they do require a conscious and deliberate 'turning our thoughts upon them' in relation to the world in which we now find ourselves. But they stand nonetheless as a primary and crucial resource and frame of reference for all further deliberation. They stand to test and stretch all the theologizing which follows.

CHAPTER THREE

The Compromises of Theology

Trying to relate these demands of revelation to the categories and experiences of the present is like re-stringing a guitar. By the time one string is adjusted, another has loosened. The moment you think all six are in harmony one of them slips out again. The various strands of present-day thought and experience which need to be strung alongside the various strands of revelation are just as difficult to handle. Compromise or paradox are therefore inevitable in some degree in any serious systematic thinking about revelation and always have been, even if they are often conceded too cheaply.

This becomes evident from even the briefest survey of the historical background to this present task. This is not an historical book, but a fleeting backwards glance will not come amiss. Two elements out of many clamour for particular attention. First, we have to acknowledge the legacy of Greek thought in the way we 'turn our minds' upon these things. It is well documented and needs only the briefest summary here. Greek philosophy, vastly generalized, used categories of understanding which abstracted from the temporary, changing, varied and imperfect world of the senses to reach an ultimate reality 'beyond' or 'through' it. And although Plato and Aristotle's heirs disagreed about the relationship between that ultimate reality and the world it transcends, there was still much common ground about transcendence: ultimate reality explained the temporary world by its timelessness; the changing world by its changelessness; the multiple world by its simplicity;

the imperfect world by its perfection . . . and so on. So from the earliest days of patristic Christian thought to the heights of refinement in medieval doctrine we find the personal God of the Bible understood also as this transcendent and eternal reality behind and beyond all things. Of course the categories of the latter do not combine well with the former: how do you reconcile a timeless, changeless, self-sufficient being with a personal, responsive Father? More difficult still—and more pertinent to this book—how do you relate a timeless, changeless being with this world of time and change? This led the early apologists to adopt the notion of 'logos', a kind of mediator between a wholly transcendent God and this passing world.[1] It led Aquinas to state the matter in bald paradox: that since God is outside the whole order of creation all creatures are really related to God but God does not really relate to his creatures.[2] It leads right in the present day complaint by such as Hartshorne and Ogden that the legacy of Greek metaphysics merely contributes logical confusion and should be frankly abandoned: it is a 'maze of inconsistencies . . . it adds the burden of puzzlement at insoluble antinomies and contradictions—as when we are asked to believe, say, that God's love is so tender that he marks the fall of a sparrow 'though all the while he remains the *noesis noeseos* of Aristotle, utterly unmoved by the motions of the world'.[3]

Yet if Greek metaphysics is hard to fine-tune with the responsiveness of the biblical God, the process metaphysics advocated as its replacement by Hartshorne is just as hard to harmonize with his initiative and sovereignty—something we shall be dealing with in more detail later. Nor, incidentally, can metaphysics be entirely dispensed with: any attempt to understand or even 'repeat' the demands of faith and revelation resonates with certain metaphysical associations and assumptions, whether we like it or not: this is even true of those Protestant theologians who claim to work purely in biblical categories. This just reiterates what was said before about the nature of revelation. The point now is simply to locate these problems of adjustment within their wider historical context; willy-nilly we inherit some of the baggage of these metaphysical debates, and cannot entirely ignore them.

We also inherit a strong emphasis on the relative independence of things, a doctrine of freedom and autonomy in the world of nature. To the extent that this is only a relative autonomy, still ultimately dependent on a first and final cause, we are directly indebted to Aristotle. But Aquinas' particular exposition of that relative autonomy, with such emphasis and sophistication (over against the prevailing determinism of Arab philosophy),[4] deserves separate mention. His celebrated doctrine of 'secondary causality' allows for the world of natural events to proceed according to its own sequence of cause and effect,[5] albeit under the deliberate purposive direction of the one final divine cause.[6] To be sure, Aquinas also insists that God acts directly on occasions, by-passing the intermediary of secondary causes, to work a miracle,[7] but that is not his normal mode of operation. On the contrary, he normally acts 'interiorily in all things', rather than apart from them.[8]

This sets the scene for the crucial development of 'modern science', which is perhaps the most significant single factor in our present categories of thinking. The world of natural events around us (and possibly, by extension, of all events—historical, social, psychological) is to be considered quite independently of any other factor. Some of the first 'modern scientists' continued to use the language of final cause ('purpose'), others rejected it altogether, but chiefly it became irrelevant. Strictly speaking it was irrelevant only to the task of science *qua* science, i.e. to the explanation of events in scientific terms. But inevitably science has come to betray in incipient imperialism: scientific explanation may easily be canvassed as the total explanation of any event, so that all other factors are altogether irrelevant. This means that the activity of God is either squeezed out of all events susceptible to scientific explanation, or else he is posited only as a first cause of the general pattern of events, with no particular involvement in any details of them.[9]

When it came to viewing theological matters through this particular lens, a whole range of positions (and reactions) emerged. The story is familiar and well-mapped. The seventeenth century produced deism, the concept of a God as 'clockmaker' who had little or no involvement in the world once he had set it going. In the eighteenth century the sphere of God's activity was located more and more in moral and religious experience where it was deemed safe from rival scientific explanations. This was a tendency developed in nineteenth-century liberal Protestantism, which also attempted to speak of God working 'in and through' the whole evolutionary process more along the lines of Aquinas' model of 'secondary causality'. Unlike Aquinas, however, this was conceived without any recourse to miracle as well, and in increasingly general terms: 'God's acts ceased to be special, particular and concerned with phenomenal reality . . . Rather, the divine activity became the continual, creative, immanent activity of God.'[10] The twentieth century has added one particularly interesting chapter in existentialist language, whereby the world of natural events is consigned cheerfully to scientific explanation and God acts only in man's existential self-understanding. It is also threatening to write a final chapter to end the whole story—by questioning the whole possibility of objective scientific enquiry anyway. Other twentieth-century theological positions have been less concerned to relate to scientific enquiry at all. The heirs of the Reformation reacted most suspiciously to the whole enterprise, and for the most part eschewed the attempt. So Barth, whose God 'accompanies' the activity of his creature, accomplishing his will directly . . . in all creaturely occurrence both great and small'[11] is in direct line to Calvin, for whom a drop of rain cannot fall without 'the express command of God':[12] neither of them really attempting an explanation of how the two levels of causality operate together.

It is clear, therefore, how this particular category of thought has had to adjust to a whole range of theological concerns. A deistic solution prevents the personal involvement of God in the details of life: hence the God of religious experience and existential self-understanding. But then this may not prove adequate to play the richer music of God's activity in nature either . . . and so on. We, of course, are now left to play the same game. We cannot pretend that scientific explanation, with all its assumptions of at least relative autonomy, has never occurred: accordingly, we must deal with it in relation to the various demands of revelation as surely as we must deal with our inherited metaphysical assumptions. The call to do this effectively, and not simply 'retreat' to re-iterating the biblical narrative has been insistent and explicit, especially since Langdon Gilkey's now celebrated plea: 'What we desperately need is a theological ontology that will put intelligible and credible meanings into our analogical categories of divine deeds'.[13]

Another way of setting the historical context—the backward glance—is to chart the effect of scientific and metaphysical factors on the historical doctrines of creation, redemption and providence. To do this is to observe the same pattern: there is an ebb and flow of meaning in these doctrines throughout their history according to the way in which particular metaphysical and scientific concerns jostle with the demands of revelation. This is not the place to undertake that kind of survey in detail, but it is worth noting the conclusions of those who have done so. Scheffczyk, for example, has done much of the work for us.[14]

He first expounds the biblical notion of God's continuous creative activity within the overall economy of salvation, noting that a distinct concept of providence is absent just because the doctrine of creation was 'an actualistic, contemporary one, and providence was simply regarded as creation continued'.[15] He grants that this perspective is never entirely lost throughout the early Fathers, the Middle Ages and in Protestant Reformed theology[16]—nor, we may add, in neo-Orthodoxy.[17] Yet in the course of these intervening centuries 'continuing creation' is not always so firmly rooted in the economy of salvation as it is in the biblical material. It is central to Scheffczyk's thesis that some tension arises between creation as integrally linked to salvation, and continuing creation as an ontological and metaphysical concern, a philosophical basis for existence. With special reference to Tertullian he asserts that:

> the practical Latin mind concentrated so largely on redemption itself that the link with Creation faded into oblivion, and Creation too became an isolated truth, studied by means of a theology with a philosophical orientation. This development . . . gradually diverted the attention of Western thought from the divine plan . . . to an ontological study of the nature and essence of Creation.[18]

Later he detects a similar feature in Augustine's thought, in his battle against both Platonic dualism and Stoic monism:

> The harmony which St Augustine established at the level of ontological thought was achieved at the expense of the scriptural concept of Creation as part of the economy of salvation. The idea of a plan for salvation, beginning with Creation, yields to metaphysical contemplation of the nature and order of the universe.[19]

The same tendency also emerges in Thomas Aquinas: the direct conservation of all things by God is logically entailed by the proposition that all things are wholly of God's making, but this conservation 'implies no new activity on God's part, but a changeless, timeless continuance of the act of creation'.[20] Thus it is distinguished from the active governance of the world (the concept of providence); it is no longer to be thought of in terms of God's deeds and saving acts through history, but rather in terms of a *priori* laws of the divine intellect. Here, philosophical concerns have clearly changed and restricted the meaning of 'creation'.

But then the tide flows back. The Reformers broadened the meaning once more by reverting to a more scriptural actualism, defining the concept of creation through the concept of redemption rather than over against it. So the ordering and governance of things (the concept of providence) tended to be subsumed once more under the concept of continuing creation, as logically it must:

> A separate doctrine of providence makes sense only where the world is seen as something ontic, possessing a relatively independent being vis-a-vis God, so that God must also set it a goal and assume its governance. But where the world is seen in actualistic terms, as a thing that God is constantly making anew, there is no reason to point a special *ratio* and *executio ordinis* . . . the act of creation constantly renewed itself does all that providence would do.[21]

On the other hand this kind of actualism has its own dangers: broadening the meaning as well as the scope of divine creativity in this way may suggest that all independence of the world is sacrificed to the sovereignty and transcendence of the divine act. Thus at least some heirs of the Reformation ebbed again: Brunner, for instance, is careful to make a distinction between creation and preservation to guard against just this danger.[22]

It is the last one hundred years, however, which have seen the most significant developments of these doctrines. Science and philosophy have both played their part. As far as recent developments in science are concerned, the theories of evolution and of relativity have had most effect, on the doctrine of creation in particular. The former lays stress on the development of the world, the continuing emergence of new forms of life; the latter may suggest that God's creative activity relates to all times, not only at one initiating point in time past. Arthur Peacocke summarizes this for us:

> Here is an important feature which the scientific perspective inevitably reintroduces into this idea of creation. It is the realization, now made explicit, that the cosmos which is sustained and held in being by God . . . is a cosmos which has always been in process of producing new emergent forms of matter—it is a *creatio continua* . . . The scientific perspective of a cosmos in development introduces a dynamic element in our understanding of God's relation to the cosmos which was, even if obscured, always implicit in the Hebrew conception of a 'living God', dynamic in action. If time itself is part of the created cosmos, there seems at first to be no more difficulty in regarding God as having an innovative relationship to the cosmos at all times than in postulating such a relationship only at some posited 'zero' time.[23]

In short, the meaning of creation-providence has more or less reverted again to a kind of 'scriptural actualism', this time under 'scientific' pressure. I.G. Barbour puts it plainly:

> . . . if we take seriously the new picture of nature, it would be desirable to merge the traditional doctrines of creation and providence into a doctrine of *continuing creation*.[24]

Of this century's philosophical developments, existentialism has had a similar effect—albeit from a very different starting point. For the existentialist the question of creation is not concerned with the causal origins of the world, then or now, but what it means to be a creature, and how the belief that we are created affects our self-understanding and our understanding of the world.[25] The answer given is that of dynamic dependence, that we are what God 'lets be' at any time and at all times; so it follows that for the existentialist too 'no sharp distinction can be made between creation and providence, for we did not tie creation to a moment of time at the beginning, but rather interpreted the doctrine of creation as meaning the dependence of the beings at all times on Being that lets them be'.[26] Macquarrie, whose comment this is, goes on therefore to echo the judgement Scheffczyk made about the Reformers. He states:

> Only if creation is thought of as an event in the past is it necessary to bring forward a distinct doctrine of providence to establish God's continuing interest in his world and to indicate that he is not a kind of absentee landlord who set things going long ago and now leaves the world to its own devices. In the present system, the assertion of God's providence is just another way of asserting his constant creating and sustaining energy.[27]

We may say, therefore, that scientific insight into the nature of the world, and existentialist insight into its meaning, have both tended to recall attention to the universal scope and actualistic meaning of creation, subsuming providence within it.

As far as the doctrine of redemption is concerned it has tended to be caught up in the same sort of ebb and flow. Insofar as God's continuing creative activity is conceived as one with his plan of salvation, then redemption too has come to be conceived as universal in scope—which likewise represents a properly biblical understanding of the divine activity (though it is true that Augustine and Calvin have at times fuelled a significant party of dissent, with their doctrine of double predestination). In relation to the specific question of how redemption is *constituted*, however, its change in meaning has been more marked. Universal possibilities of redemption have been traditionally understood as constituted by a special activity of God in particular events (the history of Israel and, crucially, in Christ), but recently even this activity has been universalized. Redemption is held to be constituted universally in all experience, not particularly in Christ. Christ is only a particular picture of a universal truth. This shift in emphasis has arisen recently, and controversially. It too is made under the influence of both scientific and existentialist insights, amongst others: the same reasons which indicate that creation is not constituted only at some particular time and space in the past are said to apply to redemption. Thus Maurice Wiles suggests:

> . . . the truth of that doctrine [redemption] would stand out more clearly if it were not tied to one particular act or life differing in kind

from the rest of the series of human acts and lives . . . The heart of the suggestion, therefore, that I want to put forward . . . is that traditional christology rests on a mistake in this sense. It arose because it was not unnaturally, yet nonetheless mistakenly, felt that the full divine character of redemption in Christ could only be maintained if the person and act of the redeemer were understood to be divine in a direct and special sense. In the parallel cases of creation and fall our forefathers had to learn . . . that what they thought was a logically necessary link between the theological assertion and particular occurrences in history was not as logically necessary as they thought it to be. Are we perhaps at the equivalent . . . moment of learning the same truth about the doctrine of redemption?[28]

And Schubert Ogden makes the same basic contention from within an explicitly existentialist framework:

Every event is constitutive of man's possibility, because, while it is in no way his eternal possession, it is given to him at least implicitly in every event that is constitutive of his existence.[29]

Obviously such assertions connect closely with current doubts about the possibility of incarnational language (Wiles' essay, quoted above, is actually about the problem of Christology). They have even closer links with the longstanding theological difficulty in formulating atonement theories, for the possibility of universal redemption being constituted by the particular events of the life, death and resurrection of Jesus is intelligible only if some conception of how this is effected can be offered—a notoriously difficult enterprise!

Thus it is apparent how the cross-tides of philosophical, scientific and theological concerns have tossed and turned these doctrines, with little sign as yet that they will come to rest, and these last two mentioned theologians have brought us right up to date. But having charted this sea in a very general way, we must now look much more closely at how such as Wiles and Ogden trawl it with the net of our particular question—not so much the secondary question of the full-blown doctrines of creation and redemption, but our primary question which lies behind both: how can and should we conceive God acting at all? Can he act in specific events for us? In all—or only some? Both Wiles and Ogden do in fact address themselves to the question in these terms, and along with others from the English-speaking world they have produced a series of common answers which deserve serious attention—not least since these answers constitute one of the more radical and increasingly popular, though in my view unwarranted, compromises of theology.

Maurice Wiles

In *The Remaking of Christian Doctrine* Maurice Wiles begins his discussion of the relationship between God and the world from two starting points:[30] the sense of dependence, of radical contingency, on a transcendent reality—a 'co-determinant reality to which we trace our awareness of the ultimate dependence of ourselves and of all that is'—[31]and the sense of ultimate meaning and purpose. They are both, of course, part of those riddles of experience with which we began.

So far as the first is concerned, because it is experienced as true of the world all the time, the relationship of dependence is held to be a general one, uniformly true of all things. The second is more problematic: experience of ultimate purpose and meaning appears to relate differently to different particular occasions, implying a particular or 'special' activity of the divine will. Of course, the experience of dependence and of ultimate purpose are both particular in the sense that we are finite and particular experiencing subjects; but while this still allows the move from a particular experience of dependence to a notion of universal and general dependence, it is less clear in the case of the particular experience of *purpose*. It is freely admitted that a move from a particular experience of purpose in a particular event to a notion of universal and uniform divine purposive activity is not *logically* necessary (since the scientific account of events is not logically exhausted by regularities and uniformities); but it is also resisted by a powerful tradition of religious experience which does clearly speak of certain events as special acts of God.

Nevertheless, Wiles insists that the move should still be made, and he does so on the following grounds.[32] In the first instance, regarding events in the natural world, he describes the process by which the 'God of the gaps' is 'edged further and further out of the world',[33] and therefore, though not logically bound to regularities and uniformity, *is* thus bound in terms of what we are justified in saying of God according to his (Wiles') predetermined criteria of economy and coherence. Here the pressures of the so-called scientific world-view is obvious and admitted. God's activity is frankly reconceived in line with it. More positively, he also invokes 'religious' reasons for the same kind of reconception: he aligns himself with Bultmann in his insistence that God's action must be truly transcendent if it is not to be merely mythological, and therefore:

> The idea of unworldliness and transcendence of the divine action is only preserved when such action is represented not as something that takes place *between* worldly occurrences, but rather as something

that takes in them, so that the closed continuum of worldly events that presents itself to the objectifying eye remains untouched. God's act is hidden to every eye but that of faith.[34]

In the context of this kind of view, where God's action is hidden in all things, and where all things are apparently subject to regular, uniform and general laws, there seems little incentive to hold to a view of special divine (purposive) action.

Then as regards human claims nonetheless to *experience* that special divine action, Wiles points out they are so frequent that:

> If it were to be understood as always implying special divine causation (however possible theoretically that may be), the occurrences of such special divine activity would have to be so numerous as to make nonsense of our normal understanding of the relative independence of causation within the world.[35]

Furthermore, serious and sustained reflection on such experiences (even by the religious themselves) tends to re-assess their value and places more weight on the work of God in 'ordinary' occurrences of life—in short, on a general and uniform understanding of God's activity. We know what he means: once we proudly paraded a special religious experience or significant coincidence for all to wonder at; now, with hindsight, we are more concerned to present the 'mature' faith which 'sees God everywhere'.

But perhaps more crucially, Wiles believes it is still possible to do justice to these 'special' experiences by propounding a fundamental reinterpretation of their true meaning: he simply offers an alternative account of them which does not entail the notion of special divine activity. This holds true both for present experiences of the believer and for past events held by the church at large to be normative special acts of God, and it is obviously a great advantage to Wiles to offer some kind of account of these, rather than simply to write off so much tradition and experience. He claims that such events, and the experience of them, need not reflect a different action of God so much as a different response to God: there is no special activity of God, rather a diversity of openness and response to his uniform activity (which response, in so far as it is appropriate, provides a 'focus' for calling forth other responses); it mirrors the purpose of God, makes it visible, even 'reproduces' it.[36] Speaking of those who are 'more fully responsive to the divine action than others', Wiles says, 'since that quality of life in them . . . to which . . . others will respond was itself grounded in responsiveness to the divine action, we may rightly speak of the events of their lives as acts of God in a special sense'.[37]

This is an important and consistent theme: the sense in which we speak of God's special action in particular events depends on creaturely responsiveness rather than on any fundamental difference in the divine activity and its relation to the creation. It is most explicit in Wiles' essay 'Religious Authority and Divine Action', where it is claimed that:

> In calling them special acts of God we would not be implying that there was any fundamental difference in the relation of the divine action to the particular worldly occurrences of their situation; we would be referring to the depth of response and the creative potential for eliciting further response from others embodied in those particular lives or those particular events.[38]

In his later book, *Faith and the Mystery of God*, Wiles develops the same basic position, though with more attention to the nature of religious language.[39] To talk of God's 'action' is to use a symbol, namely that which creates as well as discloses reality. Thus when certain occurrences in human history are symbolically *seen as* God's acts, this constitutes 'the emergence of a new reality', these events then become the 'paradigms by which our own ideals are formed and our own acting inspired'.[40] This new reality 'is' (symbolically) God's action. He acts 'not by the manipulation of events but by making it possible for men and women to glimpse his purposes of love and be inspired'.[41] God's purpose, his 'aims and motives', become his action in so far as they are grasped and acted upon. It is divine action by 'final' causality rather than efficient causality, by providing the lure of a goal rather than the mechanical impetus towards it. (It seems that any talk of God's efficient causality causes Wiles 'anxiety', because of the danger of manipulation.)[42]

So far as the event of Christ is concerned all this holds true to a supreme degree:[43] Christ exemplifies above all the one who grasped and responded to God's purposes. As such he becomes the supreme act of God in history. Elsewhere Wiles offers plausible explanations as to why this event has in fact attracted a far more traditional interpretation based, he submits, on the inevitable pressures of an outmoded and untenable world-view.[44] Thus he systematically bolsters the case for abandoning the traditional account (in terms of special divine activity) in favour of this alternative account (in terms of creaturely response, and in this instance that of Christ himself)

To recapitulate: Wiles traces the relationship of God and the world in two ways, both of which are uniform relations. The first is that God is the transcendent ground of all that is (the first starting point). This is a uniform relationship, a relation of creator to creature which remains and continues equally throughout all creation all the time. It is a doctrine of creation which is also a doctrine of the continuing sustaining power of God. The other way of describing God's activity, in terms of purpose—a doctrine of redemption—is also best understood as uniform. The purposive activity of God relates to all events, is within all occurrences equally as a common factor 'X'; it is a transcendent action of God in relation to worldly events which is 'something hidden with all wordly occurrences'. In the scope of this affirmation Wiles goes even further than Bultmann in that he conceives it as absolute and universal, admitting of no exceptions, not even the 'Christ event'. (To assert otherwise would be to point to an 'additional causal factor' and so to risk 'objectifying God' in the finite, 'mythological' terms of this-worldly agency.)[45] Thus all appeal to special divine activity is misleading; it should rather be understood as special creaturely activity, the creatures' responsiveness to the 'final causality' of the divine 'aims and motives' for them. God himself does not relate differently to them except in and through their various responses to him. As we shall see, Wiles is not alone in painting this kind of picture; others have elaborated much the same relationship between God and the world, and in greater detail. But Wiles is a particularly lucid spokesman to begin with, writing as he does with such economy and clarity, and invites at least a preliminary response in his own terms.

In the first place it must be said that there is much which cannot and need not be disputed. There is no reason to question the uniformity of the world's dependence on God. As far as God's creative, sustaining activity is concerned our experience would not 'seem to justify' (to use Wiles' own phrase) anything other than a uniform relationship which could adequately be expressed in general terms. Everything *is* presumably dependent on the 'transcendent ground of being' in the same way. Nor should we dispute the 'hiddenness' and transcendence of God's redemptive, purposive activity. A truly transcendent God cannot act within the world as one agent amongst others *tout simple*: he is not an 'additional causal factor' in some occurrences of the sort which is detectable by empiricist tools. The religious grounds for asserting this are indeed as powerful (and properly so) as the general pressure of scientific method and discovery. We may also agree with Wiles' concern that God should not be conceived as acting 'manipulatively' to bring about his purposes, if by manipulation he means leaving no freedom whatsoever to the creation.

So far so good. But the conclusions and implications drawn from these unexceptionable premises are less convincing. Wiles has argued that divine activity is of a different, transcendent order, its relation to worldly occurrences is therefore hidden, and our particular experience of it should not deceive us into limiting it to particular events; rather, since on reflection we extend the range of this experience to all events, we should posit the same divine activity in all things. This move is not unreasonable. But it is accompanied by a more questionable assumption, at least in his earlier writings, viz. that this universal activity is always the same sort of activity. The assumption seems to be that transcendent activity of will and purpose, by virtue of being transcendent and of a different 'hidden' order, must be uniform or 'simple' in its basic structure (or at least we are only justified in talking of it as 'simple'). The implication is therefore that the hidden factor 'X', a quasi-causal but non-empirical factor of God's activity, is uniform, presumably because inaccessible to normal tools of empirical analysis.

We have already seen the assumption, in various forms, in the passages cited previously. In *The Remaking of Christian Doctrine*, for example, 'experience . . . of divine providence is so frequent' that, 'if it were to be understood as always implying special divine causation . . . the occurrences of such special divine activity would have to be so numerous as to make nonsense of our normal understanding of the relative independence of causation within the world'.[46] And of course it would—*but* only if the action of 'special' divine causation is taken to mean something additional to the transcendent activity of God in all events. If on the other hand such transcendent activity is in itself diversely structured, then there seems no reason at all why numerous instances of 'special providence' should make nonsense of anything.

It occurs in other forms in Wiles' 'alternative account' of the experience of special activity. Because the transcendent nature of the divine activity compromises the validity of our experience of it, it seems more likely, to Wiles, that the diversity lies in our openness to and perception of it. So in 'Religious Authority and Divine Action' he states, as already quoted: 'In calling them special acts of God we would not be implying that there was any fundamental difference in the relation of the divine action to the particular worldly occurrences of their situation; we would be referring to the depth of response'.[47] The same assumption has been made: the diversity cannot be in the activity, so it is put in the response of the creature.

Now at the simple epistemological level this would be a curious assumption, to say the least. For if, as Wiles himself presupposes, we are in some way experiencing the transcendent then its transcendent nature cannot be wholly opaque to our experience, even though opaque to strict empirical analysis. In that case there seems to be no real justification for the assumption that we can only talk about it as simple undifferentiated unity. To be sure, this does little more than raise a question. Some positive grounds for affirming differentiation within the transcendent activity of God must be found, along with some intelligible way of conceiving the diversity. But these, I believe, can and will be provided.

In the meantime the cost at the theological level must also be noted. If God's purposive activity for the world is uniform and undifferentiated (except through particular creaturely response) then it is liable to be impersonal, amoral, and relatively impotent — a conclusion which is obviously not easily squared with our initial demands of revelation. It is impersonal to the extent that the purpose itself is undifferentiated in relation to a world of diverse particulars. As such the purpose relates only generally and externally to the world so that each particular creature or occurrence within the world serves the purpose 'outside itself', and the purpose has no internal relation and meaning specifically for each particular in its own particularity. The relationship of the particular to the purpose of God is as cog to machine or citizen to law. The analogies are instantly revealing: it is an impersonal relationship; 'God' is not acting personally in relation to these particulars, for there is no differentiation in the purpose specifically for them in their particularity—just as the law of fixed penalty makes no provision for the individuality of each law-breaker.

Wiles' alternative account of special divine activity in terms of human response is susceptible to the same charge. The uniform activity of God is conceived as specially 'present' as it is made visible by human response. But the concept he uses is 'focusing' and 'embodiment',[48] i.e. the activity is already there (and everywhere) like a continual pressure in all events, made visible only when the human response embodies it. It is like dropping a log into a river and perceiving its motion in relation to a rock. Those who go with the divine tide reveal its motion in relation to those who resist it. But the tide is there in any case; it does not act in any different way. It is therefore in an impersonal relationship to the particular.[49]

God's purpose is liable to be amoral for much the same reason. If there is no differentiation of the divine purpose in relation to the moral diversity of particular creatures and events within the world, then it is hard to see how moral diversity is being properly recognized. It would appear to make of God's purpose something indifferent to morality.[50]

Most marked of all, it is relatively impotent. There is an obvious and basic sense in which Wiles' God appears to be severely hampered: if he can only be said to act specifically in and through his creatures' responsiveness then both the scope and efficacy of that action is strictly limited. There is also precious little initiative. Naturally Wiles has implied something more: God's 'aims and motives', which would presumably exist prior to and independently from any given response, do exercise some sort of influence as final causality. When a goal is presented to a creature a divine movement (even initiative?) has taken place. Yet it is still a reduced concept of effective action, arguably inferior even to human interpersonal action when we do more than present goals to each other.

Furthermore, Wiles' approach requires much more elucidation if it is not going to fall foul of its own set of conceptual problems. Just how does God present a goal to his creatures in a non-empirical way? At what point does the activity of presenting a goal to a creature imply after all some 'efficient' causation? Put another way, at what point does 'presenting a goal' for a sentient creature become as manipulative and coercive as Wiles fears it is for any kind of efficient causation? He uses the analogy of personal relationship to support his view, but does not develop it. In any case he does not seem to acknowledge that there is a role for efficient causation in even the healthiest and least manipulative human relations: we make things happen in the events surrounding each other's lives, as a legitimate and necessary part of relating to them, and so we are acting towards them not just by presenting the person with goals. This implies yet another question: how does God influence those natural events which are therefore an inseparable ingredient in interpersonal interaction? How does he present a goal to non-sentient creatures? These are not all unanswerable, and Wiles mentions that the 'symbol' of divine activity has to be understood in various senses to cope with such different spheres of divine activity.[51] But in relation to these kinds of questions he does not take the matter further (not necessarily a criticism of such an economical writer, but the job still needs to be done).

It is in the sphere of final causation that we also see how Wiles attempts to meet objections about the impersonality and amorality of his God, but thereby underlines the problem of impotence all the more. In his earlier writings Wiles was always concerned to affirm the personal nature of God, even while the scheme of his uniform relationship with the world seemed to deny it. More recently he has reformulated (or clarified) his position to remedy the inconsistency: the uniformity, it appears, lies only in the mode of causality (namely as final causality), rather than in the content of the divine purpose. Thus God does have differentiated 'aims and motives' for his various creatures, and Wiles clearly concedes, 'I think that what I have said before can and should be extended to speak of particular divine purposes for individuals in their specific situations.'[52] The trouble is, those aims and motives of final causality still remain fundamentally frustrated without creaturely response, and as such they cannot be determinative of any *'particular* happenings within the drama'.[53] And whilst it is indeed a great relief to know that God does after all regard you and me in our individuality and particularly—even better, that he has purposes for us as such—it becomes all the more crushing to discover that he can only 'regard' us and 'offer' us the aims, not execute them nor 'make things happen' to help bring them to fruition (at least not without our help).

Of course this is not necessarily a criticism for those who, like Wiles, value creaturely freedom highly, and who appeal to a particular notion of divine love to back this 'relative impotence'. More of that anon. Let it simply be said now that by yielding so much to the pressures of 'scientific' causality and creaturely freedom Wiles has reconceived divine action in such a way that, at the very least, it brings divine sovereignty and initiative into question. Talking of divine action exclusively in terms of final causality (the natural expedient for such pressures) reinforces the effect—unless the *modus operandi* of that causality is far more carefully specified. Thus a serious compromise of two of the most crucial 'demands of revelation' is clearly in the air, and with them, of course, a compromise (or reconception) of the fundamental doctrines of Christology and soteriology: for if God's 'act' in and through Christ is conceived primarily as dependent on perfect creaturely response, rather than the sovereign initiative of God, then we are presumably back in the Pelagian business of saving ourselves. The guitar is being restrung, but already sounding badly out-of-tune.

More generally, however, we should be grateful to Wiles for focusing the issues so clearly. A three-fold dilemma arises from his writings: either God's purposive activity is the same in relation to every particular event, in which case it is hard to see how it can be other than amoral; or it stands beyond the world as a generality making no pretence to relate internally to particulars, in which case it seems inevitably impersonal; or it has moral and specific, personal, content as final cause, but no account is given of its status and capacity as efficient cause. Either God's will is the same for everything, willing good and evil alike; or he has no *will* as such but is as impersonal as the law of gravity; or his will appears inefficient. It seems that Wiles steered dangerously close to the two former before opting for the latter. The question is, is there not some other option altogether?

Schubert Ogden

If we are going to be fair to the kind of option Wiles takes then some of its other exponents must also be considered. Schubert Ogden is one such. He has been similarly concerned to elucidate the relationship between God and the world, in particular what sense it makes to say 'God acts in history'.[54] And, with Wiles, he follows the general drift of Bultmann's demythologizing programme. Mythological language 'objectifies' i.e. it represents God and his action 'in terms of space, time, causality, and substance';[55] as such it is theologically inadequate (God would be 'but one more item within the world')[56] and, of course, open to scientific criticism. So Ogden, like Wiles, is anxious to represent God's activity as 'hidden', transcendent in some sense.

However, Ogden's analysis of the nature of this transcendent relationship has been carried out in more detail, and this is made possible by his heavy dependence on Charles Hartshorne's metaphysics (Wiles, incidentally, is suspicious precisely of such detail).[57] He first criticizes Bultmann on two counts, namely that his 'fragmentary and undeveloped' analogy between divine and human action is 'one-sided' in favour of the human (and therefore in danger of reductionism),[58] and that he fails to carry through his demythologizing programme consistently.[59] Then he turns to Hartshorne for help. Hartshorne, he claims, offers a consistent doctrine of analogy which will both meet the challenge of reductionism and enable the reinterpretation to be carried through the whole range of Christian doctrine without exception.[60] The analogy is the 'strict' analogy of God to the human self, though this is relaxed somewhat in his later writings. It is therefore an *analogia entis* in which becoming as well as being must have a place, in which subject as well as object, relativity as well as absoluteness, must all be included. The category of freedom is paramount throughout the analogy—a 'key concept' (deriving, one suspects, as much from the concerns of existentialism as from process metaphysics as such):

> Process metaphysics is the metaphysics of freedom, which insists on the application of its key concept to literally everything that can be actual at all, from the least particle of so-called physical matter to . . . God.[61]

Further, since a doctrine of God should include all the ultimate categories, the analogy is given fuller metaphysical expression in a series of polar pairs:[62] the divine reality is thus a dipolar reality described variously as absolute/relative, object/subject, being/becoming, abstract/concrete, necessary/contingent, actual/potential. This dipolar concept of God is designed not only to 'make up' the deficiencies of Bultmann's doctrine of analogy but also to provide a metaphysical rationale for overcoming the bald contradictions of classical theism in its account of God's relationship to the world (Ogden's chief complaint against Aquinas being that his absolute and necessary God may be really related to the world, without the world being related to God—whereas a dipolar God can 'absorb' a real relationship in its relative pole).[63]

As this concept of God is applied specifically to God's action in the world we begin to see how the analogy works. God relates to the world as the 'supremely relative self'. As such he constitutes himself as others do, simply in virtue of relating to other objects or selves. This indeed is the very meaning of 'action':

> . . . human action is . . . the action whereby the self as such is constituted. Behind all its public acts of word and deed there are the self's own private purposes or projects, which are themselves matters of action or decision. Indeed, it is only because the self first acts to constitute itself, to respond to its world, and to decide its own inner being that it 'acts' at all . . . all its outer acts of word and deed are but ways of expressing and implementing the inner decisions whereby it constitutes itself as a self.[64]

As such, when God is considered in relation to the events of this world, it is apparent how God's action may be consistently conceived in a transcendent mode: just as 'our own inner decisions as selves are not simply identical with any of our outer acts of word and deed, but rather transcend or lie behind them',[65] so by analogy God's self-constituting 'action' lies behind worldly events, not to be simply identified with them in a mythological 'objectified' way, nor reduced to a mere 'human attitude or perspective'.

It is also apparent how, indirectly, every particular historical event can nonetheless be spoken of as 'being' God's act. A further analogy helps illuminate this, namely that of our own relationship to our bodies. Just as every bodily movement is, in a sense, our activity (in spite of a certain relative independence of our bodies) as well as being transcended by us, so every worldly occurrence is God's activity (in spite of a certain relative independence) as well as being transcended by God.[66] Thus it is clear that nothing whatsoever lies outside the compass of God's activity in this most general sense; it is part of the definition of God as the unsurpassable self that he relates to, and is constituted by, all events.

However, as with Wiles, this general relation to all things is not the whole story. For within the meaning of that relative independence of worldly events lies the creature's own responsiveness and, more particularly, man's special capacity to grasp meaning—the meaning of his own existence and the divine relation to him.[67] And in so far as the creature perceives and responds to that meaning, and gives expression to it in speech and action, he 're-presents' (Ogden's word) the divine action. In this case man's action 'is' God's action in a special way. Such actions are peculiarly expressive of God's transcendent activity, just as some human acts are peculiarly expressive of their own 'transcendent' or 'inner' selves. Ogden's conclusion, then, is notably similar to Wiles'—in his attempt to do justice to the experience of 'special action':

> what is meant when we say that *God* acts in history is primarily that there are certain distinctively *human* words and deeds in which his characteristic action . . . is appropriately re-presented or revealed.[68]

The picture is, perhaps, of clear glass which refracts more light than frosty glass: what seems like the special activity of the light actually depends on the state of the glass.

As far as the 'Christ event' is concerned, Ogden is true to his intention of carrying through his demythologizing consistently. The analogy holds: whereas Bultmann felt compelled to represent it as a fundamentally different type of divine activity, Ogden represents it simply in terms of special 'transparency': it is 'simply a transparent means of representing a certain possibility for understanding [all] human existence'.[69] That is to say, the 'Christ event' is peculiarly expressive of the transcendent self of God (and so a special action of God) primarily in virtue of the special responsiveness of Christ—the state of the glass. Thus even here it seems as true to say that human action (including Christ's as human) determines divine possibilities in specific matters, as that divine action determines human possibilities in general matters.

The meaning and scope of the relationship between this divine and human action is developed by Ogden in various ways. In his later writing it is located especially within the traditional doctrines of creation, redemption and salvation. Because freedom (as self-creation) is a fundamental category of his metaphysics 'nothing whatsoever, not even God, can wholly determine the being of something else',[70] and therefore God's prior creative action can set only minimal constraints on creaturely freedom, namely 'such that were the limits other than they are the ratio of opportunity for good to risk of evil would be unfavourable'.[71] Hence that work of creation which is solely God's work is confined to 'the fact that there is some world for us and our fellow creatures to exist and to act in' and the 'relatively fixed and stable order to the world which allows for the possibility of more good than evil being realized through the exercise of our creaturely freedom'.[72] By contrast the 'details' and 'local orders' of the world (i.e. societies, culture) are established by the creatures themselves, in their response to the saving, 'emancipating', will of God.

As far as redemption is concerned, this is conceived as a particular mode of that necessary divine relatedness to things. Even God is determined by others in some sense, for 'to be actual at all is to be really, internally related to other things' in the sense that they are 'being synthesized into one's own actuality'.[73] Redemption is this synthesis, specifically of transient, sinful creatures into the ever-lasting perfection of God, giving them meaning they could not have on their own.[74] It is an 'acceptance of things into himself'; and an 'embracing of all things into his own everlasting life'.[75] However here too that which belongs solely to God is strictly limited: it is precisely and only the acceptance. Because his final intention is the fullest possible *self*-realization of each creature (which is the ultimate meaning of salvation and emancipation), God 'does nothing that any creature does or even can do for itself'.[76]

But Ogden has also developed a more detailed account of the mode of the divine action, that is, the actual nature of divine causality. Here he says more than Wiles and, as elsewhere, draws heavily on Hartshorne. As we have seen, Hartshorne's metaphysic requires that we conceive of the divine reality in polar pairs, one of which is concrete/abstract, another potential/actual. And on the basis of the *analogia entis* with which he is operating (viz. the human self), the concrete reality of God is potential, open to the future. However, as the divine reality, there is also an abstract pole: God is, abstractly, the actuality of past and present. Thus God 'sums up' the past and present in his abstract pole, and con-cretely is the potential one who faces the future as the experiencing subject of that past-present actuality.[77] As such God is clearly 'effect', and it is concretely that he is such: everything that happens is experienced by God concretely and makes him what he is. The sense in which he is 'cause', however, is more complex. In so far as God is, abstractly, a resource, a fund of past-present reality, then he constitutes the conditions within which future possibilities may become actual: one might say that he 'sets' the conditions for all possibilities—expounded above as Ogden's doctrine of creation. This is a primary conception of how God acts in process thought: God acts by 'presenting to the creatures the unity, the richness and the limits of possibility as ordered by his vision'.[78] This is efficient causation of a sort in so far as this resource of reality is a necessary condition for bringing other things about because they have to 'take account' of him.[79] It is also a kind of final causation in that this abstract actuality of past-present, that absolute 'summing up' of things which is God, provides meaning and direction to any further occurrence.

A distinction also needs to be made between the eternal possibilities that God sets, and the specific possibilities of time and space. Because the concrete contemporary reality of God is being constituted (and changed) by the contingencies of the world, then the specific possibilities set by God also change through time and space; the 'fund of reality' is itself a changing reality, and therefore sets new and changing possibilities at each particular occasion in time and space. The picture is of a God who, being the summing up of what has previously happened, uniquely constituted up to any given moment, is a 'special' cause in any given time and space in a way that eternal possibilities cannot be. Thus 'We must distinguish between "pure" or eternal possibilities, and spatio-temporally localized possibilities . . . what is possible here and now depends upon what has previously happened, including the arbitrary decisions previously made'.[80] This is particularly important: it appears to provide a way of conceiving differentiated divine activity (special action) in relation to particular spatio-temporal events, namely by positing a changed God as the source of ever changing possibilities. We have already seen how this is reflected in Ogden's doctrines of creation and salvation, where the 'details' and 'local orders' of creaturely creativity are particular, contingent, and mutable constituents within the overall possibilities of the divine structure. It also provides a more theocentric basis to his overall account of special divine action which, as we have seen, might otherwise collapse into creaturely response and nothing else.

At first sight all this is an elaboration of how God acts which sounds promising. The premises of a scientific world-view and the requirements of existentialist philosophy are fused in a comprehensive metaphysic, illumined by analogy. It enables Ogden and others to conceive God's activity transcending all events, and hidden within them, but also provides some sort of causal account of specific as well as general divine action: 'process theology understands better than most how God can act individually and so novelly to each particular occasion'.[81]

There are, naturally, difficulties, and qualifications of the basic analogy need to be made. For instance, it may be thought that God's 'inner', private self which is 'behind' his public acts of the world's events implies a mind-body dualism of the sort which would be hard to maintain in the present philosophical climate.[82] In fact the relationship between mind and body in process views is probably more sophisticated than straightforward Cartesian dualism, but it remains problematic (though it would be churlish to quibble in too much detail: all our talk of God struggles with its analogies at some point!). There is also a range of problems, falling for the most part beyond the scope of this discussion, concerning the internal coherence of Hartshorne's metaphysic and logic; these relate to his dipolar conception of God in particular.[83] What must concern us most, however, is the point at which these problems impinge on theological matters. For in spite of, and in some cases because of, the elaboration, many of the fundamental questions about the efficacy, initiative, and sovereignty of the divine action remain—especially in relation to particular occurrences.

The root of the problem is the degree to which Ogden's God has to be passive. The tendency is obvious in so far as God depends on creaturely response to 'represent' him. But it is also betrayed by the specific elaboration of special causality explained above. If God 'causes' by setting a certain range of possibilities for creaturely response then he would seem to cause as a 'condition' is cause: that is, he causes by being 'past', 'prior', or 'static' in relation to us, and therefore irremediably passive in relation to particulars—rather as rough ground 'causes' a bowl to deflect from its course, or heavy atmosphere 'causes' a cricket ball to swing in the air. Even granted that God is setting new possibilities for each new ball (via his own prior response to previous occurrences), it is still a passive stance to the extent that his own resources for setting these possibilities depend to a considerable extent on prior creaturely activity which has constituted him previously.

One way in which this charge may be rebutted is through Hartshorne's conception of the divine 'summing up' of the data it receives from the world. This is a strong conception: God does not just 'receive' the events of the world into his being, but 'organizes' them, in Ogden's words 'synthesizes them, into a new unity'.[84] This must be so, of course, in so far as the divine reality is not simply identical with 'all that is and has been' but has an abstract identity of its own (rescuing it from simple pantheism); it is a certain (divine) way of viewing all that is and has been. Hartshorne even describes this in terms of 'ignored' events:[85] as certain events occur they are ignored (or 'forgotten'), and therefore excluded from the divine actuality or 'memory'. Thus there is something of a transformation of reality as it enters the divine reality,[86] and by so ordering this to specifically set the conditions for future possibilities God's causality could be conceived in a far more active way. Hartshorne is, at times, very concerned to assert God's freedom to act in this way:

> I should argue that God is self-moved and the chief agent of change in existence, in that the total antecedent condition of his present action, and of all other present action, is contained in his own antecedent being.[87]

The trouble is, it is not easy to see how this admirable doctrine of divine freedom is squared with the overall conception of a God who is concretely constituted by creaturely response. The symmetry of the dipolar conception of God does not seem to allow it. If God changes himself (is 'self-moved')[88] this presumably could not occur within the abstract actuality of God which is past and immutable.[89] The only other possibility is that the constitutive contents of divine knowledge are transformed as they enter the divine reality. However, such a transformation would then have to occur within the concrete pole which appears to have been passive within the polar balance (the 'receiving' face of God). Thus the polar balance is upset and the internal coherence of the edifice flawed. God's activity either has to be 'abstract', or inconsistent with the metaphysic which undergirds it. Colin Gunton has made substantially this criticism, and very forcefully. Ogden's own reply, chiefly on behalf of Hartshorne, properly points to Hartshorne's references to the freedom of God to change himself, but without really meeting the point about the polar balance.[90] Furthermore, even supposing the dipolar concept could sustain such concrete divine initiative, it is still arguable that God is, so to speak, always one step behind, at least with regard to specific action: 'God changes us by changing himself in response to our previous responses to him, and to the divine response to our response we subsequently respond'.[91] So be it, for the sake of argument, but it must still be noted that God is required to undertake this transformation of himself out of the resource of what has previously constituted him, namely creaturely self-creation over which he has no specific control. The only other resource which belongs solely to God is that general structure of universal possibilities which belongs timelessly to his abstract identity, but which, as already indicated, do not and cannot relate specifically to particular occurrences. As regards such particular occasions, and so as regards the special action of God in relation to them, there appears therefore to be an infinite regress of passivity, making it hard to find purchase for any idea of initiative. In relation to particulars God has perforce to wait on us and react to us.

Thus, as with Wiles' approach, this tendency to passivity high-lights some serious theological deficiencies. The spectre of Pelagianism hovers close at hand. More generally, the very person-hood of God is under threat, for the question inevitably arises as to whether the God who is concretely patient to such an extent, who appears to act by passive influence, is fully personal. The most appropriate analogies, paradoxically, still resist the language of personhood: the surface may change under the impact of bowls, and so set new conditions (specifically determined by that impact, accor-ding to a *generally* willed structure of eternal possibilities), but we do not readily attribute specific will, intentionality and purpose in relation to that event, especially not with regard to particular occasions. It is paradoxical, of course, because Ogden begins his theological enterprise with a 'strict analogy to the human self'.

Supposing, however, we stay with Ogden and do attribute per-sonal categories to the divine reality,[92] a related set of theologically motivated questions emerge, which may take us neatly past one aspect of Wiles' dilemma of God's relationship to evil, but lead straight into another. Because Ogden's divine reality is a different reality in relation to different events, then God may be held to relate differently to good and evil because it is a changed reality which relates to each particular event, thus absolving him from undifferentiated responsibility for good and evil. So much the better. The trouble is, he is also limited in any sense of respon-sibility for worldly events: since he is acting only out of the resources of his pastness, constituted by the world and the prior determination of abstract possibilities, he can barely exercise his will on specific events at all, and is not therefore responsible for the course which worldly occurrences take even though he may 'view' them differently and organize them into his pastness in a certain way. As we have seen, the extent to which this vulnerability goes is considerable; it is limited only by the abstract possibilities which are set by the divine reality as the conditions for any state of the world. This is reflected in Ogden's theology not only in the concept of divine action as dependent on creaturely re-enactment, but also in the general meaning of his doctrine of divine lordship: Ogden is willing to talk generally about the promise and demand of God (which is of freedom and love), but makes no connection between this love and actual specific facts of our social, political, economic life.[93] And how acceptable is this, theologically, if we are still to be talking about God? Ogden appears to have surrendered much of what is normally meant by God's sovereignty; God is certainly no longer a 'monarch'. Of course it will be argued that genuine love (which influences but does not impose) requires such vulnerability, and this is something, already promised, to which we must indeed return (re-stringing to stay in tune is a lengthy and often tortuous business!). The chief point now is simply that the issue of divine power and sovereignty is inescapably raised by Ogden's position. It must be added to the issues of personhood and initiative already raised, and to which it is of course integrally related.

It is also important to concede that Ogden writes of God's specific influence on particular occasions as more personal, more active and more effective, than this account may have suggested. For instance, he does talk of God's creative and redemptive 'decisions' in prior relation to every individual decision of his creatures, in terms which are not simply identical with the general decision of eternal possibilities.[94] Perhaps Hartshorne's insistence that God can and does organize specific possibilities by transforming the data of reality as it 'enters' God, however difficult this is to conceive, justifies these kinds of affirmation; though it may also suggest that Ogden is interpreting Hartshorne's ambiguous and difficult passages more under pressure from theological considerations derived independently of process metaphysics, than from the logic and metaphysics of Hartshorne himself—which, as already indi-cated, appear to falter at this point and may not sustain all that Ogden needs to have sustained.

Taken overall, therefore, is there really any advance on Wiles' position? Certainly Ogden has attempted a bolder and more detailed concept of special divine action. Armed with the categories of process metaphysics he has insisted that the divine reality can and must be conceived as fundamentally different (or variable) in its relation to particular worldly occurrences, and therefore God acts 'specially' even when the tools of empirical analysis fail to detect the diversity. But in the end the theological price is high, and not so very different from the dilemmas which Wiles bequeathed us: these particular occurrences can have no concrete relation to the initiative and efficacy of God; he can bear precious little respon-sibility for them. And though a vulnerable and significantly passive God in relation to particulars may seem easy to live with and easy to absolve, it will be a major contention of this book that we are deceived in this: to absolve God too much in relation to too many particulars would raise just as fierce a question about his love and goodness as to burden him with a total and undifferentiated responsibility.

Peter Baelz, D.D. Williams, W. Vanstone and the logic of love

Clearly the notion that divine love and action is necessarily vulnerable must be given a fair hearing, and there is no lack of recent theology about it with which to engage. It has become a fashionable bone to chew on, and a good thing too.

In the 1966 Hulsean Lectures Peter Baelz was beginning to pursue this notion, specifically in relation to the problem of special divine action.[95] He was also concerned, just as appositely for our purposes, with the interrelation of these issues with that particular problem which underlies Ogden's theology: the relationship between personal and 'transcendent' categories in God (how can God be truly personal, yet also in some sense eternal, changeless, timeless and so on?). It led Ogden to a sophisticated process metaphysic and a dipolar concept of God with its corresponding concept of divine activity, as we have seen. By contrast Baelz's theology is, in his own words, more 'impressionistic': the lectures are not intended as part of a detailed systematic theology of God's action, being, love, or anything else; nor does he claim to base them on a particular metaphysical system. In spite (or perhaps because) of this they remain suggestive, with an uncanny power to illuminate issues in a general way. They repay close attention.

In common with such as Wiles and Ogden, Baelz sees human response as determinative of special divine action:

> God remains eternally the same God; but in and through the obedient response of Jesus [and any other response][96] his activity is more fully discerned, because more fully expressed. And since it is more fully expressed, there is a very proper sense in which we may speak of God's *special* activity.[97]

At the same time he shares the view that this special responsiveness has meaning only in the context of a universal dependence on God's prior, general activity.[98] It is thus inevitable that the ultimacy of God implied in such universal dependence should find itself in tension with the independence implied in the world's responsiveness. So does this make God vulnerable in some way (for the sake of love and freedom)?

In the last lecture, entitled 'The Faithfulness of God' Baelz begins firmly with a personal analogy for God and states the problems: a fully personal God involved in a world of relative independence must be subject to it in some degree which calls his immutability, his transcendent 'God-ness' into question.

> What, for example, are we to say about the ultimacy and omnipotence of God? If the processes of nature and history are a real becoming . . .

> If God respects man's freedom, and waits upon his prayers and
> works together with him in the world, then he himself is surely
> involved in change and in a real sense dependent upon man for the
> achievement of his purposes. His activity in the world is matched by
> a certain passivity. But if all this is so, is God still God, perfect being,
> beyond the vagaries of change and chance? Or has he become one of
> us? We may still love him, but can we still completely trust him? He
> will, no doubt, do his best, but is his best good enough?[99]

Baelz first rejects a 'classical' answer, which is that God is able to
'take in', 'foresee' the whole spatio-temporal process, and therefore
acts 'already' in our future in one timeless and sovereign activity.[100]
This would be a spatial analogy of time: God 'sees' the whole of
reality, past, present and future, as if it is already laid out in space
before him—and so he has 'already' taken into account our future
acts as well as present ones. If acceptable this view might ensure
that God meets and overcomes every eventuality thrown up by the
relative independence of the world and the freedom of his creatures. However, it is not acceptable to Baelz, who feels the notion
of a future already known, yet not pre-determined, is meaningless
and logically improper (we shall be returning to this later). Baelz is
thus reconciled to a notion of a real indeterminacy in the world
process over which God's control is really limited. However, this is
immediately qualified in a number of ways. There is still an ultimacy
in God in so far as he wills this indeterminacy in the first place.
Further, the indeterminacy itself is not absolute: it is set within
certain limits of possibility, governed by general laws. Baelz
acknowledges that this is more obviously evident in nature than
human history (where necessary evolution is no longer fashionable), but points out that 'there are factors even in the human condition which urge man in the direction of justice and peace. If he is to
survive at all, he must learn to exercise a common humanity.'[101]
Yet this would be a picture of a world governed by general laws
only, with little or no reference to the special activity of a personal
God. What ultimate 'lordship' does God exercise over the individual in specific ways in particular situations? A possible answer for
Baelz lies in the religious experience of grace and forgiveness. God
comes to the particular soul with special grace, guides and fortifies
it through the vicissitudes of a world governed by general laws (and
their inevitable unpleasant side-effects). The world is thus, generally, willed by God as a 'vale of soul-making', and the experience of
the individual within it is so textured as to be receptive to the
comfort and guidance of God.[102] Baelz acknowledges the
inadequacies of this view:

> But does God care only for a man's character, and is he always
> testing our endurance? If this were the case, one would have expected
> at the very least that the tests would be more obviously proportioned
> to a man's attainments[103]

So he goes beyond it in this way: primarily he appeals to the important religious dimension of God's presence with us in the world—
not just as a fellow-sufferer, but (*qua* God) a uniquely *creative*
fellow-sufferer with infinite power to transform those sufferings
and evils into good (the supreme instance, of course, being the
cross and resurrection of Jesus).[104] Pursuing this line of thought
Baelz then paints a picture where the structures of the world do
indeed throw up indeterminacies, evil as well as good, over which
God has no control except as ultimate author of those structures;
nevertheless, God's love does all it can within these necessary limitations (for love cannot coerce); and, suffering evil with us, creates
new good out of it. To this end God may be conceived as anticipating every possibility, even though he cannot predetermine it.[105]

However, Baelz also goes one important step further in his quest
for theological adequacy. This God is clearly a suffering, mutable,
and temporal God, even if actively overcoming evil with good, and
Baelz wants to do justice to his transcendence, timelessness and
impassibility as well, for as he says: 'There is no going back on the
ultimacy and transcendence of God.'[106] His proposal is put
forward tentatively at the end of the lectures, as a 'platonic myth'.
Having first rejected recourse either to the bald discontinuity of
language (advocated by D.Z. Phillips)[107] or to even balder
'paradox' (D.M. Baillie),[108] he proposes a 'hierarchy amongst
analogies':

> On the one hand the transcendence of God seems best expressed by
> the impersonal analogies of timelessness, impassibility and univer-
> sality. On the other hand the immanence of God seems to call for the
> personal analogies of temporality, involvement and particularity. Is
> it possible to retain the essential insights of both, while subordinating
> the one group of analogies to the other?[109]

Baelz attempts just such a structuring, albeit sketchily. Personal
being is the primary category; transcendent categories are sub-
ordinate but not ignored; and God's relationship with time is a
particularly significant feature of how this works. Since it belongs
to the very definition of personal being that it moves from one state
to another (the present and the future) this must be predicated of a
personal God: it is not in itself an imperfection (by contrast with
other characteristics associated with temporality and personality
such as the dichotomy between what we are and what we ought to

be). Thus God does have temporality in the sense that he moves
from one temporal state to another. Yet if we also speak of this
movement in one particular pattern, a giving and receiving back
again (a movement of love), then we can also speak of a timeless,
changeless, universal pattern of movement—a perfection of the
transcendent God in classical terms. Here, proposes Baelz, is a way
of doing justice both to personal analogies of divine involvement
and particularity (which seeks new objects of love through time),
and to analogies of divine transcendence. There is change and vulnerability in God's movement in relation to the world, but also a
timeless perfection which is invulnerable and sovereign.

We may say, then, that Baelz has acknowledged an independence
in the world, born of creaturely freedom and divine love, and
embraced the vulnerability it implies. *Yet* he still genuinely
struggles with God's ultimacy. This is expounded as the ultimate
dependence of all structures (and their relative independence) on
the divine will, the infinite power of love to engage with every
possibility and work creatively with and in every event to trans-
figure it, and the changeless and faithful character of this love.

But is it adequate? Certainly what he has done on the way to this
conclusion is helpful to a point: the attempt to reconcile polar
opposites without recourse to process metaphysics is useful, if
embryonic; the account of the transfiguring power of love is
moving. Yet it has to be said that the package as a whole is still
leaky, and at one crucial point which Baelz himself seems at times
to acknowledge.

The problem again lies in the generality of God's action in the
ordinary structure of the world. For inevitably in such a world
there will be unpleasant side-effects, there will be 'accidents', and
individuals within it will suffer an injustice beyond the capacity of
God to avert. Baelz himself states:

> A further difficulty, however, in such a conception of God's
> providence lies in the fact that it is so general. What of the countless
> ill-starred and unfortunate by-products of this over-all purpose? The
> suggestion that God exercises a general control over all things is of
> little comfort to the man who finds himself the product of one of
> nature's less successful experiments. The notion of God's general
> providence threatens to become a blasphemous mockery if it is this
> and nothing more. God sacrifices the individual on the altar of his
> cosmic plan.[110]

That is why God provides something more in the way already described, by his transfiguring presence with us, meeting us in these

vicissitudes and transforming them in individual experience. But is even this really sufficient? Empirically we may have to say it is. *Prima facie* our experience is hard pressed even to concede this much, let alone anything more, except for *some* of its riddles with which we began. But theologically we cannot rest satisfied. We must have more than half an eye on those demands of revelation, namely universal and special activity, which constitute divine sovereignty. Are they really stretching a conception such as Baelz's? For the implication of this position is still that there exists for God a distinction between the main plan and its unintended but unavoidable by-products. Certainly this kind of distinction is true of our finite experience of creativity, but can it also be true of the master-craftsman? Are any of the supreme painter's 'bad' effects (and good effects) purely accidental? In the divine symphony, are any of the discords merely unfortunate—or any of the harmonies purely fortuitous? May we not rather suppose that the divine artist has no mere by-products, that every note will be present for its own sake and not solely for the sake of other constituent parts of the work?[111] Universal and special activity, purposive divine sovereignty writ large and small, must have something to say to this, and it may well be suspected that in Baelz's 'hierarchy among analogies' the dominant analogy of personal being has actually swallowed up God's transcendent sovereignty more than our theological considerations allow.

But what again of Baelz's proposed answer, that all such by-products are transfigured, made into the main plan as it were, that means are transposed into some further end: could not this constitute an adequate account of ultimate lordship? Certainly it does constitute *an* answer. But it is important to analyse more closely the relationship proposed here between means and ends, and see clearly the options available. There is a significant difference between making an unfortunate event serve some further end as a contingency plan, and having no accidents in the first place in the sense that there is always some end related internally to every event. In the first instance there seems no sense in which the event is intended for its own sake, even though it may be made to serve some further end, and therefore there is no guarantee that it has any value in itself; in the second instance there is some intended end in every event, it exists in some sense for its own sake and not just for the sake of something else (though in neither case, incidentally, is anything being said about the necessity—or otherwise—of the event: even in the second instance the intended end need not be tied to that particular event and none other).

The distinction may be sharpened if it is set in a difficult personal

context. If I know the cancer germ in myself, or my wife, is purely
and simply an unfortunate by-product of God's world which may
nonetheless be made to serve some further good end (for someone,
somewhere), this tells me one thing about God's lordship. If on the
other hand I know that the cancer germ is in some sense bearing an
intended ingredient of God's activity of love for us in that
particular situation, then that tells me something else about his
lordship. Of course it also tells me, at least *prima facie*, something
else, less palatable, about the nature of that love. It calls into
question God's goodness, and the ancient dilemma rears its ugly
head: how can God be both all-powerful and all-good in the world
such as it is? Does the one have to be sacrificed for the other?

This dilemma provided precisely the pressure under which Baelz
has sacrificed the former, if indeed he has. He seems to admit that it
has been sacrificed, in spite of a moving statement of faith that the
transfiguring power of love will triumph. The ambiguity lies at the
various points where the 'weakness' and vulnerability of love is
also stressed:

> Faith in God's providence and hope in God's future will always
> remain a venture . . . The tragedy that threatens to break man's spirit
> and destroy his world is a constant reminder of Love's weakness.[112]

But as already indicated Baelz' argument is too impressionistic for
us to be sure of his precise position. The point at present is simply
to insist that the distinctions outlined above are real, and so highlight the choices to be made. Naturally the extent to which the choice
Baelz appears to have made may be criticized as an *unnecessary*
compromise will depend on whether or not any alternative account
can do any better.

At all events, Baelz has usefully set a further agenda. It will be
recalled, for instance, that Baelz built a good deal of his insistence
on the divine disability on the basis of God's temporality, the
meaninglessness of any 'spatial' analogy for God's eternity. Further
discussion of this will clearly be necessary. Likewise, with regard to
the meaning of sovereignty, the categories of 'accident', 'by-
product', and the relation between means and ends will also require
further consideration. Before this, however, we should return more
specifically to the recurring theme of love, to which Baelz seems to
have appealed both as the crucial strength and the crucial weakness
of the divine activity, and which surely requires more analysis.

To talk of the 'necessary weakness' of love is not new, but neither
is it precise. It has been one of the most significant contributions of
process theology—and those influenced by it—to offer a serious

analysis of the meaning of love and its 'weakness' when it is affirmed as a defining characteristic of God and his action. Thus D.D. Williams,[113] amongst others, attempts to show what it means to say that a loving action is always by definition vulnerable to frustration. If this is not the case then we are not dealing with authentic love; to *guarantee* that the lover's will succeeds is in fact to reduce that 'love' to mere manipulation. Williams expresses this in terms of two categories of love: the freedom of love means that 'At the heart of every human love there is a dependence upon freedom which cannot be either bought or compelled';[114] and the causality of love is such that 'intentions are alterable in the very process of their exercise . . . any absolute determinism is excluded'.[115] Thus: 'The traditional assertion that the will of God is the ultimate cause of every event cannot be preserved without qualification, because a will which allows no effective power to any other cannot be a loving will.'[116] In more recent writing, strongly influenced by process theology, W.H. Vanstone spells out the implications even more explicitly.[117] In his phenomenology of love he defines authentic love as necessarily 'precarious' and 'uncontrolled':

> . . . the activity of love is always precarious . . . That which love would do or give or express may fail to 'arrive' . . . Love may be 'frustrated': its most earnest aspirations may 'come to nothing' . . . The activity of love contains no assurance or certainty of completion.[118]

> When one who professes to love is wholly in control of the object of his love, then the falsity of love is exposed. Love is activity for the sake of an *other*: and where the object of love is wholly under the control of the one who loves, that object is no longer an other.[119]

A more veteran process theologian, Norman Pittenger, summarizes the point by characterizing love in traditional Christian theology as having to be 'backed up by force', whereas in fact the real triumph of love will not and must not be achieved by 'changing love into coercion'.[120]

On these grounds it is therefore deemed perfectly proper, indeed necessary, to talk of God's creative act as bringing into being a world of creatures in which there is no guarantee that the creator will have his way in particular matters: it is a world in which he may be frustrated, and as long as he acts in genuine love this frustration is beyond his power to eradicate. This may be supported by appealing to the familiar analogy of human procreation:[121] we bring children into a world where there is no guarantee that we can secure their best interests or response, where the initiatives parents can take in that respect are limited in scope and efficacy; and such parents who do decide to bring children into such a world are not to be considered unloving, rather the opposite.

This is a compelling analysis of love and is often movingly expressed, especially in Vanstone's influential book. Yet there are a number of issues which need to be disentangled and examined more closely if we are to see clearly. To begin with, the analogy may be misleading. It is actually questionable whether parents do bring children into the world armed only with hope that circumstances will be kind and the proper response forthcoming. For instance, remember that riddle of experience Peter Berger identified as a sense of ultimate order:[122] a sense which may be deeply buried but which still surfaces revealingly in those situations like a mother's reassurance of a frightened child (*'Everything* is in order, *everything* is all right').[123] The grounds for this sense or 'belief' are not for the moment at issue; what is significant is that such a sense exists, so the love involved in procreative decisions is not simply grounded on hope. And it is at least arguable that without it procreative love would be a questionable love.

This leads us to examine more closely the question of vulnerability and precariousness as essential features of love. If we are to take seriously the point above, then vulnerability in procreative love is only attached to the immediate perspective. That is, the child may of course be struck with disease, or 'turn out bad', unresponsive, and so on, and of course the parents have little or no control over these things; but this is a limited perspective on an enterprise which in fact depends on a deeper security. This deeper security is not always specified, articulated, nor indeed is it fully conscious, but presumably depends on some form of belief in another world in which all things are made right. Translating this to the love of already existent interpersonal relationships, the corresponding intuition is expressed in countless love songs: it is the sense in which true love seems to presuppose that nothing in the circumstances of life and death can shake the security of that relationship; at least, nothing except perhaps the will of one or other of the lovers.

This brings us to a most important distinction. We need to distinguish between that kind of vulnerability which is open to rejection only by the will of the beloved, and the kind of vulnerability which may also be defeated by other circumstances beyond its control, i.e. the conditions in which the beloved exists. For both Williams and Vanstone the force of their position seems to depend chiefly on the former. The logic of love is such that it cannot force acceptance on the beloved (and remain love), and with this we must agree. Certainly the infinite patience and resources of divine love *may* in fact freely win the acceptance and response of all;[124] but it certainly does not do so, as far as is empirically observable, in this life (a fact which biblical teaching fully recognizes). And the logic of love no doubt lies behind this fact. Nevertheless, both writers imply much more than the strict logic of their position seems to require, for in practice the divine disability seems to have been extended to the conditions surrounding any individual and his response. Thus Williams is unable to conceive of every evil being made to serve a good end for an individual,[125] and Vanstone is again more explicit:

> The activity of God in creation must be precarious . . . control is jeopardised, lost . . . regained . . . Evil is the moment of control jeopardised and lost.[126]

That 'creation' here refers to more than the will of individuals and includes the circumstances surrounding them, is made clear by subsequent reference to the Aberfan disaster:

> We believe that, at the moment when the mountain of Aberfan slipped, 'something went wrong': the step of creative risk was the step of disaster: the creative process passed out of control.[127]

The reason why love cannot guarantee the conditions suitable for the beloved is not stated, but is implied. It rests on underlying assumptions about freedom in the world as a whole. If the world is a complex interaction of creaturely responses at different levels, and if no actual response can be guaranteed even by a divine lover, then when any errant response impinges harmfully on another creature, it might seem that God, because of love, would be helpless to intervene (without compromising the freedom and integrity of those errant responses). So the individual may suffer certain conditions for the sake of others' freedom and integrity (whether of the natural or human order), and a truly loving God can do nothing except suffer with the unfortunate victim and provide some spiritual resource of grace and strength with which to grow through it (the kind of position implied by Baelz). Vanstone is quite clear on this: there is no sense in which God intended some conditions of suffering for the sufferer; there is no intention of God in the mountain slip of Aberfan; it is pure accident, something 'gone wrong' with creation; God does not act in the slip itself but only 'received, at the foot of the mountain, its appalling impact',[128] standing in the same position as the children. But he will 'in the extremity of the endeavour', find 'yet new resource to restore and to redeem'.[129] So, as with Baelz, we are faced with the possibility that God can make tragedies into means to further good ends (the business of redemption), but in no sense at all has God exercised intentional control in relation to the tragedy itself: he *cannot* if he is to remain faithful to the logic of love, its freedom and necessary weakness.

It is tempting to capitulate to this sort of account, if only because it seems to mesh so well with our own experience of love and its limited possibilities. Consider again the challenge: even if it is only the individual will of the beloved to which the divine love may necessarily be vulnerable, the circumstances of any individual's existence are always composed of other potentially errant wills (which are themselves frustrating the divine will), and therefore God is necessarily frustrated in his activity towards the individual in wider terms than the individual's own will. Is this not precisely our frustration, as we seek to do the best for a child, a friend, a lover?

But therein lies the rub. The analogy is being drawn closely from human experience, rightly and inevitably, but is it not staying too close? Has it been sufficiently stretched (as all religious language must be) by the demands of revelation? Our scope of loving action is, naturally, limited; but this is because we are finite. That is, it is not just the constraint of love which limits our capacity to achieve ends through the action of others, it is the constraint of finitude. But the divine activity, *qua* divine and infinite, is universal in scope, as well as specific in intent, so if we can reasonably conceive God's activity in these terms we may after all be able to affirm God's capacity to 'incorporate' any event (including the errant responses of other creatures) into his purposes. This would mean that though the context of an individual's existence is indeed composed, in part, of other creatures' errant wills, God's love need not be frustrated in his action towards that individual in his circumstances. Instead, granted the universal and specific scope of divine action, the context of an individual's life may always be conceived as the action of God towards him, because that context is already woven into God's purposes. If it is Judas' will to betray Jesus, so be it; there is no compromising of Judas' freedom in this respect; the logic of love is intact. Yet God's initiative and sovereignty in ordering the whole web of events are such that even Judas' rebellion is 'placed', and made to carry God's purposes for Jesus. How this universal scope of action can be properly conceived belongs to the rest of this book. The point now is simply to alert us to this possibility that it is not so much the logic of love that frustrates the divine action in particular instances, as a merely finite conception of the *scope* of that activity.

To reinforce the point it may be helpful to further expose the under-lying assumptions of Williams' metaphysic, which both explain the route he has taken, but equally suggest the flaw in it, namely, a weak use of analogy. This is easily done. Williams assumes love as a fundamental metaphysical category, for whatever is present in the inescapable structures of human experience must *ipso facto* be present in being itself.[130] His task is then to ask what conditions of 'being' would be required for love (in human experience) to be possible—and God's being as love would naturally be the supreme exemplification of these conditions. Thus we have a *via eminentiae* which is clearly determined by what we find possible (in principle) in our human activity of love. The analogy tends inevitably to be univocal; as analogy it has largely collapsed.

By way of response we should insist instead on some distinguishing feature for divine action, so that it may be truly identified as divine. This is a minimal requirement for religious language, whether as model or analogy. Under pressure from the demands of revelation, therefore, we should at least try to conceive an action which has perfect efficacy and universal scope. This is not simply a *via negativa:* we could have some conception of what perfect efficacy and universal scope might mean, though it certainly does transcend our experience of human activity. Actually it may even transcend our conception, strictly speaking, lying only in a 'determinate direction' beyond it.[131] But as such it is not merely a supreme exemplification of some feature of our experience, and has much less tendency to collapse into univocalism.

All this must of course be developed in more depth, and it will be. The point now is simply to be able to sketch the countercharge against Williams and Vanstone in this way: their analogy of love (and therefore their application of its logic), has become too univocal. We should say that precariousness and vulnerability belong necessarily to the meaning of love only in respect of the creaturely response; only contingently do they belong to the circumstances and conditions which love is able to provide. This contingent meaning of the nature of love belongs only to finite creativity, limited as it is in scope and efficacy. It is by pressing that analogy of love to univocalism, thereby denying its unlikeness with divine creativity, that Williams and Vanstone are led to ignore the distinguishing possibilities of a divine love with its resources of a universal scope of action. (The point is directly parallel to a comparison between limited human creativity and the possibilities of divine creativity.)[132] In short, we should beware of trying to understand and analyse divine love in isolation from the other demands of divine action, and the full demands of revelation. Every string needs tuning, and although Baelz struggled nobly to harmonize with the authentic note of ultimacy, it is *not* being properly heard in the likes of Vanstone and others.

Furthermore this does not mean that love is qualified (in the sense of 'weakened' or 'compromised') by these 'other demands'. Indeed, it is a most important part of staying in tune that these other considerations positively enhance our understanding of divine love, rather than weaken it. We have already seen reason to affirm this, implicitly, by consideration of the procreation analogy. Parental incapacity to guarantee the best circumstances for their children (which *prima facie* does not seem to constitute a denial of true love) must be seen against the background of a deeper sense of order and faith, however buried or inarticulate. Even if we cannot secure the right conditions of well-being for our children, there may be (somehow, somewhere,) a principle of ultimate order and justice which will 'make it all right'. The implications are clear: if God is God then he has no further reference for faith than himself. He is that 'somehow', 'somewhere'. The logic of love for him *does* mean the capacity to guarantee right conditions for his children. If he cannot guarantee this then, since there is no further reference of faith, the question might be put to him in a way that need not be put to human parents: should he have created? Thus, to turn Pittenger's comment on its head, love which is *not* backed by this kind of force may not be love—it might be self-indulgent irresponsibility. For if love is genuinely seeking the best for the other (as Vanstone rightly insists), then God's authentic creative love must include the capacity to order right conditions for the beloved, a guarantee that no individual will be merely a hapless victim of circumstances which are not in any way woven into an end for him. God 'ought not' to have created with that sort of risk if his is a truly loving creation, even if we must leave open the logical possibility of that individual's self-willed frustration of God in respect of himself alone.

Process critics should thus consider the purpose of love as well as its mode of operation. If the purpose is willing the best for the beloved then that not only includes freedom (to reject or respond), but also the right conditions for that response to be made and the best to be realized. Love must include providing those conditions. If it cannot do this because of some kind of metaphysical or logical constraint then we in turn must ask whether that kind of precariousness and vulnerability in creative love is commensurate with real, responsible love.

Let us put the matter more starkly: which is morally (not pastorally) more acceptable? To say to the innocent man who screams with pain that God knew this kind of thing would happen when he set about his creative enterprise, and knew he could do nothing about it specifically (except, perhaps, with our help, to be driven by it to greater endeavour in the future), yet that he still proceeds with the creative task. Or to say God knows it, specifically in relation to that man, as an inevitable part of the business of creation, and stays with it because he also knows he has 'already' forged the end to which the pain and crying is related: viz. some unimaginable good which the screaming serves, for him as well as others. Of course we would *say* neither—at least not like that. We weep with those who weep, just because it hurts, and just because the end is often unimaginable at that time. But which should we *believe*? The latter is desperately hard. But the former is even harder when it begins to look, as we have seen, more like creative irresponsibility than creative love.

Finally we should also recall that other feature of love which we can consider more simply, and not necessarily just in relation to the horrors of life. Is not love, by definition, bound to take initiatives? What lover *simply* waits on his or her beloved for the longed-for response? True and committed love rather makes every effort to elicit the response, by creating the best conditions for itself, within which it will have greatest effect. As such this initiative of love surely requires a bolder structure of special divine action than the process theologians and others have so far provided. Thus we maintain that the logic of love is a double-edged sword which cuts more than one way in theological discussion, on more than one side of the debate about God's action in the world. The biblical pheno-menology of love has already alerted us to this: ultimately it has more to do with possibilities than limitations, whatever pain and struggle it encounters on the way.

Summary

I have suggested, therefore, that there is a significant strand of contemporary English-speaking theology struggling to articulate a coherent account of divine action in the face of the various demands of revelation, tradition and modern thought, but which consistently compromises its specificity, its initiative and its sovereignty. We have Wiles, rightly insisting on a truly trans-cendent, non-mythological account of divine causality, but then finding it so hard to move beyond a uniform and merely general conception of it: apparent diversity (in our experience of divine activity) is shifted onto our response instead, so in relation to particulars God remains relatively passive. We have Ogden's deft use of process metaphysics achieving some conceivable diversity actually in the divine activity; but this is hard-won, and at the same theological cost: the freedom of the world and the logic of love conditions and drastically reduces the efficacy of the action. We have Baelz struggling harder than most to maintain God's sovereignty (his 'ultimacy'), particularly in his concern for an adequate theodicy, but ultimately he too falls by the same theological wayside. The reason for much of this compromise surfaces from time to time, and very specifically, as the problem of reconciling polar opposites: any attempt to conceive of a transcendent God acting in special ways with personal initiative and perfect efficacy is liable to require a God outside as well as inside the spatio-temporal process. Ogden's use of process metaphysics and Baelz's 'hierarchy of analogies' propose alternatives to the starker contradictions of classical theism in this respect, but do so at the same theological cost.

And of course there are other modern statements of God's action joining the chorus: conceptions of God's relationship with the world in which the law-like nature of the world, the logic of love, and so on, duly exert their pressure but where the special action of God is rendered problematic or ineffective. Wiles, Ogden and the others represent but one part of a wider 'retreat' from what has been termed the 'red-blooded' theology of special divine action of former days. For even a writer like John Hick, with his paramount concern for divine sovereignty and creative initiative, displays his confidence only in relation to the world as a whole; it is a generalized conception of divine activity, with little room for special acts in relation to particular events:

> The whole process, comprising the evolution of the physical universe, the emergence of intelligent life and its development towards the end-state of perfected existence, is God's creative act . . . The difference, then, between human action and divine action is that a human being is part of the world, acting as one part upon other parts, whereas God is the transcendent holy will enacting the entire world process . . . The entire mysterious interweaving of light and shadow comes ultimately from God; and no one detail, in contradistinction from another, is directly arranged by God.[133]

Hick also says much that is helpful about the personal nature of God and his final fulfilment of all things, which mitigates the price he has paid on the way; but it remains high—and familiar.

Do we have to pay the same price? After all, such a theological position as that represented by these and others is hardly discreditable according to most reasonable canons of theological adequacy. It takes on board a fair amount of revelation and tradition, and interprets as many of the riddles of experience as it can. I have little doubt that, psychologically, even logically, it is as creditable and credible as many other attempts. Yet I have already indicated that I believe it to be, in the end, a 'theological wayside', a capitulation, an unacceptable compromise. I believe this chiefly because it is not stretched enough by those demands of sovereignty and personal initiative (and therefore, as argued above, by the demands of responsible creative love as well); and also, I suppose, because it leaves too many of the riddles of my experience on one side. It does not say enough that is significant about the very small, very specific, even petty, events of personal life which I find I 'must' refer to God: it is not enough to talk of God's action only in evolution in general, for your life and mine and the sparrows' will not reduce simply to an expendable part of a whole. And I do not believe this is just the plea of a wistful egocentricity.

Perhaps the most pointed commentary on this whole trend of theology comes from Michael Goulder who, as we have already noted, himself retreated from 'red-blooded' theology but is equally dissatisfied with this proposed compromise. In his reply to Hick he writes:

> Perhaps the first thing to strike the reader accustomed to traditional Christianity is how little, in John's view, God does . . . It is close to the view known as Deism, which retained belief in God as creator, but dispensed with original sin, the election of Israel, the divinity of Jesus, providence and so on . . . John's clear eyes see that the red blood of traditional theology will not save the souls of men in the 1980s; and like the Deists before him, he is saving what he can from the wreck. But the deistic God was sacked in the nineteenth century for doing no work; and we may reasonably enquire how much work the God of John's theology does. The greater part of his chapter is to explain what God does *not* do.[134]

Of course Goulder is hardly a comfortably ally, for his own God does nothing either: he has retreated, honestly enough, to frank atheism. And if our judgements against this current trend are not to go the same way they are obviously going to require something else, viz. the backing of some positive alternative; a conception of divine action which does a better job of compromise, which can portray a universal and specific action of God with initiative, sovereignty, and with some credibility in relation to contemporary thought. To this attempt we now turn, with no illusions that it will be an easy task: 'it is hard to tell a theistic story of divine activity', says David Brown in a recent contribution to the subject,[135] and I can only agree. Certainly I shall be leaning heavily on other sources for help: notably, Austin Farrer.

CHAPTER FOUR

Another Attempt:
A Structure for Divine Action

The agenda for any successful account of divine activity has been set already by the terms of the preceding discussion. We have to conceive how transcendent divine activity can be diversely structured to relate to specific worldly occurrences with initiative and sovereignty, without compromising divine love or demands of creaturely freedom, and without making nonsense of modern world-views.

Some preliminary comments may help to make the scope of the task clearer. Naturally the nature of divine agency will be at the heart of the discussion, but not the question of miracle if this is understood strictly as the occasional breach or by-passing of natural processes. This is not meant to imply that God does not or cannot act in such a way; but if he does it is still no help in conceiving whether and how he may be acting in and through *all* life. For to restrict God's special action to the occasional putative miracle hardly answers those persistent riddles of experience which detect him round every corner of life, and certainly does not meet the full demands of biblical revelation which records many more acts of God than the strictly miraculous.[1]

Furthermore, although every possible effort will be made to conceive and illumine the fact of divine agency, the precise means by which the divine intention has causal efficacy will remain, for the most part, outside the scope of discussion. The reason is simply that I suspect the means or 'mechanics' of causality by divine intention are in principle impossible to discuss sensibly. More of this later.

Taken together these two points also raise the (only) sense in which the 'Christ event' is not directly determinative of all that follows. In all important senses the nature of the life, death and resurrection of Christ will be exerting its pressure: as chapter two made consistently clear, the business of conceiving divine action as universal and special is demanded above all by this event; likewise the initiative, sovereignty and efficacy of that action as it operates through freedom, suffering and love. (And this means that any subsequent references to the Christ event are not merely illustrative of a general point, but constitutive of it.) Yet the precise means of causality in the Christ event is another question. It may well have involved (by choice or necessity) a unique means, and that is certainly what the doctrine of incarnation has traditionally presupposed. But as such it could not, by definition, help explicate the mechanics of divine causality elsewhere, except possibly for other occasional miracles, the spreading signs of the kingdom, some of which may involve similar means but which then lie outside the main concerns of this discussion.

In general, therefore, I am more concerned with the business of conceiving that God is acting universally and specially, than identifying the exceptional occasions when he employs different and extraordinary causal mechanics.

How then may transcendent divine activity be conceived as diversely structured? The discussion which follows will rest on three axioms. These are more or less familiar positions which are taken to be reasonable and defensible. They will be sketched out here, though no attempt will be made to argue them fully. The first is that divine action may be taken throughout as analogous to human action: in short, that human agency is a proper, reasonable model for transcendence. R.H. King in *The Meaning of God* adduces three reasons for this, the historical, conceptual and existential.[2] A more recent book by T.F. Tracy deals in even greater depth with the same contention, defending it mostly on logical and conceptual grounds.[3]

Historically, of course, there is precedent enough within the Judaeo-Christian tradition, which we have already identified in chapter two. Here God is understood primarily, though not exclusively, as agent: he identifies himself in Israel's experience as the one who 'brought you out of the land of Egypt'; he is also identified as the ultimate agent in creation and, in the prophets, as active everywhere in nature and history; in the teachings of Jesus he is the agent of the kingdom; and in the church's reflection on the life and death of Jesus he is the agent, through him, of salvation. Hence King's conclusion, already quoted: 'The model of personal agency is the dominant biblical model for 'God'.

Existentially, too, the model of personal agency is compelling. It is, suggests King, 'congruent with one's own sense of identity . . . An action I myself intend is one that I can personally identify with . . . Intentional action is an important way, possibly the only real way a person has of extending his identity and relating himself to the larger world.'[4]

But it is the conceptual reasons for the model to which we must give most attention. These are good reasons, though naturally there are also considerable difficulties. To begin with, if we are to conceive of God as in any sense personal and so 'subject' (and the logical connection noted by Ian Ramsey and others between the words 'I' and 'God' provides some grounds for that),[5] then we must have some access to that subjectivity in order to talk intelligibly about him. It is precisely the notion of action which provides such access, at least in our experience with others: to know another I observe his actions; action in this sense is intersubjective.

To be sure, we need to exercise great caution here, for when using the analogy of human action we are using an opaque and much disputed notion which may never be settled into a single satisfactory theory.[6] Nevertheless it does seem possible to maintain the basic contention that action is intersubjective—with a few cautionary qualifications that follow from considering some of the objections to it.

The primary objection to meet is that, far from having access through action to another's subjectivity, we merely infer from it to an antecedent intention and so can hardly claim to 'know', only to surmise; intention is thus posited as some antecedent cause of the purposiveness of the action. This represents the 'introvert' tradition.[7] Yet of course in the more recent 'extrovert' tradition this idea of action as a bodily event brought about by some mental occurrence ('volition') is considered far from satisfactory.[8] Rather, action is one event, mental and physical, not a composite of two events. Thus, terms like 'will' and 'intention' do not help to explain the notion of action but depend on it for their own sense; they are connected not causally but logically and conceptually. After all, we could not infer the intention unless it was already implicit in the 'outer' event of the action; and to explain the purposiveness of action by some antecedent 'causal' event of intention is to be driven to an infinite regress of cause to explain the intention.[9]

So an extrovert position naturally helps sustain the view that subjectivity is made accessible through action. On the other hand it is not necessary to adopt the fully extrovert tradition uncritically. First, it is important to make clear that intention is not thereby simply *reduced* to the 'outer' event of the action.[10] An action is defined by the element of intentionality (and distinguished thereby from mere 'occurrence') as that which, in the experience of the agent, distinguishes the event from those events simply to be explained by antecedent causes.[11] The agent, when acting with intention, is transcending his situation to the extent of envisaging alternatives, and is in a real sense original. The action with intention is uniquely his, the agent's, and it can be truly said that his identity is in his action. More will be said later in defence of this view of intentionality.

Further, it is by no means clear that the notion of action is exhaustively described either as one mental-physical event or as two distinct events, one mental (and interior), and the other physical (and external). These may not be the only alternatives. It may be possible to conceive of intentional action as proceeding from a certain kind of mental state (rather than event), and in such a way as to guard against the argument of infinite regress. Thus 'If it is accepted that volitions are not motions of the mind, but states of the mind, then . . . it can be allowed that voluntary action is action issuing from a volition without this having any implication that volitions must be preceded by volitions *ad infinitum*'.[12] This kind of view mediates to some extent between the 'introvert' and 'extrovert' traditions; it might still allow that the subject is approached through the nature of publicly observable behaviour, but would also allow more weight to the subject's own account of what he was doing (arising from that mental state). This should be considered a salutary correction of any tendency to make too large a claim for access to subjectivity through the 'outer' event alone, certainly guarding most vigorously against the simple reduction of inner to outer.

With such qualifications in mind we may therefore proceed with a basic view of action which does indeed provide real access to an agent's identity. To then talk of God's action, by analogy, is to talk of God's identity. It is the primary way his identity is intelligible. His purposes are known primarily through his action. We should not look for a further, elusive subjectivity of God behind it all, even if the qualifications mentioned above do also lead us to take some note of what God has, putatively, *said* about his action.[13] In this sense action remains a reasonable model with which to talk about God.

The model may, however, be criticized on other conceptual

grounds, namely that some bodily reference is required to make sense of the concept of action, and God does not have a body. This is a particularly forceful objection if we are not allowed to resort to a simple Cartesian dualism of mind and body; it has also been lodged against non-dualist attempts to conceive a non-bodily person.[14]

One obvious response is to embody God; that is, to conceive the world as his body, and his mind or spirit expressed through the world's events. Ogden, and especially Hartshorne, come close to this and a more recent book by Grace Jantzen explicitly advocates it.[15] Such a move, incidentally, need not imply dualism: God and the world could be conceived as a psychophysical unity comparable to ours.[16] However, it is a conception which has its own problems: it would require that we see the universe as an organic whole, like our bodies, a 'single operative unity', like an individual. This is difficult to square with our actual knowledge of the world, and even if it were possible it would then raise the related problem of creaturely freedom: the world's unity would necessarily be too tight to allow the relative independence of creaturely activity in its interaction with God.[17] An even more fundamental difficulty is that such a God, on this definition, would be finite, for his life and being and possibilities of action would be limited by that structure of worldly reality in which he is grounded and constituted. Human bodily life includes processes beyond the reach of human intention ('sub-intentional' processes of the body, as Tracy calls them); by analogy God would be similarly limited.[18] Miss Jantzen counters this by stretching the analogy, so that we conceive God's control over his body differently to ours: his is absolute, involving no 'sub-intentional' processes.[19] Yet even if this is allowed the concept of God remains one in which he is constituted by and dependent on a finite world, and in theological terms this involves a high price: God is no longer a self-sufficient creator with a life of his own—he needs the world for his very being.[20] The problem is eased somewhat if the world is infinite, so that God and the world are dependent, but co-eternally: nonetheless God would still not be self-sufficient creator *ex nihilo*, and the existence of a world as "creation" would not be a matter of grace but of necessity. That too is a high theological price to pay. (The view that God is not necessarily embodied in the world, but willingly embodies himself, may be more acceptable: but since it still presupposes a concept of God who could logically have constituted himself otherwise, that is in a non-bodily way, we still need to demonstrate the viability of the concept of a non-bodily agent.)

King's response is simply to deny the need for bodily reference in our concept of agents.[21] He makes two points in this respect: first, he argues that we do not have to observe our own bodily behaviour to know our intentions; second, whereas bodily reference is normally required to identify other agents (except possibly in the case of telepathy or telekinesis), with regard to God there are other distinguishing features, namely the universal scope and perfect efficacy of his action. This may not satisfy those who require more strictly empirical terms of reference for identifying God, but then even the world (as a whole) is not strictly identifiable in those terms.

The defence can also be staked out further back, in the more general concept of God is incorporeal, and also in the nature of religious language. Such a concept is often adjudged meaningless on the grounds that we have found nothing like it in our own experience,[22] and this criticism has to be met on its own grounds. To that end it still seems to me that a longstanding argument of Ian Crombie's constitutes an adequate reply.[23] That is, we may not be able, strictly speaking, to conceive of a bodiless spirit, but the duality of our own nature, the applicability to ourselves and our experience of concepts which are not needed for the description of the material world, does at least give us a 'reference range' of such difficult statements as 'God is a bodiless spirit'. It may not strictly speaking constitute a conception of such a being (because such concepts which are not needed to describe the material world are nonetheless always tied, in our experience, to the material world), but it does lie outside the range of our possible conception 'in a determinate direction'.[24] Incidentally, this need not imply that we go back on the previous insistence that there is no dualism between intention (one range of concepts) and action, in the sense of outer event or bodily movement (another range of concepts); it is rather to reaffirm that though they may not be considered as separate events, which are causally related, neither are they simply to be identified, the one reduced to the other; they are properly distinguished, requiring a distinct set of terms and concepts.

So 'bodiless spirit' may be tolerated, and accordingly the specific concept of a non-bodily agent should also be tenable, for personal spirit is known in action, as we have already maintained. Indeed when the concept is scrutinized (more closely than King attempts) it does prove at least arguable, and at best a most illuminating concept. It may even be easier to conceive than the more general notion of 'spirit' or 'mind'. Thomas Tracy's rigorous analysis concludes that although personal agents as we know them are always psychophysical (embodied) units, the concept of a purely mental agent is entirely possible: for whereas it would be a category mistake to speak of 'mind' as a subject of predication, there is nothing to stop us speaking of an agent to which various mental predicates can be ascribed.[25] Obviously there is much complex debate lying behind such a contention, yet the general point can still be made with considerable force and plausibility: namely, that the view that bodily reference is needed to make sense of the concept of action may depend more on our actual bodily experience than on the concept of action itself. P.J. Donovan summarizes the point like this:

> The feeling that there must be some bodily movement at the basis of all human actions may be considered to arise not from any requirement of the notion of *action*, but from the fact that we are speaking of humans, who are basically individuated and located in time and space by their physical bodies . . . But so far as the concept of an intentional action itself goes, having a body would not seem to be a necessary condition for being an agent.[26]

Thus in talking of a God who is not individuated and located in time and space by a physical body, we may still talk of him as an agent.

Here, then, is the first axiom which it is as well to have identified historically, existentially and conceptually, even if not fully argued: namely, that we are speaking of personal action as the model for transcendent divine agency. We therefore extend what we know of personal agency by analogy to divine agency in order to conceive how the latter may be structured in relation to the world.

The second axiom follows immediately. The conceptual reason for using human action as a model for divine action will depend on a certain understanding of human action as defined by intention. This needs further explanation. It is already clear that intention is not seen as an antecedent event causing action, but rather as bound up in the action; yet it is not reducible to action simply in terms of the outer event, but distinguishes the occurrence from the system of cause and effect which precedes and follows it. But how exactly is it distinguished? Wherein lies the originality of action as distinct from 'mere event' or 'occurrence'? What, in short, does 'intention', which we use to define action, *mean*?

We may certainly begin by saying that when an intention initiates an 'act', it includes various causal processes which bring about events that 'carry the act to completion'.[27] In this sense it is important to realize that the intentional act is inclusive of causes and events, not in competition with them. To say more than this we need to turn to Elizabeth Anscombe's treatment of the subject. In her monograph *Intention*, she set out the view that intention is, as already indicated, neither an antecedent event nor merely descriptive, but a form of explanation with its own logic, answering the question 'why?'.[28] Action is therefore defined by intention in the sense that it is identified within a context of meaning. To act with intention is to act with meaning. Moreover, as the question 'why' is pushed further and further back, the context of meaning is enlarged until the process ends on the generally perceived basis of completeness; in other words, when the action is considered self-explanatory (something which is never true of a mere 'cause'). This, of course, is an end, a goal. Intention therefore defines action in terms of meaning and purpose. It is a rationale, as explanatory as causal explanation but operating at a different level Thus we find a definition of action with intent as a 'succession of activities ordered towards an end. Its unity consists in an intention to realize a goal'.[29] The second axiom is, therefore, that we are accepting this understanding of action with intent as an explanatory account operating at a different level to (but inclusive of) natural causal explanation.

Naturally this too requires further explanation and qualification. Even if intention is not an antecedent even (in Gilbert Ryle's crudest sense) may it not still be a phenomenon which can itself be fully explained in terms of antecedent causal conditions? Put another way, is this 'form of explanation' simply a way of speaking about causally determined neurological events in our brain which *appear* to require a distinct set of terms and concepts, but deceptively so, for really it arises only as an 'epiphenomenon' of those events? This kind of reductionism naturally arises when it is claimed that we can, in principle, give a complete causal account of neurological events in the brain corresponding to all mental processes.

In fact the claim is arguable: the relationship between neurological and mental events need not be a causal one (indeed it is hard to see how that could ever be conclusively demonstrated one way or the other) resulting in a reductionist explanation. Other kinds of relationship have been suggested, some of which certainly allow for the originality of the mental processes.[30]

It should also be pointed out, by way of further clarification, that this view of intentional action need not exclude the explanatory power of 'ascriptivism', so-called. H.L.A. Hart's insistence that ascription of responsibility (i.e. *'who* did it') *explains* may not be sufficient of itself, but could be incorporated in this broader notion of intentional explanation.[31]

Perhaps most importantly we should be clear that this view of intention as a different kind of explanation from the web of natural cause and effect surrounding any event by no means implies it has no causal efficacy. Far from it: from the point of view of the agent the causal efficacy of intention is central to its meaning: 'we do have it in us to make things happen, and the principal way in which we do this is by intending'.[32] As King also remarks: 'The aspect of efficacy really becomes apparent . . . when an action fails, when I do not accomplish all that I intend. Then I become aware of just how dependent I am on the efficacy of intention'.[33]

We should note, however, that even this does not necessarily give us any insight into the precise *means* by which intention 'makes things happen': I have already hinted that this may be impossible to tell in any case. The reason revolves around those fundamental kinds of human action for which no explanation in terms of means is called: these are the 'basic' actions, 'originating members' of a chain of cause and effect which, as we have already noted, may not themselves be explained by preceding causes, for there is no necessary causal story to tell, e.g. speech acts, raising an arm.[34] These physical and neurological events which occur at the initiation of human action without a complete set of physical causes (except for determinists) therefore imply a significant opaqueness in the explanation of causal means for both the dualist and non-determinist physicalist. (Incidentally, the objection that one can at least offer a causal account of the human agent's body which relates to the effects of the basic action, but which cannot be applied in the case of God who has no physical body, at which point the analogy would break down, has already been defused: it is not the notion of action itself which requires this kind of causal account, but only the fact that man has a body.)

If, for the sake of completeness, the analogy is pressed to the point of asking, if not the precise causal means, at least the point of initiation in God's action, then a number of possibilities have been canvassed. For instance, it could be argued that indeterminacy is a fundamental feature of the universe and so provides that category of 'uncaused' events within which the divine agency operates.[35] In fact I suspect this is dangerous: to talk of indeterminacy as the point of divine causation risks re-introducing a more subtle and sophisticated version of 'mythological' action, a new God of the gaps.[36] Alternatively it could be suggested that a 'panpsychist' theory of reality offers the point of purchase and initiation,[37] though this is a metaphysical theory open to its own particular problems. The most satisfactory account will probably depend on a 'timeless' view of God's creative activity, such that every point of time is a point of creative activity (a view which will be explored further below). Within this picture perhaps the best we can do to explicate the 'causal joint' is to conceive God's impinging on the animate and inanimate world as a kind of telekinetic basic action— not implying any bodily mediation, but still allowing the basic analogy of God as an originating, intentional agent 'alongside us'.[38] Yet still no claim is being made to have penetrated exactly how causal efficacy is achieved on either the human or divine side of the analogy. The chief point remains that just as we make things happen by intending (without knowing precisely how), so we may conceive God intending effectively the things of the world.

Once again, therefore, the axiom may stand with due qualification: human action is defined by intention which is causally effective, and as such can still function as a proper analogy for divine action. Its implications for our understanding of the relation of transcendent divine activity to worldly occurrences will emerge shortly.

The third and final axiom can be dealt with more briefly. It is simply that any account we do finally offer of God's relationship with the world must indeed concern the world as a whole, and not either nature, history, or the individual human subject, exclusively. Traditionally, as we have seen, God has been conceived as acting in all these areas, but in the first by intervention and miracle. This concept is now, to say the least, out of fashion; and yielding to the pressure of empirical world-views, which seem to uncover at least a relative autonomy of the natural order, much contemporary theology has divided the world up. Nature has been 'conceded' to impersonal necessity (or, if there is indeterminacy at the sub-atomic level, at least to 'statistical probability'; or to chance). It is only in history, through God's interaction with the human will, that he acts, and his purpose can be unveiled.[39]

But such a division of the world will not do, and fortunately there have been voices raised stridently against it. Briefly, it will not do for two types of reasons. First, there are theological reasons. By any stretch of the imagination it is not a faithful interpretation of the biblical account, and once again we refer back to chapter two and the pressures of biblical revelation. The creator and redeemer God did not simply inspire Moses, he brought plagues on the Egyptians and parted the Red Sea; he did not just reveal himself in Jesus, he stilled the storm and made the fig-tree wither. More fundamentally, man was raised from the dust and in Hebrew thought has remained, ungainly through it sounds, a body-soul unity such that it would be most arbitrary to conceive God as acting in only one constituent aspect of that unity.

Then there are also what might loosely be called empirical reasons. History cannot be divorced from nature just by observation. Natural events have historical consequences; historical events are grounded in a natural context. The two are inextricably intermeshed. And if the intention is to restrict God's activity to the realm of history because it is considered less vulnerable to the reductionist, then this is foolish: the modern historian (or historicist) has as little need of reference to God in his explanations as the modern natural scientist. This is not to deny the opaqueness of history, but it is to admit that it *can* always be attributed to the opaqueness of human personality and will, rather than to God.

We may therefore agree with Gordon Kaufman's judgement, that 'it is a measure of the desperation of contemporary theology and faith, in the face of the power of the modern scientific world view . . . that this way out [of divorcing history from nature] was attempted at all.'[40] I certainly do not wish to attempt it, and so intend to rest squarely on this third axiom throughout the rest of the discussion, namely that we must give an account of God's activity in relation to the whole world, and not just a part of it.

This, then, is the groundwork. In fact a good deal of it would not necessarily be disputed by much contemporary theology, including the likes of Wiles and Ogden. But its implications have not always been fully pressed into service, especially in relation to Wiles' assumption that transcendent activity must be uniform and therefore not specific; also in relation to the assumption that divine sovereignty will always have to be compromised. It is on the basis of these axioms that we are now in a position to challenge such assumptions, and go on to venture an alternative account.

It will be recalled that Wiles' assumption was made primarily under pressure from the quite reasonable observation that empirical science has uncovered a general structure in the natural (and historical) orders within which regularities and contingencies occur that need no specific reference to God in the explanation of particular events; in which case, the creaturely experience of special divine activity represented in the Judaeo-Christian tradition is better understood as a particularity of creaturely insight and response rather than of divine activity in relation to the creature. To put it another way, the apparent autonomy of the whole world process within these general structures, ordered by regularities, may be the single action and purpose of God, but as such that purpose could not be said to be specifically related to particular events within the whole (apart from specific creaturely response). The theological adequacy of such a notion has already been questioned. We can now go further and overturn the underlying assumptions. To that end we offer two preliminary points.

First, if we take the analogy from human action seriously, the mere fact of regularities and general structure does not exclude the possibility that they carry specific meaning and purpose in relation to particular events, and are therefore specially related to the agent;

they can indeed be conceived as special actions. This arises precisely from the fact that action is defined by meaning and purpose, not by its form as an 'outer event': 'an action differs from bodily movement. A given bodily movement (for example, moving my arm outwards) may represent a variety of actions (such as mailing a letter, sowing seeds, or dealing cards)'.[41] Thus, for example, the same rainfall, explained in terms of the regularity of laws governing the evaporation of water and its precipitation under the force of gravity, *may* have quite a different meaning in a different context: it may water one man's garden—and wash out another man's cricket match. Of course, that is not yet to *establish* it as a special action, as purposive in these particular respects, but that is not yet the point: it could be. The mere fact of its explanation at one level in terms of regularities within a general structure is not sufficient to preclude that possibility.

Second, it follows that the 'hiddenness' of such action to tools of empirical analysis is perfectly intelligible. Just because action with intent is a different order of explanation from that of the empirical sciences and not causal in the same way, the scientific account of the world may be untouched and unbreached by this different order of explanation. There are no gaps being filled. Of course the hiddenness is only complete in respect of strictly defined tools of empirical analysis. Intentions are not observable in the same way as scientific laws, nevertheless, as we have insisted, they are implicit in the events and can be identified. But the identification, according to this logic of explanation, will require a larger context in which its meaning can be interpreted, and may require observation over a considerable period of time. (Theology is concerned precisely with discerning and explicating this larger context.)

So far, then, the suggestion is simply that what is transcendent and hidden within all worldly occurrences need not, merely in virtue of that hiddenness and the general structures and regularities of those events, be uniformly related to them. Rather, the alternative account could in principle be offered of a divine agent realizing specific ends in and through these general structures and regularities; specific ends relating to particular events. This is made possible by the recognition of intention as a defining principle of action which may be expressed transcendently, yet quite specifically, in and through general structures and regular causal sequences.

This is hardly a new thought, at least in its general form.[42] It owes much to Austin Farrer's position worked out in his later works *Faith and Speculation* and *A Science of God?*[43]—which Wiles has been accused of ignoring.[44] Farrer's much quoted summary of this way of understanding God's action in and through the observed structures of the world, speaks of 'the grid of causal uniformity' which 'does not . . . fit so tight upon natural processes as to bar the influence of an over-riding divine persuasion'.[45] Again, this does not imply any particular theory of *how* that persuasion occurs; for instance, as Brian Hebblethwaite properly comments, it does not mean that God is re-introduced into the gaps of (for example) sub-atomic indeterminism,[46] but suggests rather that 'the whole web of creaturely events is to be construed as pliable or flexible to the providential hand of God—in quite another and necessarily wholly inscrutable dimension'.[47] In Farrer's own terms, there is a necessary hiddenness in the 'causal joint'; both with respect to the interaction of divine and human agency,[48] then with respect to the interaction of divine agency and natural activity.[49] This hiddenness, for Farrer, arises out of the analogical nature of the language of divine action: God's causality is of a 'higher' order than ours,[50] and so the modality of divine action in its interaction with creaturely action is necessarily hidden to us.[51]

Admittedly this could, on its own, sound simply like an evasive appeal to mystery, abandoning precision to hide behind the voluminous skirts of 'stretched religious language' (particularly since Farrer frequently denies the need for further enquiry on the grounds that it is not necessary for 'religious practice'). Wiles certainly complains of this.[52] Yet if, as we have suggested, we can and must accept in human experience the hidden causal efficacy of human intention in physical action, without knowing its precise causal modality, then we can surely affirm by analogy the hidden causal efficacy of divine intention on creaturely activity without knowing its modality. Furthermore, agnosticism about the modality of divine action need not muzzle us against further exploration into the meaning of the basic analogy of divine action through others.[53] Thus while Farrer's basic point may have needed bolstering by more discussion of this kind, it still stands: the hiddenness of the 'causal joint' does not of itself discredit the notion of divine activity, nor does it preclude the realization of specific ends by means of that causality. In this general sense, then, his point is the same as ours: we may conceive of a divine intentionality transcending the outer events, yet implicit in them, which has causal efficacy, though of a different kind from the causal explanations of the empirical sciences. Specific ends, such as the emergence of new forms of life or growth to human maturity, are realized by this divine intention, and may be called special acts of God within the overall purposes of creation.

There are also some connections with a view of God's action worked out by Gordon Kaufman, at least as far as the relation of

God's specific and overall purposes is concerned. There is much in Kaufman's account which is at odds with ours, but also some useful terminology and clarification of concepts. This is particularly true of his essay 'On the Meaning of "Act of God" ',[54] where he distinguishes between the 'master-act' and its constituent 'sub-acts'. Just as constructing a bench includes a variety of 'sub-acts', including sawing, hammering, chiselling etc., each of these involving its own unification of activity towards a particular end and therefore an act in its own right, so Kaufman suggests that the whole course of evolutionary development can be considered as one all-encompassing master-action unified by God's intentions, within which there are various constituent sub-actions: he lists, for example, the emergence of sentient life, of man, the growth of agriculture; also the history of Israel and the life of Christ are 'acts through which God moved human history and consciousness toward a fuller awareness of who he is'.[55]

In fact this view does not commit Kaufman to seeing every natural or historical event as a distinct sub-act of God, but 'only those events which move the creation forward a further step toward the realization of God's purposes'; many processes are only functioning as 'fundamental rhythms or orders that support and sustain the more complex processes of the teleological movement'.[56] It is at this point that Kaufman's conception may not be sufficiently bold. But at least his terminology enables us to see a unity in God's overall action and purposes, *and* a diversity within that unity: God's relation to the world is a unity in terms of the consistency of the action in carrying out the overall purpose (the 'master action'), but this in no way serves as the basis for a deductive argument to the conclusion that there is no special action in relation to particular events, even individual lives, within that overall purpose; on the contrary, the master-act includes within itself sub-acts, the realization of specific ends, though these are of course woven into the fabric of the whole. To that further crucial question of how widely the net is spread, what proportion of what kind of events are suitable candidates to be considered as the realization of specific ends of God, Kaufman gives no answer to satisfy our initial demands and we must go on to tackle it ourselves. But we have now laid the foundations, however skeletal, of a structure on which to build: the bare conception of transcendent divine action acting in and through the events of the world to realize specific ends is by no means impossible to conceive or articulate.

However, these foundations now have to be tested and made to carry a heavy load of demands. The most pressing arise from one of our initial axioms, as well as the exigencies of revelation, which insist that we apply this structure of divine activity to the whole world, history as well as nature, while retaining the notion of sovereign efficacy. God is to be conceived as working effectively to encompass *all* creaturely activity within his specific intentions. Is the notion still intelligible in these terms?

So far the model of agency has enabled us to conceive of God acting in and through the world primarily in the way that a human agent can 'take up' physical events (such as bodily movement) and invest them with meaning and purpose. Thus there are two levels of explanation being canvassed, one in terms of intention, the other in terms of natural causes. However a thoroughgoing account of God's relationship with the whole world is not simply an account of the transcendent mind and will expressing himself through the physical events of the world (in this sense the world *would* be best conceived as God's body), but rather of a transcendent agent acting through other agents; an action in and through a world with a life of its own. For, as Farrer points out, the world is a complex inter-action of many different kinds of 'activity systems'.[57] At the lowest level there is barely any 'activity' at all (in atomic and molecular structures); and even where there is more flexibility and movement there is not in the strict sense any action (i.e. there is no inten-tionality, for example in the movement of the waves); but higher up the scale movement and self-determination increase until in the animal world it is quite proper to talk of purposiveness, and in the human world there is of course agency proper, in the full sense of intentionality.

At the lower levels the problem of effective divine action working through the world, without compromising its own existence, *is* adequately served by the model's two levels of explanation. God's intentions encompass the structures and movements of these lower activity systems without excluding or overriding their own existence as they are—just as we can encompass our heart-beat or the movement of our lungs without undermining their nature as acti-vity systems in their own right. But at the higher levels there are more difficulties. Is it equally possible to act effectively in and through another agent with will, intentionality and purpose of its own—without reducing the agent to something less than agent, to pure patient?

Here the appeal to two levels of explanation is less helpful. It seems that the same level of explanation is being canvassed. It is not just that one event is explained first in terms of natural cause and effect, and then in terms of an agent's intentions, but that two agents, two sets of intentions, are involved in an action. Farrer speaks of the 'paradox of two agents for an identical action', the paradox of 'double agency'.[58] The full extent of this paradox can be appreciated when we realize that we are being asked to conceive not simply of one agent fulfilling his purposes in and through another in general terms, but of a primary agent acting specifically through the event of a secondary agent's own (free) action. The meaning and purpose of the primary agent's action is to be found in the secondary agent's action, but with no guarantee that they are meaning and intending the same thing:

> Everything that is done in this world by intelligent creatures is done with two meanings: the meaning of the creature in acting, the meaning of the Creator in founding or supporting that action. Subjectively considered, there are two doings; physically there is but one event.[59]

Now is this kind of interaction conceivable, without sacrificing either the sovereign efficacy of the primary agent or the relative independence and freedom of the secondary, in this specific action?

It should already be clear that at least we need not be concerned with the 'how' of this phenomenon, in the sense of trying to penetrate the mechanism or modality of the causal joint between primary and secondary agent. Nevertheless, to accept the bare conceivability that it is the case, even if no attempt is made to understand the how, some work still needs to be done. There are various ways in which this might be attempted.

The first is by simple analogy with the interaction of human agents. For there is a limited sense in which I can effectively act through another's action without imposing my will on his, reducing him entirely from agent to patient. This is especially true in intimate personal relations where the straightforward category of cause and effect will not contain what actually happens. In making my intentions plain it does seem as though I can elicit a response in another which is nonetheless a free response originating in that person. Or, even where another has no intimate knowledge or connection with me, is it not in some degree possible *to so order events around him* that his action (whatever it is) may carry my meaning and purpose? For instance, trustees are charged with this kind of enterprise on behalf of another: to make sure that a client's wishes are carried out in and through changing circumstances they may have to initiate events themselves—investing, selling property—and thereby ensure that others' actions still carry their meaning and purpose; likewise, businessmen are sometimes in a position where market forces can be manipulated to serve their own purposes, however consumers react.

On the other hand it has to be admitted that, whether in close interpersonal relationships or acting 'at a distance', these sorts of enterprise carry a high degree of risk and uncertainty. The other person may not respond to my advances in the way I intend. And is it really ever the case that we can contrive a situation where *whatever* the action of another it can convey my meaning and purpose? If it is then maintained that divine omnipotence and omniscience ought to be able to guarantee and underwrite precisely that area which is subject to risk and uncertainty in our finite experience, can we be sure that the risk and uncertainty is in fact inherent in our finitude and not rather inherent in the very concept of interacting free personal agencies?

If this last point were conceded it might be said to constitute a question mark against traditional ideas of divine sovereignty, though need not count against the conceivability of double agency *per se*. It could simply mean that divine action through our action is conceivable, but subject in principle to the same risk and uncertainty as our action through others, and we would find ourselves back in the same framework of divine action conceived under pressure from the presumed logic of love: action with vulnerability.

In fact we need not be driven to this conclusion so soon, if at all. Even apart from any general dogmatic assumptions about sovereignty and 'theological adequacy' it also seems, paradoxically, that the notion of double agency itself may require a strong view of sovereignty—for its own coherence. For if there is no distinguishing feature of *divine* agency over against human agency (such as absence of risk or uncertainty), then an analogy of human agency as a model for transcendence is in danger of collapsing into a univocal way of speaking. That is, we are in danger of forgetting that we are using human action as a model for transcendent divine action, and that our quest for conceivability is ultimately a quest for conceiving of divine agency operating through human agency, not human through human. (This is a parallel point to that made before with respect to the logic of love.)

The question then takes this two-fold form: are the distinguishing features of divine action such as to eliminate the element of risk and uncertainty, and can an appropriate analogy be found to sustain the conceivability of that sort of action operating through human agency, without, again, reducing our agent to patient?

King touches on these questions primarily in relation to the problem of identification.[60] If we are to identify divine action it must of course be in ways quite different from those whereby other agents are identified, not least because God is not normally identified by his body. This has to be the case: to be transcendent he cannot simply be one agent amongst many as he would be if he were a bodily agent; he cannot be restricted to a particular perspective on the whole. I have already indicated that this need not undermine the analogy with personal agency altogether[61] but it does mean we need further ways of distinguishing and identifying his actions, and King suggests three.

First, the actions must be universal in scope, not limited to a particular sphere of influence or a certain range of effects. This is sufficiently comprehensible within the analogy of personal agency; we are not without a certain ability to conceive of actions beyond our bodily limitations, even to the extent of entering into another's perspective. For:

> In order for God's action to be universal in scope, he must be in a position to intend for each agent from within the agent's own particular perspective and for each in relationship to the whole. The interrelatedness of agencies being what it is, that is the only way in which he can effectively act on a universal scale. If this ideal of agency is not entirely conceivable to us, it is surely not entirely inconceivable either. For it is an ideal to which we all more or less aspire. We would like to comprehend more of the world than we do, and to comprehend it in greater depth, in order thereby to act more effectively in it.[62]

Second, the action of God is to be distinguished by its perfect efficacy.[63] God does all he intends. There are no compelling conceptual problems here either in terms of our ability simply to conceive it within the terms of the analogy of personal agency. Certainly we do not do all we intend, but we have some idea, some conception, of what it would be like to be the perfect agent. We, being limited by our own bodily substructure and the regions of our subconscious, and being ignorant of the wider structures of the world, may often be blinded both to our own intentions and their possible consequences; a non-bodily God need not be. But of course it does pose enormous problems when this efficacy is being conceived in relation to our agency: how can God be conceived as doing all he intends through other agents, without doing violence to their own agency? It has to be said that this second proposed distinguishing feature, the most closely associated with traditional ideas of sovereignty and omnipotence, merely restates the agenda for further debate if the analogy of double agency is going to be successfully employed.

Third, King distinguishes God's action by its originality.[64] It originates with him, is utterly his own; he is the sole and sufficient basis of all he does. (This is actually the doctrine of aseity, open to serious questioning on conceptual grounds in many of its forms, but for the moment let it rest simply as 'lying in a determinate direction' beyond our conception of human agency.)[65]

Is it now possible to combine these distinguishing features in an appropriate analogy by which to elucidate the paradox of double agency where God is the primary agent? Or do they have to be seriously qualified—particularly the second—in any such attempt? One of the most powerful analogies presented by Farrer,[66] which Dorothy Sayers had also used and developed to greater depth,[67] is the analogy of the artist, author and playwright, in their relation to what they have created. The good artist constructs the movement of the plot of the credible behaviour and interaction of characters within the situation he has conceived and brought into being. Dorothy Sayers would actually claim that the characters take on a life of their own in this creative process, to the extent that the author cannot, if he is to hold to his creative integrity, interfere arbitrarily with that development (though it has to be said that other literary critics, notably J.-P. Sartre, disagree).[68]

In this picture the originality and scope of the artist's agency in relation to the novel or play certainly cannot be denied. However, the efficacy of the analogy, as we suspected, is still problematic. In so far as the divine author, unlike the human, posits real agents in a real world, capable of going their own way, the analogy would seem to break down. Can he be sure of achieving his ends in the same way as a human author can? Or, to the extent that we accept Miss Sayers' claim that the artist's creatures really do take on a life of their own in some sense, then the analogy holds, but only by conceding precisely this point: by apparently compromising perfect efficacy. Thus it seems again merely to restate the problem as to how the divine intention can work effectively through human agency: it is hard to resist the implication that either the notion of perfect efficacy as a mark of divine action, or the genuine free agency of creatures, has to be abandoned if the paradox of double agency is going to be intelligible.

Yet I have already suggested that if a strong view of divine sovereignty is abandoned we not only pay a theological price which may be too dear, we also lose an important distinguishing feature on the divine side which would weaken the basic analogy. Clearly a way out of this impasse will have to be found. I believe it can be found, but it will require closer consideration of two aspects of the discussion which have not yet been fully pressed into service: the meaning of divine sovereignty in terms of the universal *scope* of divine action (through time and space), and the analogical nature of the model of double agency.

With respect to the meaning of divine sovereignty, its problems in relation to creaturely freedom ease significantly to the extent that perfect scope is allowed to explicate perfect efficacy. Here the artist analogy *is* a useful one. Commenting on Farrer's use of the analogy, Hebblethwaite aptly portrays this perfect scope of divine activity. Farrer compares the way a good author constructs his work to God's universal action 'in and through the law-governed behaviour and interaction of natural substances at every level of complexity from elementary particles right up to human brains and the mental, inter-personal and spiritual life which they sustain', and so, further, 'through the historical and social life of mankind in all its ramifications and developments'. Thus God's action in relation to any one human being at any one time will be a complex affair: 'Not only must the many threads going back into the past, shaping the whole cultural and spiritual context of a man's life, be borne in mind, but also the many levelled nature of divine activity in the present has to be reckoned with.'[69] Quoting now directly from Farrer: 'While [God] thinks out the orderly life of a man's mind, he must at the same time think out the action of the minute physical underlyings which carry the work of his brain'.[70] With such universal scope of action God thus can and does embrace the whole of our environment. It is directly implied by the doctrine of God as creator and Lord of creation, and calls to mind Karl Barth's ringing insistence:

> . . . His [God's] will is accomplished directly and his decisions are made and fulfilled in all creaturely occurrence both great and small. He would not be God at all if He were not the living God, if there were a single point where He was absent or inactive, or only partly active, or restricted in His action.[71]

This universal scope of action could have far-reaching implications for the efficacy of action (though Farrer himself does not seem anxious to press this point as far as we shall be doing). For example, using Farrer's language, if I could 'think out' the condition of my wife's total situation, and furthermore, if I have equally 'thought out' the condition of every conceivable situation which might be locked into hers, or which might be locked into hers by any action she undertakes, is there not a sense in which I could by my actions so 'load the dice' that whatever she does (though still as a free agent, acting from within herself and with her own intention) can nonetheless be woven into the fabric of past, present and future to carry my meaning and purpose?[72] It could be something as simple as ensuring she met the kind of person to persuade her in a particular course of action: for with unlimited scope of action in other people's situations as well as her own I could guarantee this without risk or uncertainty (which would be seen to belong to our finitude rather than to the notion of interacting free personal agency itself).

But what would this mean for her freedom, or the freedom of any agent? To what extent does this imply an unacceptable manipulation? Here an important distinction must be made, for there are two distinct ways of construing the business of 'loading the dice'. It could mean so arranging and ordering reality that a creature has to act (and, also, to intend) in a certain way; so constituting his nature and the nature of circumstances surrounding him that he intends what you want him to intend: his act is your act, in a one-to-one correspondence. *Or*, it could mean so arranging and ordering reality that whatever intention the creature has, and indeed enacts in his particular context, carries your intention in a wider context of meaning. In short, so acting that his real act is a sub-act within your master-act (to go back to Kaufman's terminology), but you are playing a different drama. Thus we can return to Judas and insist again that if it is in him to betray Jesus, so be it, but it will carry a meaning within God's intention other than Judas' intentions: Judas' act will be a sub-act in God's overall purpose. It is of course the latter of these two alternative senses of 'loading the dice' which is being canvassed here in support of the paradox of double agency. The former seriously compromises the sense in which the secondary agent remains free agent, yet of the latter it can still be said that whatever the agent freely does is encompassed without risk in the primary agent's action.[73]

To further support this picture, another objection must also be dealt with. It may be argued with some justice that it is very hard to see how that reality which is to be ordered around an individual (so that the divine intention will in any eventuality be fulfilled) is sufficiently pliable to the divine hand for the overall conception to be sustained. After all, the context to be arranged is constituted both by other natural activity systems proceeding under a general pattern of uniformity (or indeed with a measure of indeterminacy at some levels), and free decisions of other human agents. Both kinds of activity are to be respected. And even to *know* what every 'necessary' and contingent interlocking event will be is not yet equivalent to arranging those events. Most difficult of all, to the extent that the reality which is to be 'arranged' around the individual and his free decisions is constituted by other contingencies (whether of human or 'natural' activity) it may be argued that there is insufficient stability, no purchase for the divine hand to weave the necessary pattern, only an infinite regress of creaturely contingencies.

In fact this kind of objection reflects an inadequate grasp of what is meant by the universal scope of the divine action. When it is being claimed that God 'thinks out' every activity and its inter-action with other activities, this is not simply a statement about what God knows; rather, we have to conceive of every sequence of activity arranged 'from the beginning' according to its 'future' interaction with other activities. 'From the beginning' does not here imply that all effects are present in the first single cause of the world, but rather that the world is a continuously woven mesh of newly emerging activity sequences, and at every point of inception (and continuance) God's creative intention is exercising its hidden causal efficacy. That the world is such a mesh of newly emerging activity sequences is most visible from the human perspective by analogy with human action at the juncture of 'history' and 'nature'; human intention changes the course of natural sequences, whether it is the building of a dam or the binding up of a wound. From the divine perspective we have to conceive of *every* sequence begun and continued with God's creative will, developing by interaction with other created sequences so that it develops both in accordance with its own nature and the divine intention which knows what each interaction will in fact produce. In the case of knowing subjects the divine will may indeed be known (in experience and revelation) to be presenting itself persuasively (but not coercively), and so be specifically known to affect some sequences; but that human know-ledge is secondary to the prior divine knowledge as to whether in fact the human agent will respond—and if there is no response all other relevant interlocking sequences will have accommodated this fact 'from the beginning'.

Thus we have a conception of a complex interaction of activity systems, some no doubt reaching far back and forwards without particular moments of development and creative interaction, but at every point known and arranged 'from the beginning' to accom-modate the divine purpose, without being 'forced' or 'faked',[74] and not 'steered' in any empirically verifiable way. The much quoted instance of the successful Dunkirk evacuation is useful by way of illustration. (It is often quoted because of its rare, putative, status as a specifically intended act of God *already clearly visible from within the human perspective*, combining an extraordinary coinci-dence of unusual factors but without recourse to the 'breaking' of natural laws.) Assuming for the sake of argument that it was a specific divine intention, we can now say this: God knew that in this instance Hitler would respond to all sorts of interlocking pressures (themselves known and steered by God at all moments of their creative development) by 'unaccountably' halting his Panzer divisions. He also knew and in like manner 'placed' Allied decisions to evacuate at a certain time. From the beginning of all relevant causal sequences he also 'thought' the fine weather to interlock with these decisions—and the 'miracle' of Dunkirk was actualized. Why he chose Dunkirk and not other events to make this kind of activity so luminous relates no doubt to wider purposes as yet opaque from the human perspective, but that is not for the moment our problem.

It is of course a difficult conception, stretching imagination to the limits, and possibly beyond. This is in large measure due to the pressure it places on our normal experience of time and tense; for in this picture future free decisions, and the inception of future sequences of activity, must be conceived 'already' in terms of how they interlock with present and past sequences to an extraordinary degree of complexity. Thus the meaning of 'future' event is already circumscribed by what has happened and is happening. God has 'already' acted to provide the context of 'future' events. In short, both the extraordinary complexity of the conception and the grammar by which it must be described suggests that only a God acting creatively from outside our temporal perspective can create and order such a world as this. This simply confirms our suspicion, raised specially by Baelz's discussion, that God's relation to time lies close to the heart of any reasonable account of his activity. The job of conceiving the kind of relationship between time and eternity required by this account obviously cannot be shirked, and belongs to the next chapter.

The second consideration to ease this problem of relating two free agencies, and ascribing perfect efficacy to the first, refers us back to the analogical nature of the language we are using: it is a plea that we remember that this language is used analogically *throughout*, in an effort to express the truly transcendent. The analogy being proposed is, in effect, that the divine-human relationship (of double agency) is like the relationship of human agency to lower activity systems; the 'higher' level of agency can take up and encompass the 'lower' without destroying its status, simply in virtue of being 'higher'. But we should further remember that within this basic analogy all that is being referred to as divine action is itself depicted by analogical language. Yes indeed, it is divine agency we are talking of, and therefore in some sense, divine causality, even more specifically a kind of efficient causality as well as final causality; all that has already been made clear. But we should not therefore be beguiled into forgetting how stretched this language must be. We should not, for instance, tacitly assume that the divine action and causality is defined by intention in exactly the same sense as human action is defined by human intention: it is done so in an analogous way. That is, divine intention defines divine action in a higher sense than human intention defines human action, just as human intention defines human action in a higher sense than animal purposiveness defines animal activity, or than a web of causal laws defines the movement of events in the inanimate physical world. This means that in the case of the former relating to the latter in each pair (i.e. when divine intentional activity relates to human, and human relates to natural sequences) the correspondence is not one-to-one, but is that of a higher, more complex reality to a lower and more simple one. This must provide significant scope for the assertion that the higher can in this case 'take up' the lower in such a way that it may *always* carry its own meaning and purpose.

A further analogy may help: divine intentional action may be likened in some respects to the 'higher' reality of three dimensions, as compared with human intentional action of two dimensions. The relationship is then something like that between the reality of a village street and a pencil drawing of it.[75] As such, the higher reality is 'doubly' analogous because it is more complex in more than one sense (for instance, three-dimensional depth makes a difference to both shape and size), but because this is the case, it can and does always express itself in the two-dimensional: *some* aspect of the more complex reality is always capable of being represented by the more simple reality. For instance, a pencil line on the drawing can always be said to represent more than one plane of the actual village street (the roundness of a spire, or the edge of a building). Thus it is the very complexity, the 'otherness', of divine intentional action which reassures us that some aspect of itself can always be expressed in our more simple human action, whatever it is.

We should also be reassured that all this is not merely a retreat into mystery. To insist on the full measure of complexity and unlikeness on the divine side of the analogy is perfectly legitimate as long as we are providing corresponding analogies from within human experience (such as the relationship between three- and two-dimensional reality, or indeed the relationships between human and animal activity and natural events: it is the kind of unlikeness which relates these). It is also, as has already been suggested, not only legitimate but necessary if we are truly to be talking about God who must be identified in some distinguishing way. Nor should we forget it was the failure to maintain this unlikeness in analogy which produced the flaw in both Vanstone's and William's work.

Furthermore, none of this means we have taken leave of that basic model of human action as defined by intention, accepted from Miss Anscombe, which we are using to explicate divine action. Our model is still a statement about divine action in terms of meaning and purpose, even though it is also, quite properly, a statement about the transcendence of the divine intentional meaning which does not just allow of a 'larger number of purposes', but utilizes a 'higher', more complex understanding of what purpose means.

One final point in connection with this: it should be made clear that the sense in which the relationship between divine and human agency has been conceived as analogous to the relationship between human agency and physical events of other activity systems is strictly limited to the way in which the higher can in principle take up the lower, without destroying the meaning of the lower activity system. It is certainly not equivalent to the actual exercise of human agency over lower activity systems, which, in practice, is characterized as much by disruption and violence as by respect.

Clearly this second consideration is concerned much more with the formal possibilities of conceiving divine efficacy within the basic model of double agency. But taken together with the more substantial discussion of the first, it surely presents a firm enough basis with which to proceed. Due regard both to the universal scope of divine activity, and to its transcendence, does indeed warrant this contention—that whatever happens within creaturely activity may always be caught up to serve the divine intention. And all this, it should be recalled, is an attempt to defend the intelligibility of the paradox of double agency (where one side of the paradox is the transcendent God), which in turn serves to explicate the notion of God acting in and through particular events of the world sovereignly and effectively, to secure specific ends within his overall purpose. As such it has provided us with a basic structure of divine activity within which we can conceive how whatever happens is encompassed without uncertainty, within a higher meaning of God's intention.

This is a very strong claim: there is after all a vast range of possibilities within which human agents act freely and the contingencies of the natural world are actualized, but still the extraordinary complexity of their interaction in every case and at every level is guaranteed to be encompassed within the divine action. Consequently, so strong a claim can only benefit from more detailed exposition and defence. What does this *mean*, in more precise terms? What does it mean to claim that *every* event is caught up to serve God's intentions? What does this mean in relation to 'evil' and 'frustrating' events, in relation to the contingency and necessity of the world? In what sense is this universal divine action still special? Above all, what does it mean, in much more detail, about God's relation to time and temporality? In the exposition which follows, these problems will be addressed. What should also emerge more clearly is the extent to which the theological demands of divine initiative and sovereignty have indeed been fully met.

CHAPTER FIVE

Taking It To Extremes

Whatever happens is caught up to serve God's intention? Could this mean *every* event of nature and history, including my personal life? What, for a start, constitutes an event? Tackling these questions seriously may well take us to extremes, but nothing is ever gained without venture—especially in the world of theological compromise.

'Event' might be defined as any change from one state of affairs to another (though it is doubtful whether we have an adequate concept of change to make this particularly helpful).[1] Alternatively, it might be defined simply in terms of the activity of being, whereby being itself is conceived as event in the sense that energy is the physical ultimate (and therefore everything *is* by virtue of its activity).[2] But it may be misleading to dwell too much on this kind of definition, for in terms of this discussion the primary issue is not so much the meaning of event *per se*, as its meaning when it functions in the theological proposition 'every event is caught up to serve God's intention'. That is, however event is defined, we are concerned with the extent to which any occurrence, any change, any 'being', any constituent of reality, however basic in structure (or however apparently 'surd' or 'evil'), can be viewed as action and specifically as God's action.

The initial problem lies in the common-sense proposition that most events we know about and can talk meaningfully about are composite (i.e. divisible into sub-events). A harvest, for example, is divisible into a large number of constituent sub-events, natural and human, down to the action of sun and moisture and the movement of man's hands. And it is normally easier to see how the 'larger' event is capable of being described as action (defined by 'end' and intention) than its constituent sub-events. This is also true of purely natural events; the storm can quite easily be seen in principle as an action of God, with its own end and rationale, whereas its constituent sub-events of evaporation, the molecular and sub-atomic movements, are barely known, let alone seen as acts in their own right. How far, then, can these constituent sub-events be viewed as 'action'?

As we have already seen, Kaufman rejects this question at the outset. For him not every natural or historical event is a distinct sub-act of God, but 'only those events which move the creation forward a further step toward the realization of God's purposes'.[3] By implication, not all events do. Many processes are only functioning as 'rhythms . . . that support and sustain . . . the teleological movement.'[4] P.J. Donovan would agree. In his *Philosophical Analysis of the Doctrine of Providence*,[5] he considers it 'inappropriate' to talk of many events, changes of states of affairs, as action; after all, digesting, falling down stairs, the action of dripping water, and so on, are not intentional. And the fact that such events might be activities which are part of some 'ultimate purpose' (like Kaufman's rhythm supporting a teleological process) is not sufficient warrant for viewing them as 'action': 'an action . . . is an entity in its own right . . . an episode in which activity is directed to the achievement of a particular goal . . . an action is not simply a slice of activity'.[6]

As a definition of action this is helpful and will be referred to again below. But it does not of itself settle the issue as to whether all events (even digesting, dripping water and so on) may or may not fall within that definition when viewed from a different perspective and from within a different context of meaning, i.e., it does not settle the issue of whether such events—all events—may be seen as action of God. After all, 'digesting', 'falling down stairs', 'dripping water' are already descriptions of events presupposing a certain perspective and occur within a certain context of meaning; they could quite easily be viewed under a different description, for example as 'maintaining a particular life-support system', 'learning an important lesson', etc. Whether or not this sort of description is still disqualified as action because it is still only 'part' of some 'ultimate purpose' will be dealt with further below. But it is not relevant to the present point, which is simply that the question is not settled by the definition alone. Another act-description from a different perspective and from within a different context of meaning can always be offered.

In fact Donovan admits this: 'one may of course re-focus one's conceptual viewpoint, and treat as acts what one previously treated as elements within some activity'.[7] He gives the example of building a ship, which can be sub-divided down to the hammering of each rivet. However, like Kaufman, he still goes on to deny that this sub-division can be carried beyond a certain (though unspecified) point: it is impossible to further sub-divide to the action of lifting the hammer, taking aim, and so on; to go further and suggest that even these are 'made up of a series of muscular and nervous actions, each complete and with its own rationale and purpose', is 'absurd'.[8]

But the question must be pressed as to why it is necessarily absurd when viewed within the widest possible context and from an eternal perspective: that is, if God is the agent concerned. Certainly from a limited human perspective there must come the point of *reductio ad absurdum*. Events occur within human action which cannot be intended because they are not even known.[9] As such, though they might support and undergird action, they cannot possibly be abstracted from the action and meaningfully conferred with the dignity of that title in their own right. And of course events lying outside human activity cannot be intended, even if known, simply because they lie beyond the scope of human activity and willing. Yet here lies the rub: those elements which are absent from certain events within the human perspective, and thereby disqualify such events from being classed as possible actions— namely, consciousness of all events and unlimited scope of activity—are precisely the elements which normally *define* divine agency: that is, universal scope and (integrally) divine knowledge.

It is hard, then, to see why any event, however basic in structure, should not in principle be intelligibly described as a divine action, as long as we are defining the meaning of divine action according to its universal scope. Of course, in practice that description may also require much more to make it intelligible, not least some indication of how a loving divine purpose relates to certain kinds of evil, baffling or 'surd' events. More of that anon. So far all that is being maintained is that in principle it is not just the composite event but *every* event which is capable of this kind of description.

To recapitulate: hitherto, an examination of the nature of action-language and the paradox of double agency has suggested (a) that regularities within general structures are still capable of expressing specific intentions of a transcendent agent, and (b) that neither contingencies in the natural order, nor human action in the historical order, exclude that same capability. This has been maintained on the grounds of a truly universal scope in the divine activity, where

God is conceived as active in every circumstance and within the widest possible context, and because of the analogy whereby we are bound to speak of divine intention as a 'higher', more complex, reality than human intention. Now we can further claim, very precisely, that every event in the natural or historical order, however basic in structure, may be conceived as an action of God, at least in principle.

However this does sharpen other problems. For a start, if indeed every event may be described as an action of God, how can we differentiate the ways in which various events relate to God's intentions? It is crucial that we resolve this difficulty. Not to do so would risk falling foul of an objection raised by Donovan. He considers that a notion of universal action (i.e., one where every event is an act of God) evacuates 'action' of real meaning. Because 'action' is relative to a context which includes non-action, it requires an antithesis, that which is 'mere activity'. Therefore, Donovan maintains, we need to differentiate events which in themselves constitute an action of God from those which do not.[10]

Yet in fact we do not have to abandon the notion of universal action altogether to meet Donovan's point: actions do not have to be differentiated from mere events or activity to gain their meaning, but may be differentiated by the different kind of relationship each event has to the various ends of God's intention. And indeed this does need to be done. Obviously this is not a requirement that the 'content' of every purpose of God for every kind of event should be specified (an impossible task!),[11] but rather that a different kind of relationship between events and purpose can be intelligibly described. To fail to show what this relationship might be, and to resort only to the 'complexity' of divine intention, would constitute a significant weakness in the quest for intelligibility. It would also be a desperate blind spot in a world where events do present themselves so diversely to our moral sense and our sense of purpose. We therefore need a much closer analysis of the relationship between different kinds of events and their ends within the divine purpose.

There are at least two ways of conceiving such a relationship, and the difference between the two turns on their response to the particular pressures exerted by contingency (and, indeed, inflexible regularity) in the natural order and freedom in the human world, where these constitute an apparent frustration of the divine purposes. Both may be conceived and analysed in terms of the concepts of 'means' and 'ends'. It will be recalled that the need for such an analysis was suggested particularly by Baelz's position.

One way relates events which constitute a *prima facie* frustration of God's purposes to his intention by referring them to a further, overall purpose, an end which lies beyond the event itself. Thus it would not be appropriate to talk of a specific end intended by God as internally related to all those people involved in such events: each event bears no end in itself, for anyone, but gains meaning as an action of God only in so far as it is made into a means to a further end. By virtue of exercising a capacity which belongs to their being (perhaps the actualizing of some contingency in a certain way) such events frustrate specific ends intended by God for those involved, but are incorporated into a larger purpose by being *externally* related to other ends. So the tree blown over in a gale which kills a man is made into a hiding place for small wild-life, and firewood for his dependents, and so on. So too the car accident which kills the foetus and injures the woman is made into an opportunity for the car driver to amend his ways through shock and chagrin. These further ends are served by *means* of the event (and could in principle presumably be served by any number of other means), but there is no end intended in the event itself specifically for the man, foetus or woman. As far as *they* are concerned, the end of God 'in' that event is only general and external, to at least some of them.

The significant feature of this view of things is that the contingencies (and regularities) of the world which provoke such events force the divine intention into a different relationship with those individuals involved in them: the events are transposed from ends to means. Remembering Vanstone's view about Aberfan, cited earlier, we could not say there was *any* sense in which the event was intended (or even permitted) for the man or foetus or woman as an end (as one might easily say with the actualization of some other possibility, such as the successful birth of the baby); we have rather to speak of it as transposed into a means to some other end—and this is the result of the activity of 'secondary' agents within the paradox of double agency. In Kaufman's terminology one might then say of this view that the so-called accidents and frustrations in a world constituted by other interacting agencies are necessary features of the world which have the characteristic effect of turning intended acts (or, more properly, sub-acts) of God into mere events constituent of other sub-acts. Donovan would agree: some events are 'mere' events or activity.

This tendency, to see particular events forced into a different relation to specific ends of God, is clearly related to the tendency to push talk of God's special activity in relation to any particular event back to some general, overall purpose, and so push it right away from at least some particular events. A certain hesitancy in talking about God's special activity in relation to particular events is re-introduced. It does not constitute a full-scale abandonment of the notion, but does tend to prefer speaking in generalities rather than specifics. So we find Kaufman, though insistent that God is to be conceived as realizing some specific ends within the overall course of nature and history, nevertheless cautious and grudging about God's specific action towards individuals:

> God's subordinate acts here are governed largely by his over-arching purposes and ultimate objectives, not simply by the immediate needs or the prayerful pleas of his children ... Doubtless we men, both as species and individuals, have place within those 'purposes, and certain of his subacts are responsive to our acts ... But the place we have is his to determine and assign, not ours; at the very most our lives are but almost infinitesimal constituents in his all-comprehending act, and his responsiveness to the particularities of our activity must be understood as a function and phase of his master act ordering all human and cosmic history.[12]

The tone of this is precisely of one who seems unable to conceive of God's special action in relation to all particulars as fully intentional for them, as well as being some 'function and phase' of an overall purpose (which, of course, it is as well). It is a conception where some particular events are *only* understood through reference to further, general purposes. This is the characteristic conception of a world in which the complexity of interacting activity systems, and especially their resistance, is considered an insuperable obstacle to 'universal' special activity. The same tendency was explicit in Donovan's contention that action cannot be universalized and seen in relation to every constituent event 'merely by its being part of some ultimate purpose'.[13] This means for Donovan precisely that we should be wary of talking of God's special action, his realizing specific ends, in relation to certain particular events. This way of conceiving the relation between frustrating (or insignificant) events and the end of God thus constitutes a reversal of the direction we have been travelling before. The meaning of the proposition 'every event is caught up to serve God's intention' would revert to a much looser and more generalized way of speaking both of 'events' and of 'serving God's intention'. Specific ends could be conceived as being realized only in relation to some particular events; for other events the ends of God are related only generally and externally.

It is easy to see the attractions of this way of conceiving the relationship. It meets Donovan's need to distinguish event ('mere activity') from action, and it certainly provides a real and easily handled differentiation in the relation of divine intention to 'frustrating' (evil) events: they become pure means to other events. And it still claims in some sense to relate whatever happens to God's intention, *via* this more circuitous route of ends related only externally and generally to the event. It is, in fact, a fairly familiar way of conceiving the relationship: it might be re-expressed in terms of the distinction between consequent and antecedent will: i.e., in the actual circumstances of a concrete situation (such as the actualization, within the necessary condition of contingency in the actual world, of a frustrating possibility) what is intended by God in the event is still freely and really intended (by virtue of its relation to some other end), and this is his consequent will. But this is to be distinguished from his antecedent will, which is the prior choice and intention of God in the ideal circumstances.[14]

Yet there is another way of conceiving the relationship between events and the ends and purposes of God, one which insists that the end is always *internally* related to all those involved in any event in such a way that every event is in some sense 'end' and never purely 'means'. In terms of the conceptuality with which we have been operating this further implies that the 'accident' and 'frustration'. the apparently unfortunate interactions of natural and human agents, do not transpose the situation from ends to means-to-a-further-end alone (though they may still do that); rather, they are already woven in as ends, realizing an end as a sub-act within the master act. As such the intended action of God can be spoken of both more universally and with far great specificity than in Kaufman's account. In terms of the examples suggested above, it means that I may after all treat the fallen tree, or the car accident, as in some sense an intended action of God in relation to those involved, bearing some intended end for them. These events are not simply made a means to some general and external end, rather, those involved may find some specific end within the event for themselves.

Of course, an end which any event bears 'within itself' still derives meaning and value as an end from a wider context of meaning which includes the interrelation of that event with other events (and, indeed, other ends). But the significant feature of this account remains precisely in the fact that the meaning gained through this wide context has the status of 'end' (as well, no doubt, as means-to-some-further-end). Thus the event conveys intended meaning 'within' or 'through' itself, even though that meaning and value depends on a wide context, and this value is to be notionally distinguished from the value of 'means', which also depends on a wider context of course, but which conveys no intended meaning at all within itself. It is the difference between saying of the crucified Christ that here there is constituted something valuable of faith and courage and saying that here is nothing but pain and cruelty. In the first instance what is constituted may still relate to the resurrection which follows, and derive some meaning from it; nonetheless it is 'already' constituted *there*, in the actual event of crucifixion. It enables the cry 'Truly *this* man was the Son of God.' In the second instance there is nothing in the crucifixion, solely in the resurrection. It can only provoke the cry 'If you are the Son of God, come down from the cross.' (Note that the latter actually depends on a notion of 'pure' means, which one may well suspect is an abstraction in any case, thus supporting this view that every event should be conceived as internally related to an end of God, not requiring the category of pure means.)

Such, then, is this alternative way of conceiving the relationship between events and the ends and purposes of God. But what of the demand for some differentiation in the relation of divine ends to different kinds of events? In the first account it is obviously afforded by the clear distinction between ends and means. Some events are only means, others ends. Here that distinction is vitiated, for there is always some end. Yet in fact, as already indicated, we may simply argue that the differentiation lies in the kind of end to which the event is related. By virtue of the wider configuration of events and relations within the wider context of meaning, God achieves different kinds of ends in the crucifixion and resurrection, in the death of a child and its birth. This may well provide a much firmer basis for differentiation than the unreal distinction between ends and means.

It will already be clear that we are beginning to choose between the two accounts. The choice depends on a number of considerations not least those explicitly connected criteria of theological adequacy. More of that later. Here we may simply recapitulate those points from the accounts given above which might be considered as aspects of 'internal' coherence, as distinct from coherence within the wider theological context.

First, as already noted, the first account does tend to reduce some events to the category of 'pure means', and it is hard to see what meaning can be given to this—especially when applied to God's agency.[15] Further, to the extent that it does employ the concept of 'pure means', that concept is bound to be applied to events in personal life. *There could be no special exemption in this scheme of things for events in an individual's history (indeed, his history as a whole) being constituted simply as means.* This risk we have already seen to be implicit in Kaufman's account. Certainly this may seem merely to correspond to empirical reality as we know it *prima facie.* It does seem part and parcel of a necessary indeterminacy and indiscriminacy of the world, constituted as it is, that some persons should have to suffer as means to further ends. If God does not interfere to stop volcanoes, or Hitler, then those who suffer the consequences—for the sake of the integrity of the natural order, or the integrity of Hitler's freedom, or whatever—are in some sense 'sacrificed' for a 'higher purpose'. Yet we should be clear that such an account can only be offered either at the expense of God's sovereignty (i.e. God *cannot* bring about intended ends in relation to every individual, in every particular event, but only in relation to some generalized sub-acts within the master act), or at the expense of his goodness (for how could a good God ever consign individuals to the category of mere means?): a familiar enough dilemma, to which we shall be returning shortly.

Furthermore, this same concept of 'pure means' is invoked by the first account to deal with another notion which may prove theologically difficult to live with: namely 'frustration'. According to this account, there is a class of events in the world which forces the relation of the divine intention into a relation of means; such events 'frustrate' the specific end, and transpose it into the means to another end. This is a difficult concept in relation to divine activity because it implies a class of events which seem to be beyond the scope of intended activity, and unless some sort of dualism is being expressed at least some account must be given of how this class can be related to the divine action.

The obvious candidate for this is the category of 'consequences', 'concomitants' and 'side-effects'.[16] So it is argued that the divine creative activity, like any creative activity, entails unwanted consequences; such consequences are the frustrating circumstances which have to be coped with, and for which the concept of means needs to be invoked. To carry out a plan will, it is assumed, entail by-products and it is part of any creative endeavour to have to deal with them. This is a familiar assumption, already noted in Baelz and Vanstone's views. Again, the distinction between a consequence and an antecedent will may help to clarify what is meant here. It is the actual circumstances, the total circumstances of the world, to which the divine will must be related. And they include much that is consequent on what is not antecedently willed, but exists or occurs as a by-product of it.

Yet it is doubtful whether this sort of account can be sustained when applied to *divine* creativity and agency. It seems to apply categories (of undesired consequences, concomitants, side-effects) which we only grudgingly apply to finite human endeavour, because of limited scope in human activity. After all, the circumstances of human endeavour always include elements beyond the possible field of human activity. I plan to harvest a crop, but the rain frustrates me; such circumstances are none other than the consequences of some other endeavour (providing warmth elsewhere, evaporating and recycling rain over this field and so on), over which the farmer has no control. But is it then proper to apply this category to God for whom there is no limit in the scope of his activity? P.T. Geach raises the same point, again in terms of the distinction between consequent and antecedent will. Consequent will implies circumstances beyond control, which is precisely what cannot be predicated of an almighty creator God: take 'the merchantman's captain who throws his wares overboard in a storm: antecedently he wills to bring them into port, consequently upon the storm he wills to throw them overboard. But the captain only does not will rather to allay the storm because this is not open to him; he is not one whom wind and sea obey.'[17]

The point is reinforced when we realize that it is not always impossible, in principle, to talk of consequences, concomitants and side-effects as intended even within the endeavour of limited human agency. In a careful analysis of what is meant by such terms Anthony Kenny concludes, cautiously enough, that under certain conditions concomitants and side-effects of an action may be foreseen, desired, and adopted as such (and therefore intentional).[18] Of 'consequences' he admits that they may also be wanted enough to be brought about in any case independently of the end of which they are the consequences, and as such we can certainly hold the agent responsible for them. And though he suggests it is wrong to talk of consequences as intended in so far as they 'do not form part of the chain of practical reasoning which leads to the initial decision to bring [an end] about',[19] elsewhere he notes that the consequences of one act may appear as the result of another act (and so intended).[20] He also reminds us that there is another concept of intention according to which all the foreseen consequences of one's voluntary actions are intentional—a Benthamite principle which supports the traditional presumption in law that a man intends the natural consequences of his acts.[21] So if it is intelligible to talk of responsibility and even intention in relation to at least some consequences of the acts of finite, limited, agents, then it is surely intelligible to talk of intention in relation to all the so-called consequences in the unlimited scope of divine activity (they will 'accord' with ends of other divine acts within the universal scope of the divine action); there need be no 'accidental' consequences in the creation of this world.[22]

Such a world as this, where God is able to relate his intention in such a way to all events, where there is no class of events which frustrates him as mere accident or consequence, is the kind of world envisaged in the second of the two accounts described above. It can lay claim to being intelligible, and being intelligible it must carry a great presumption in its favour when it obviously sustains a far stronger doctrine of God's sovereignty than the first account: there is no class of events which frustrates him. It must also be preferred, as already indicated, because it evades the moral problems posed by the other account, namely the notion of a God forced to use consequences only as means and not as ends (peculiarly important when personal life is at stake).

Finally, by returning to consider specifically the nature of *creative* activity, this affirmation of God's capacity to relate ends to all events is lent even firmer backing. Consideration of finite human action in general suggests that the distinction between the main plan and the by-product may not be absolute. Consideration specifically of human creativity, which we have already seen to afford the best analogy for the universal scope of divine activity, suggests that the distinction can and must be wholly vitiated in the case of the divine creator. For the distinction is contingent, depending on the scope of the artist (and, of course, his degree of wisdom), not necessary to the actual business of creation. The point is stated succinctly by C.S. Lewis:

> I suggest the distinction between plan and by-product must vanish entirely on the level of omniscience, omnipotence, and perfect goodness. I believe this because even on the human level it diminishes the higher you go. The better a human plan is made, the fewer unconsidered by-products it will have and the more birds it will kill with one stone, the more diverse needs and interests it will meet; the nearer it will come—it can never come very near—to being a plan for each individual. Bad laws make hard cases. But let us go beyond the managerial altogether. Surely a man of genius composing a poem or symphony must be less unlike God than a ruler? But the man of genius has no mere by-products in his work. Every note or word will be more than a means, more than a consequence. Nothing will be present *solely* for the sake of other things . . . The great work of art was made for the sake of all it does and is, down to the curve of every wave and the flight of every insect.[23]

In opting for this view I am only too well aware that we are going well beyond most accounts of providence. Even Farrer would not admit the full extent of the edifice we have built on his foundations. He cannot bring himself to abandon the category of accident, even from the divine perspective: 'Accidentality is inseparable from the character of our universe'. An accident may be 'foreseen, provided against, discounted, or profited by', but 'it cannot be intended or arranged';[24] if it could, as argued above, it would of course cease to be an accident. I am also well aware that we may appear to be straining the demands of a reasonable theodicy to breaking point, and so creating other kinds of compromise. In what follows, however, I shall attempt to clarify and defend still further the implications of this view, and in the final chapter show how the theodicy question can and must be turned on its head: I believe that *only* this kind of picture provides the opportunity of a reasonable theodicy. In that sense I shall therefore attempt to show why we must maintain this most strict and precise version of the contention that 'whatever happens is caught up to serve God's intention'.

Further clarification involves four areas which specially deserve more attention. Three of them are considered here, the last is to be dealt with in a separate chapter. They concern the implications of this account for the nature of evil, for necessity and contingency in the world, for the sense in which such 'universal' action is still special, and for the relationship between time and eternity.

The nature of evil

As it stands the contention that any and every event is caught up to serve God's intention appears to put God's ends in intrinsic relation to evil events. If God has ends in all events and some events are evil, then we appear to be in grave trouble.

We cannot live with this, and we do not have to. God does not have ends in intrinsic relation to evil events, in the first instance because the whole notion of an event being evil 'in itself' crumbles under analysis. To begin with, as we have already seen, the concept of 'mere event' is something of an abstraction. In one sense 'event' is an important constituent of reality (perhaps, with Farrer, the prime constituent). Yet it is empty of value, unless it is related to a wider context of meaning.[25] More specifically, within the conceptuality with which we have been operating, it is a relative, negative counterpart to the notion of action. That is, every 'event' occurs within a wider context of meaning in which, by its relationship with other events, it can and must be properly described as an action of God. As such, an event cannot be abstracted and considered simply 'in itself' as evil—or good.

Now of course there are evil events, in the sense that we can and must speak of certain events in the world within a wider context of meaning in which they are just evil (and others good). But this is never the *whole* context: this context of meaning is itself only a relative, negative counterpart to a still wider context, the primary context of God's action. Thus 'event' and 'evil' gain their meaning compositely from a wider context, and may then find it changed in a still wider context. (This corresponds to a familiar theological insistence, normally associated with a more orthodox ontology which sees the fundamental constituent of reality in terms of substance rather than event, that evil is essentially parasitic; evil derives what being and meaning it has in relation to what is good: the function of this point in theology is, of course, to guard against ultimate dualism.)[26] The point is perhaps best made by example: the event of an earthquake (and its constituent sub-events) is not itself evil, but only in so far as it gains that meaning in a certain, wider, context of meaning (involving, for example, human pain and loss); likewise the mere 'event' of exercising the human will for its own sake can never be evil in itself, but only in so far as it gains meaning within, say, the context of harming other agents. But then these wider contexts can themselves be broadened as well so that the pain and loss and harm are likewise related to a wider (possibly eschatological) context as potential or actual constituents of greater goods, such as courage, pity, compassion. The possibility of actually conceiving this last point for certain kinds of evil and horror will be dealt with later.

Admittedly it might seem at first sight that this analysis has not advanced the case very far. After all, if it is being proposed that within the primary, wider, context of meaning there may be a good end in an event which, within a secondary and more limited context, is evil, the fact remains that God would still seem to have ends in intrinsic relation to that which is evil (unless it is being suggested that the meaning gained within the latter context is somehow 'unreal'—an expedient we must surely reject summarily for reasons I will mention briefly below). But in fact the problem has been eased. For by shifting the source of meaning of the reality of evil from 'events-in-themselves' to a wider context, it is possible, in principle, to speak of God's ends in intrinsic relation to all events without speaking of God having ends in that which is intrinsically evil. The end God has within events which, in the limited context, are really evil, may indeed constitute a good end within the larger configuration of the divine perspective. That particular *configuration* within which evil is really present is not an end of God, but then that particular configuration is not an exhaustive description of the situation; by definition it is only a limited (though real) context. Thus as regards the relationship of this particular configuration to God's intentions the question is not so much whether God intends it as an end, as whether 'it' has any proper meaning in the context of God's intention. He certainly intends every constituent event within the configuration, but the configuration itself, in its particular context of meaning, is inseparable from the wider configuration in God's wider context of meaning.

It should also be made clear that the limited configuration may be identified explicitly as the aspect of reality constructed by creaturely activity. Here if anywhere we are entitled to speak of the real but limited extent to which creaturely activity is given a 'temporary' hold on reality, a derivative creative function (for good or evil). As we have already had cause to note, Judas is given the choice to do what he wants, and the configuration around the cross is formed. But there is still no need to talk of the configuration of events around the cross within a context of meaning in which the betrayal is only a betrayal, and death only death, in relation to God's intention. For each event of the betrayal and death is already related, in a wider context of meaning, to ends of God involving a far wider configuration of events (involving, for instance, atonement). Similarly, to return to the event of an earthquake, the creaturely activity of the earth's crust exercises its capacity of 'being what it is', and a particular configuration of events is formed. But again, because the meaning of the constituent events is not exhausted by that particular configuration but encompassed within another wider context, it is still appropriate to speak of them in relation to divine ends. It is thus possible, in principle, to take every event of the earthquake and find some good end within it, such as the courage and pity evoked in some, and the merciful release into new life for the victims. The same could be true in principle for any exercise of the human will in an evil way, such as unwarranted aggression. Within God's perspective the very exercise of the will (and its effects) may constitute the possibility of self-knowledge—and reform—in the evil-doer.

Naturally we must also clearly insist that this limited configuration of events, the context in which evil is real, is not left out of the divine perspective entirely. If it were, it would mean that evil itself is not real to God and could mean nothing to him. This would be conceptually impossible to square with any significant doctrine of incarnation and atonement. It would also make a mockery, existentially, of his love and personhood in relation to ours. Furthermore, the very fact that evil events do have to be referred to a wider context of meaning before they can be spoken of in relation to divine ends indicates that there is real differentiation between and good and evil events, and therefore a real perception of that differentiation within the omniscience of the divine perspective.

However, granted the reality of evil as conceived above, the crucial feature of this account must be the fact that evil is a certain limited configuration of events which is but an arbitrary and 'temporary' aspect of reality, and which even as it presents itself to human experience already contributes part of a wider context of meaning in which a good end is being realized. John Hick expresses something similar in this way:

> Seen . . . in the perspective of a living faith in the reality of the great, ongoing, divine purpose which enfolds all time and all history, evil has no status in virtue of which it might threaten even God Himself. It has an interim and impermanent character which deprives it of the finality that would otherwise constitute so much of its terror.[27]

In this sense one might therefore say that the status of evil is ultimately tenuous; it crumbles when taken apart for scrutiny from the widest perspective. It has been found possible to sustain this kind of view precisely on the grounds set out above, namely that constituent events cannot be abstracted, called evil in themselves, and then predicated of God as intended ends. Evil only exists in a certain configuration of events which can always be seen from a different perspective, and as such may never have an ultimate hold on reality.

The necessity and contingency of the world

Thus far, our account of God's relationship with the world may also provoke misunderstanding about its necessity. Having 'explained' every event in relation to an end of God it could well seem that we have described the world as a wholly necessary world; that is, a world of which no part could have been otherwise; and, therefore, as the 'best of all possible worlds'. It is important to be clear that this is not the case.

To begin with, the sense in which every event has been 'explained' is limited. Certainly, to find in every event a direct relation to an end of God is in one sense to come close to 'ultimate explanation' or the 'self-explanatory'. That is, by referring every event to the personal will of God it seems that an ultimate source and rationale has been found. Yet precisely because God is characterized by 'personal will' the emphasis is more on having found 'ultimacy' and 'source' than on having found a necessary 'content' to the rationale. According to G.F. Woods' exposition of the notion of ultimate explanation, by analogy with the human will, one is saying little more than what one says when encountering human decision: I choose to do what I choose to do and there is an opaqueness in the mystery of that personal choice which it is impossible to penetrate.[28] Thus to say that every event has a direct relation to the purpose of God is to say little more than that the world has a purpose in its every respect; it is not to say much, as yet, as to what the purpose has to be: it says nothing about the necessity of that particular choice in each respect. The personal will of God is an opaque fact which we encounter in the world's events which no further explanation can penetrate, not a logical necessity,[29] and it will be recalled how characteristic this is of the biblical God's *inscrutable* compassion and grace. This limited notion of explanation helps cut the link which is often forged between 'explanation' and 'necessity'. It leaves plenty of room for God to choose events which are contingent or freely willed by creatures, and even because they are such; it can also embrace all events.

This last point can be illustrated with reference to Keith Ward's discussion of this problem.[30] He is unhappy with a limited notion of explanation. He argues that it is too weak by comparison with Thomist or rationalist ideals of explanation. On the other hand he is equally unhappy with these latter precisely because they do tend to necessitarianism. So there may appear to be only two options, either that all existent realities are such that each part entails the existence of and is entailed by the existence of every other part (in which case all is necessary), or, if existent realities are only sufficient (not necessary) means to a necessary end, then other means would have done as well, or better, or more economically.[31] The former is rejected by Ward because of its conclusion that all is necessary. The latter is favoured because, while preserving an ultimate end (of goodness), it evades the conclusion that there is only one, necessary, path to that end. Thus when 'explanation' is linked to 'necessity', the price of supposing there is an explanation for everything is that everything is necessary; and because this is unacceptable some events are left unexplained or 'expendable' in terms of the ultimate end ('other means would have done as well, or better, or more economically'). They may only be accounted for in terms of the *general* necessity of their randomness and/or counter-adaptivity (i.e., as instances of the general character of the world which must perforce include such elements of sheer randomness, accident and so on). Seeing only these two options, and favouring the latter, the price Ward has to pay is thus a familiar one. He has to allow that some other way might have been better in some respects and that the actual world contains within it events that may be wholly random and counteradaptive in relation to the divine purpose. So again it would become impossible to talk of God's specific action (with intent) in relation to all things, but only in relation to some things and ultimately to an overall purpose.[32]

These alternatives (of a wholly necessary world, or a world incorporating wholly random elements) have coloured the assumptions of other writers, as we have seen.[33] They are surely false alternatives, which do not take full account of the nature of explanation as we have described it.[34] Explanation by personal will is not the same as absolute logical necessity, but neither does it have to be understood as the categorizing of some events simply as instances of a general principle of necessary randomness. An event may resist the category of sheer necessity without being classed as wholly random (or even 'necessarily' random), for there is this further category, namely the contingent (in the sense that it could have been otherwise) which is not random (in the sense of being wholly without purpose), and which is still directly linked with the divine will and purpose. It is precisely this category which allows us to 'explain' every event by referring it to the divine will, though without any great pretensions for the 'degree' of explanation being canvassed: it enables us to talk of all specific events in terms of their relation to God's will without consigning the whole world to iron necessity in all its detail.

We may therefore agree with Ward that there might be other ways of realizing ends; there is a genuine contingency such that things could have been otherwise, and which is linked no doubt with the real measure of freedom accorded to the creation. But this does not commit us to the view that other ways could be better in the sense that this way includes wholly random and counteradaptive elements which might have been better ordered or should have been avoided, when viewed from the widest possible perspective. Instead, with the aid of a particular notion of the relation of God's eternal perspective to our time—to be envisaged below—it is possible to conceive of free creaturely decisions and responses as already known and woven in with other events from the beginning to serve God's purposes. The particular web of this world's history, in all its detail, was certainly not the only pattern possible, for the responses could have been otherwise. In this sense the creaturely response of faith, for instance, does have significance; it makes a difference to the way in which events are ordered 'from the beginning', and to this extent we have no disagreement here with Wiles and Ogden in their view that God's action is affected by creaturely action. But unlike their scheme of things, the priority here remains specifically with God who has 'placed' those responses from the beginning to serve his purposes. Furthermore we may also say that this web of events is from beginning to end a pattern which is perfectly directed and could not in that sense be bettered.

Naturally this sort of perfection is largely invisible from within the historical perspective, and can only be appreciated from the perspective of the eternal whole (but more of that later).

In this way we come to qualify the sense in which it is the 'best of all possible worlds'. It is not a unique perfection of creativity. It is one of an infinite number of patterns, all of which might, within the divine ordering, lay claim to that perfection. To link it uniquely with perfection would indeed be to link it with necessity, and would constitute a failure to understand the nature of creativity—which can produce multitudes of good things with no possible choice between them. This is something that both the human artist and the parent can understand in principle as they consider the 'work of their hands'—even if they have to look wistfully to the infinitely wiser and more effective creator to see it in practice.

The sense in which God's action is special

Another clarification which may be needed concerns the sense in which God's action may still be said to be special. Does the proposed concept of universal action, that is action which encompasses every event, effectively dissolve its speciality? For by suggesting that all events are the special action of God it could, paradoxically, appear that none are special. The account would then seem to be reverting (ironically) to a generalized understanding of divine activity, more akin to Wiles' position after all. In fact there are various senses of speciality in divine action which have been charted throughout this account, and which are in no sense threatened. It may be helpful now to draw these threads together in one place, recapitulating points already made.

In the first instance divine action is diverse or 'special' in the sense that the divine intention is realizing different ends in relation to particular events (even when, empirically speaking, these events fall within general structures of reality). Thus God may be acting specially in relation to, say, sunshine and rainfall, in realizing the different ends of making possible the harvest, and watering the crops; or, more obscurely, providing the context in which the disappointed farmer is driven to creative action with new resources, learns patience, and so on.

Divine action is also special in the sense that the configuration of relations between ends and events which form the 'wider context of meaning' is also different in relation to particular events. Thus *what* those ends are in particular instances of sunshine and rainfall depends precisely on the larger context of the state of the crops at that particular time, the state of the farmer's spiritual resources, and a whole cluster of other needs (obvious and less obvious) related to the situation; in short, the configuration of relations between ends and events which form the wider context of meaning.

Having established this we may now note that there are also at least two senses in which God's action can be said to be uniform as well. First of all, since in this account all events are constitutive of an end, it would be possible to describe God's action in relation to all events under a single heading: for example, Ogden talks of all events constituting the possibility of 'authentic being'.[35] Then there is also a sense in which one metaphysical category, one type of account, is being offered for all (or nearly all) events; namely, divine action through other agents (the paradox of 'double agency').

However it should be clear that as far as the first is concerned that 'one' end of, say, 'authentic being' is a generalization. Within the overall unity and integrity of God's purpose it is indeed possible to generalize the content of that purpose, as well as the fact of it, in such a way as to give it a single name applicable to his every action: thus God's action towards us, even in punishment, is always 'love' or 'providing the context in which we can realize authentic being' or 'glorifying himself'. But different kinds of action serve that very general purpose in the sense that different specific ends are being realized to achieve it. Further, that general purpose of God is conceived in this account as internally related to each individual and therefore specific in that sense too. It is not a general purpose standing outside the world to which the individual relates purely externally. Thus although every event serves the general purpose of 'glorifying God', it is also an event of love to serve the creature; the purpose is 'for us', in addition to the fact that we are serving some purpose for God. So the tendency to generalize and externalize God's purpose, noted particularly in Wiles' account, is resisted in this account. God can be conceived as realizing specific ends in relation to particulars. We may even say that God realizes specific ends 'tailored' to individual needs in every event. In short, for action to be universal does not entail that it is also general (to assert or imply such an entailment is to confuse the categories of universal-particular and general-specific).[36]

As far as the second point is concerned we should be clear that the 'one metaphysical category' of divine activity should not necessarily exclude the traditional concept of miracle in occasional events. I would simply reiterate the point made earlier, that our chief concern here is the concept of special divine action 'normally speaking'.[37] The question of miracle, when defined narrowly as a certain means of causality which by-passes natural agents, is simply another subject; it is not to be conceived as the normal mode of divine activity. As already indicated, the incarnation may certainly have to be conceived as an exception, and that too is a subject for another book.

Thus divine action is special in that different ends are being realized through the wider configurations of ends and events, whatever we can or cannot say about the causal mechanics of some of them. And this, of course, is entirely compatible with the central claim of Christianity that some events have unique significance. There is no reason at all, within the terms of this account, why we should not talk both of all events bearing a special end *and* some events bearing a special end which is particularly significant for the whole historical process. While all events are potentially or actually creative and redemptive for some, and at least one, some events may be creative and redemptive for all, and therefore more significant. H.R. Niebuhr, amongst others, offers the analogy from human creative endeavour to show how this might be conceived. The crucial act in a play may cast a different light onto the rest of the drama; it may 'redeem' and resolve hitherto unresolved elements in the plot, set discord and tragedy in a new context of meaning, and so bear unique significance for the whole drama.[38]

This last point highlights the sense in which this account might differ from Ogden's generalization that all events constitute the possibility of redemption and 'authentic being'. While agreeing that every event is the action of God of a redeeming kind, even that every event is the action of God creating for us the possibility of 'authentic being', nevertheless it is not necessary to reduce the Christ event (whether causally odd or not) simply to another event alongside every other, nor even just as a 'decisive re-presentation' of all such other events. For though redemption may be given in 'all life', it may still be correct to affirm that the very potential of all life in this respect is constituted by the special action of God in one particular event (viz. in Christ). Thus it would be more correct to talk of the possibility of every event-constituting-the-possibility-of-redemption itself being constituted by the Christ event (at which point, incidentally, we would be more in line with Bultmann's insistence that the Christ event does have unique 'constitutive' significance for redemption—which is precisely the point at which Ogden takes him to task for failure of nerve).[39] This view restates the analogy, from human art and drama, of the specially significant theme or act which gives new possibilities to the whole. It also quite accurately restates the biblical picture outlined in the earlier chapter, helping to satisfy those demands of revelation perceived there. Certainly, as noted in that chapter, an adequate doctrine of atonement (broadly understood) is needed to sustain this sort of picture. But I do not feel this is impossible. It would require a doctrine which sees God in Christ taking into himself (*qua* transcendent God) the experience of perfectly overcoming suffering, sin and death (*qua* man), so that out of that particular experience he may help us use the general possibilities of redemption presented to us in all life. But this too is another subject, requiring another book.

Summary

What, then, of the task originally set for this alternative account of God's relationship with the world? The demands were that God should be conceived as acting transcendently and with sovereignty, yet without compromising creaturely freedom; that he should be conceived as acting 'diversely' or 'specially', with personal initiative and concern for particulars within the general structure of the world. In principle, I suggest, these demands have been well met within this conception of God's activity which is universal in scope, but with one large conceptual gap to be filled: we have already had more than one occasion to note that such a conception may only be sustained with at least some explication of how that transcendent God, with such a scope of action, can be related to time; how polar opposites can be reconciled particularly with respect to time and eternity. To this we now turn.

CHAPTER SIX

Time and Eternity

The picture painted thus far of God's relationship with worldly events presupposes much about the relationship of God to time. It is high time to expose these presuppositions and consider how well they can be sustained in the face of various criticisms. We should remember, for instance, how Baelz isolated the issue of time as crucial, and rejected one view of God's relationship with the world precisely because he could not accept a certain view of the divine relationship to time. The subject is so vast that what follows can only be a sketch of past and present debates as they impinge on our account. I will therefore offer fairly detailed references to these debates in the course of this discussion so they can be followed up in more depth elsewhere.

The sort of relationship between God and the world which is being envisaged here is one where God not only knows what future events will be (in our future, that is), but also acts to arrange circumstances according to a certain pattern in that 'future'; whatever contingencies are actualized by freely taken decisions (or by 'random' selection in the physical realm) are known and already accommodated within the divine action. This is all presupposed by the way in which we have expounded the view that 'whatever happens is caught up to serve God's intentions'; the universal scope and perfect efficacy required in such an exposition could only be sustained with such 'fore' knowledge and action.

Now this sort of view could conceivably be supported by a God relating temporally to the world, but knowing the future infallibly in every detail by 'prediction'—that is, having created structures in which all future effects are present in their causes and so, in principle, predictable (the sort of world envisaged in Laplace's famous claim).[1] In fact this sort of view is not easy to sustain in the face of modern physical theory. Heisenberg's claim, embodied in his 'uncertainty principle', is that much of the information required for the prediction of the future from the past (in the sort of terms that Laplace envisaged) is actually unavailable in principle (not just available in practice due to human ignorance). Actually, this too is open to question.[2] But whether or not Laplace's view of predictability stands or falls as a physical theory it must surely fall on any assumption of human freedom—not because foreknowing a future 'free' action is of itself strictly incompatible with the genuine freedom of that action, but because it is foreknowledge based on what would appear to be a wholly deterministic view of causality: applied to human agency it would be difficult to see what kind of freedom might be left to us.

Thus if theists reckon with a God who relates temporally to the world they more usually reckon with a God who has created a world with a genuinely open future in which creaturely freedom and physical contingencies may be actualized in a way which is unpredictable even to God.[3] As in the process view, God might indeed know the range of possibilities of the future, may indeed have constituted and circumscribed that range of possibilities by his creative act in such a way that no future state of affairs could fall outside them; he may further know what sort of response he will make to the actualization of all such possibilities; but the specific content of these possibilities, and therefore of his future acts, remains unknown.[4] The final outcome, incidentally, may or may not be guaranteed.[5]

However, this view simply will not support the kind of picture we have painted. Even if final success is guaranteed, a God who must 'wait' on the actualization of a multitude of physical contingencies and free human actions cannot easily be conceived as already acting within all the surrounding circumstances of those contingencies in such a way as to encompass every event within his meaning and purpose in the sense required (that is, ordering events in direct relation to an end, and not just as means). Rather, it is precisely the view with the characteristic effect of forcing the ends of God back 'at a distance' from particular events, generalizing them in relation to those events, and realizing them only by employing certain events as means to these external ends.[6] It is the view characteristically implying frustration and accident which we have considered to be neither necessary nor desirable.

Do we then have to resort to a view of God as one who relates to worldly events from outside the temporal sequence? This is far more likely to sustain an account where both 'future' contingencies and the circumstances which surround them (these also being constituted in some measure by contingencies) are known, and both are so woven into the pattern of a larger context as to bear the divine meaning and purpose in the strict sense required.

The notion of a God beyond time, and who thus relates to the world from outside time, can be traced, in seminal form, probably as far back as Parmenides, through Plato and Augustine, but receives its first thorough treatment in the Christian tradition from Boethius.[7] For Boethius eternity is experienced by God as a *totum simul*, and it is from that standpoint that God experiences the temporally structured creation:

> If you reflect on the immediate confrontation by which God discerns all things, you will judge that it is not foreknowledge of something as future, but rather knowledge of a never failing present.[8]

Aquinas adopts much the same view: 'The eternal has neither beginning nor end' and 'contains no succession, being all at once' (*total simul existens*);[9] Of the Reformers, Calvin in particular supposes something very similar;[10] as does Schleiermacher.[11]

However, in understanding what is meant by a 'never failing present' and 'being all at once' it may be necessary to make an important, though provisional, distinction between the experience of God 'in himself', in his own life, and his experience of and relation to the creation[12] (for the present discussion it is the latter which is of primary importance, even if ultimately no wedge can be driven between the two). What is being maintained in this so-called 'classical' view is that what we experience as past, present and future, is experienced by God only as present (whatever may be said about the nature of God's own experience apart from creation). In respect of this distinction, then, the passage quoted by W.C. Kneale from Boethius makes the point more clearly than that from St Thomas: in the 'confrontation' by which God discerns this world, he knows 'all of it' as a 'never failing present'. On the other hand, the citation from Aquinas does also convey a notion commonly associated with this 'present awareness', namely that it 'contains no succession'; that is, for God to see past, present and future as present, is to see all things 'simultaneously'. It is not difficult to see how such a notion supports the sort of view which is being canvassed, which requires precisely that God should know what lies in our future and should be able 'already' to have acted.

But of course such a view immediately raises a whole range of serious problems. It is true that at first sight it might seem to gain support from recent theories of space and time which trade on the relativity theory. Thus time may be regarded as a fourth dimension, bound up with space in 'space-time', a single continuum experienced by finite beings only along a particular 'temporal' path within that continuum, but in fact already existing as a whole.[13] But such a conceptualization, while providing a way of talking about God's 'simultaneous' vision of all things, does so at some cost. For instance, Geach insists that if this sort of view is held too rigorously it must imply that time is unreal.[14] For if God really does see things simultaneously, either he is unaware of the temporal aspect of things (and the theory is theologically inadequate) or things really are simultaneous. This second alternative not only offends against common sense (which insists on the reality of time), but is philosophically unacceptable on more specific grounds:

> . . . temporal succession itself cannot be an illusion, since the so-called illusion of successiveness is already a real succession of experiences: just as misery cannot be an illusion, because to be under the illusion of misery would be real misery.[15]

Further problems arise when it is considered whether a God beyond time could actually have created a temporal order, and once having created it act within it; moreover, since action within the world presupposes knowledge of the world as it is experienced from within the world, there is the problem of whether God can know things as they are experienced while it is being supposed that he knows them simultaneously (i.e., he would need to know the temporal order as it is experienced, even if it were granted 'unreal'). For according to Nelson Pike, the timeless creation of a temporal order is absurd, because to produce something is to effect its beginning in time;[16] and to act within that creation, whether it is conceived as active 'sustaining' or more positively 'intervening' would seem to presuppose that God's causation is in, not beyond time;[17] as for the knowledge which would seem to be a necessary precondition for effective action, this is denied by R. Coburn who argues that the truth of a particular temporal location ('today is the 12th May') cannot be known by one who has no location in time.[18]

Another range of problems clusters around the question of human freedom. Any sort of foreknowledge of a person's actions is deemed by Pike to constitute predetermination of those actions, when the foreknowledge is essentially (and not contingently) certain, deriving from absolute, infallible omniscience.[19]

Finally, there is an even more wide-ranging set of problems which relate back to the being of God-in-himself. For despite the initial distinction made between the life of God in himself and his experience of the world, the two may be ultimately inseparable. The whole notion of a *personal* God 'beyond time', however he may be conceived as relating to the temporal order, needs clarification. Indeed in one sense this question is prior to all other problems of his relation to the temporal order, since there would be no meaning or purpose in relating to the world unless personal categories could be used. Pike enumerates the following problems in asserting that a God beyond time could also be truly personal:[20]

1)   Reflecting and deliberating take time, so a reflecting, deliberating God would appear to require temporal extension.

2)   Anticipating and intending require temporal location: '. . . to act purposefully is to act with thought of what will come about after the beginning of the action'.[21]

3)   Remembering requires temporal location and extension.

The point is that these mental abilities, which seem to require an individual who could not be in any strict sense beyond time, may also be considered to define personhood. The conclusion may therefore appear irresistible, that God could not be beyond time and truly personal.

In the face of such problems it might seem necessary to bring God into time, at least from the moment of creation and in respect of his relations with the creation.[22] There does not seem to be any fundamental incoherence about this, at least in so far as the notion of time beginning with creation is concerned.[23] Yet, as we have seen, to sacrifice God's place beyond time is to give up the kind of specific action of God in all events which we are concerned to defend and expound. It is very hard to see how anything other than an extra-temporal God could act within the world in the way being suggested. Thus some attempt must be made to consider these objections and meet them as far as possible. No claim is being made to settle these questions, nor even to discuss them fully, but only to indicate that they are still open questions and by no means closed by the kind of considerations that Pike and others have advanced. To this end it might be helpful first to consider each objection in turn, then to offer some alternative way of conceiving the problem.

The first objection concerns the alleged unreality of time which is not really 'past, present and future' to God, and the offence this causes—not only to common sense, but to the fact of successiveness in our experience. But in fact the phenomenon of successiveness as a defining characteristic of temporality needs to be analysed more closely. For instance, if McTaggart's distinction between 'past, present and future' series and 'before and after' series is adopted it may be possible to retain some notion of successiveness in the before-after series of relations even though the experience of past-present-future is excluded (from God's eternal perspective).[24] To justify this we would need to argue that the experience of the series past-present-future is indeed less 'real' than the fact of successiveness in terms of before-after, and so temporality is not essentially constituted by the former. This kind of argument is quite possible: after all, the experience of past-present-future is in fact only an immediate awareness of the present; the present is 'really real' in a sense in which neither the past nor future are. Indeed, the present 'includes' past and future within itself in that the 'real' present is not just an infinitesimal moment, but requires the adoption of the notion of 'specious' present (the actual present moment plus a short stretch of memory and anticipation which is experienced with present immediacy). Thus the reality of time could be described as a composite of the actual present moment (which would be an abstraction if considered alone) and a short period of 'past' and 'future' experience, experienced together with present immediacy as one 'present' experience. This is an analysis which admits of the successiveness of before-after, but not of past-present-future (where the past has 'slipped away' and the future is yet to come).[25]

This distinction between the 'before and after' series of relations and the 'past, present and future' series of relations is developed by A.C. Ewing along the lines described above—and further.[26] He suggests in fact that an extended specious present might be conceived as the way God experiences the world, 'so that there might conceivably exist a being for whom the whole time series were present and there was no such thing as future or past . . . [but] an event would be apprehended as before or after another'.[27] This is advanced by Ewing himself only as a tentative theory, and is used here in the same spirit, but it does seem suggestive enough in a particularly difficult area to question the finality of any 'realist' objections.[28] More generally this conception does not make time an illusion, because in this sense to perceive time under the past, present, future series is in fact to perceive only a very small part of the time series, whereas the divine perception of 'before and after' sees the whole series; our experience of time is thus not so much the perception of something illusory as a perception of only a very small part of the total reality.[29]

Incidentally, another appeal to the concept of an 'extended specious present' has been made more recently by Grace Jantzen,[30] but it is more limited and therefore possibly misleading. She employs the familiar and useful distinction between our subjective experience of time (in which its measure is variable), and objective time (in which it is not); she then allows God's subjective experience of (our) time to be like an extended specious present even though 'really' and objectively it is successive. So far so good. However, she does not allow the future to be incorporated into the analogy in any other sense than prediction. This is because she does not wish to conceive of any objective sense in which God transcends 'our' time: objectively God is simply everlasting along with the world (which is all of a piece with her view that the world is God's body). Certainly the difficulties created by God's transcendence of 'our' time are enormous, and we have more work to do in what follows if they are going to be properly tackled. But again we must insist that only this kind of transcendence will do the job required.

Continuing now with the various other objections raised previously, what of the view that an extra-temporal God could not create or act within the temporal creation? In fact it is hard to see why this has to be. The theoretical alternative is put by Ewing as follows:

> Causality is a relation and therefore it could not be in either of its terms in the sense in which their qualities are. It seems to me like asking whether the distance between London and Manchester is in London or Manchester and because I cannot answer the question concluding that I am wrong in thinking that there can be such a relation as distance between them at all.[31]

In other words, God's causality in time does not require God himself to be exclusively conceived within time. A familiar analogy offered by Dorothy Sayers will illustrate the point.[32] As we have seen, she likens the creation of the temporal world to the human act of creating a novel or drama: as such its creation (in every detail) is not an event within the time scale of the world created, rather the events of that world have their being in the one creative act which, relative to them, is 'timeless', 'extra-temporal'.[33] The argument is also taken up linguistically by R.L. Sturch.[34] Sturch argues that creating and sustaining have a 'root meaning' which can be divorced from temporal associations. He asks whether the volition of God that creation should be, and continue to be, is not a sufficient meaning to creation and sustaining (at least where God's wanting 'X' omnipotently, is necessarily bound up with 'X's *being*): and as such, as long as volition is agreed to be a-temporal, creation and sustaining can be seen as only contingently deriving their meaning from temporality.

Further, the view that God cannot know things which are knowable only by those who occupy a temporal position is also questionable. It is actually questioned by Pike himself: a 'timeless' God and a temporal individual can report the same temporal fact, even if there is a sense in which it bears a different meaning.[35] In Ewing's formulation of the problem, God 'outside' time could certainly know that one event was before—or after—another, which in fact constitutes the 'most real' relation within our temporal experience of a specious present.

The range of problems connected with human freedom may also dissolve, or at least be eased, as long as the notion of an extended specious present is held in view. Such a notion, strictly speaking, has nothing to do with foreknowledge. The 'future' is known as immediate, present, insight; it is not known 'in advance', and certainly not known by prediction from preceding causes. Boethius is quite clear about this, and its implications: ' "For doth thy sight impose any necessity upon these things which thou seest present?" "No." '[36]—and Pike concedes the point; this 'works' even if God is essentially omniscient (which, in the case of foreknowing, *would* seem to 'impose necessity').[37] Ewing pinpoints the fallacy in claiming that 'present' knowledge of 'future' acts involves determinism by insisting on the same point:

> What is incompatible with freedom is the notion that all events are fixed before they happen, but I am not suggesting that God knows them before they happen. That would be putting him in the time series after all. If my suggestion is correct, it is not true that God knew in 1,000 B.C. that Hitler would start a war on Poland in A.D. 1939 . . . he knew it timelessly . . . And supposing it was an act of free will on Hitler's part . . . [God] only knew it because he was immediately aware of Hitler . . . God would know it because Hitler did it, not vice versa.[38]

The fallacy thus lies in the fact that attempts to show the incompatibility of 'foreknowledge' and free-will succeed only by insisting precisely that it is *fore*'knowledge (from the point of view of the knower); that is, God is brought back into the temporal series, thus smuggling in the appropriate premise from which the desired conclusion follows.[39]

Finally, with respect to the nature of the being of God, some account must be offered of a God beyond time who can yet be designated as personal; that is, as reflecting, anticipating and intending, and remembering. A minimal answer to this might be to question the necessity of reflecting, intending and remembering as long as God knows. 'Knowing' as a mental act does not require temporal location or duration, nor a temporal relation between the knower and what he knows.[40] Thus simply as a knowing subject God's personhood might be said to be intact. In fact this sort of solution is unlikely to satisfy, not least because the pivot of the whole argument of the thesis has been a 'strong' concept of God's intentional action (by analogy with our own). To subsume all talk of intentional action simply under the notion of 'timeless knowing' is not adequate to that analogy. It is not enough to show that a God outside time can perceive this temporally structured world as such; we need to show how conditions in the transcendent divine life are such that he can and does *act*. On the other hand it has already been suggested that there is some possibility of conceiving a God outside time as creating and acting within the temporal order, so in that sense we are not simply subsuming all talk of action under the category of 'knowing'. Further, the possibility of talking of an a-temporal God intending, responding etc., has been defended linguistically, again by Sturch.[41] He analyses the logic of such words as intending, responding, anticipating, remembering, and suggests that the first two at least have a root meaning without necessary temporal associations. Taking the root meaning of 'intend' as 'God wishing X' (for the world), or, further, as a wish/belief that Y follows X, he grants that while Y may be temporally related to X, the agent is not necessarily thus related. Similarly, if it is suggested that an a-temporal God could not be affected and respond, then Sturch replies that if 'X is affecting Y' implies only 'Y would not be as it is were not X doing what it is', then this can be taken without temporal associations; also, in the case of response, the response of God might be conceived as laid down conditionally 'from the beginning' in the very act of creation. In short, 'timeless knowing' might be filled out in such a way as to allow at least a partial reinstatement of the action analogy.

Now it has to be said that this kind of reply, taking each objection in turn, is piecemeal, drawing on a variety of approaches in answer to a very powerful challenge, and as such it may not seem adequate. Also it does not pretend to give any positive indication as to the nature of the divine existence beyond time (God's eternity), preferring only a minimal indication of how a God beyond temporality as we experience it may still be conceived as relating personally to it. This may be construed both as a strength and as a weakness. On the one hand the nature of God's own life, of his eternity, is hardly available to adequate rational analysis and description from within the temporal perspective; therefore the less said the better. On the other hand by saying little we may appear to imply sheer timelessness, that God in himself has *nothing* to do with time. And there is no doubt that a concept of sheer timelessness sharpens those difficulties that Pike and others raise, as to how such a God can be conceived as personal, to a point at which they become intolerable. In short, it may not be enough to provide formal arguments for the possibility of conceiving a God relating personally to the world from beyond the world's temporality without also providing some positive indication as to the form of God's own 'temporality'—or 'eternity'. Reluctantly, therefore, we must now make some attempt to consider the meaning of God's eternity; that sense in which the form of his own life is temporal and the sense in which it is a-temporal, even though this can only be a perilously speculative enterprise.

Pike attends to the question of God's eternity as it functions in theological talk, and concludes that the meaning given to the 'eternity' or 'timelessness' of God by Schleiermacher, Aquinas, Boethius, Anselm and Augustine (though with some reservations about the last two) is to be taken quite rigorously: God has no temporal extension and he has no temporal location. Thus to speak of God's eternity is to say that he has nothing to do with time in himself—even though he may be aware of the created temporal order and its contents. Interpreting Boethius' comment that God 'has always an eternal and present state' Pike concludes (though with some diffidence) that this means God exists in an a-temporal mode of existence.[42] This is definitely a statement about God's life-in-himself, the form of his own experience, rather than a statement about the content of his experience, his epistemological relation to time and its objects.[43] Pike proceeds to assume this radical, negative meaning of eternity throughout his treatment of the subject. It would seem, therefore, that if we are going to attempt a more positive indication of God's eternity we will be departing from the normal tenets of classical theism (and of the 'founding father' of modern Protestantism). Any attempt to characterize God's eternity which posits not simply timelessness, but rather some kind of temporal analogy (though without going back on our insistence that he must indeed be beyond 'our' time), constitutes such a departure.

In fact, as already indicated, philosophical theologians have not been reluctant to make such a departure. Process theologians actually start from a denial of the classical scheme, particularly as it relates to the doctrine of God (though their reconstruction will not serve our purpose since it binds God—in his concrete, active, aspect—too exclusively to our temporal process).[44] The concerns of some biblical theologians have also led them away from classical norms.[45]

However, more cautious attempts than the process view are on offer. Ian Ramsey, for instance, certainly preferred to assume a more positive predication than 'sheer timelessness' to describe God's eternity, though without putting God right back into the world's time.[46] Taking over Kneale's distinction between sempiternal (endless duration) and eternal (timelessness), Ramsey examines the various concepts of the eternal elucidated by Parmenides, Plato, Augustine and Boethius, and claims that the concept only arises *through* models of the sempiternal.[47] This is not simply by a negation of these models, but by a disclosure of that which, conceived primarily as a succession of moments, completes that temporal series in a way best expressed metaphysically by some such word as 'unity' or 'whole'. The eternal is thus a disclosure of that which is temporal and 'more', rather than simply a-temporal (this 'more', Ramsey is at pains to point out, is not on 'logical all fours' with the spatio-temporal, but its meaning is still given through the sempiternal model of the spatio-temporal, not by exclusion of the spatio-temporal).[48] Thus for Ramsey the concept of God will be a concept which 'straddles the eternal and temporal . . . and to talk of the life of God will not be incompatible with timelessness'.[49]

Of itself this may not take us very far, but it does encourage us in that direction. Some similiar encouragement may be found in Alasdair Heron's reflections on the subject, though the standpoint from which he approaches the subject is quite different.[50] While not using Ramsey's particular language theory of 'disclosures', Heron still finds in Plato's later conception of eternity that which contains and includes the temporal series, that which it is as true to call 'temporal' as 'a-temporal'.[51] The particular platonic model which justifies this claim is that of eternity (*aeon*) as the simultaneous coincidence of past, present and future, of which the temporal series (*chronos*) is its broken reflection (much as light is refracted into its constituent colours through a prism). In terms of a prior distinction within the temporal series which Heron has made (between the structure of time—past, present and future—and its movement—the 'vanishing' present), eternity might still be described, according to this model, as temporal in structure.

In fact Heron finds even this inadequate to represent the time of God. A living God must also in some sense have the movement of time within his own being:[52]

> In so far as the Platonic notion of the aeon separates off structure from movement, being from action, it cannot adequately refer us to the living God, though it might perhaps serve well enough for a comatose ground of being.[53]

Of course it cannot be the same kind of movement between past, present and future which we experience. This would be to put God back into the temporal series in a way which leaves him subject to the 'vanishing present'—an imperfection. Heron seems to acknowledge this. He adds, somewhat cryptically, that both movement and structure are present 'in a different way' in God: 'they must be understood to be the possession of the eternal rather than as possessing him'.[54]

These reflections of Heron's are suggestive. Unfortunately they are also still rather obscure. It is difficult to attach much meaning to the 'different way' in which the movement and structure of time are present in God simply on the basis of the statement that, whereas we are in the possession of time, God is in possession of it, or 'contains' it. What could this mean It could mean, negatively, as already indicated, that God cannot be subject to the movement of the vanishing present. This much the process theologians might agree with, in so far as they conceive of a perfect divine memory in which past events are held in the divine consciousness with present immediacy. Since in process thought all the categories are present in God to supreme degree, supreme temporality is temporality stripped of the imperfections of finite temporality, namely imperfect memory which loses hold of past events.[55] It could also be accommodated within a limited notion of the specious present, in so far as that present includes, precisely, the past experienced with present immediacy.

Yet thus far the future is left unaccounted for, and so presumably remains genuinely future. And while it may be legitimate to conceive of God having a genuinely open future,[56] it could not be *our* future which was thus open to him; that would be to imprison God again in the kind of temporality which he must transcend in order to act in our world in the way which has been envisaged. In fact Heron might not wish to allow any kind of future open to God: a movement which is 'in the possession of God' seems to preclude the notion of an indeterminate, open, state into which God moves. Even a future structured within divinely ordered eternal possibilities (after the fashion of process views) might entail the kind of movement which this view seems anxious to avoid.

Out of this kind of impasse it may be that a choice has to be made between two broad options: reconceiving the movement of time or entertaining a notion of a 'parallel and transcendent divine temporality'. The first pursues the kind of enquiry suggested by Heron's reflections but takes it further, attempting to provide a conceptual scheme in which the movement of time is radically different and which accounts for the future. To this end it could be assumed that divine eternity is to be understood primarily in terms of the before-after series of relations. Within that series it might then be possible to posit a movement which not only holds one term of the relation ever present (rather than vanishing into the ever-receding past), but which also reduces the meaning of future to that term which lies after the preceding event. In this case 'movement' would be reconceived primarily as the experience of direction, that is, the experience of events lying in a certain ordered structure, without experiencing them 'temporally' (i.e. 'tensed') in that order.[57]

The sense in which the experience is dynamic (and not merely some kind of static contemplation) is not easy to conceive, but analogies from the aesthetic realm have often been used to help. There is, for instance, the experience of a familiar piece of music. This may be experienced as a whole, but depends for its meaning on an order of before-after (otherwise it would be experienced as a very complex chord). Yet the experience could be said to be dynamic in so far as the music is constituted of themes which are recapitulated, shedding new light backwards and forwards on earlier and later instants. This interplay between earlier and later depends on the direction determined by the series before-after, yet takes place dynamically between the instants without being bound to any one temporal (i.e. 'tensed') perspective. The instants are all 'already' held in present view, but by being 'separated out' in the structure of before and after they allow for this kind of dynamic interplay.

The advantages of this kind of picture are twofold. First, it has obvious connections with the notion of an extended specious present, and as such it is continuous with the kind of experience conceived as God's view of the world. This is both theologically and philosophically propitious; any wedge driven between the structure of God's own experience and his relation with the world is unlikely to be satisfactory. Further, there are also certain specific theological gains to be made with this kind of conception. For instance, the personal structure of God has been traditionally expressed in the doctrine of the Trinity, and while trinitarian views of God have in fact been held alongside radical classical doctrines of sheer timelessness the traditional doctrine must gain intelligibility from this kind of temporality. After all, there is a strong tradition that the trinitarian God bears within himself the movement and structure of love, and if love is characterized primarily as mutual giving and receiving then some mutual interaction of 'persons' for whom both giving and receiving is always held present would be no bad characterization of *eternal* love. It gains meaning precisely through a structure and movement of before and after which does not let an action slip away into the past, yet does provide for two terms of a relationship in which there is dynamic interplay and a sense of direction.

Divine temporality of this kind may also help make intelligible some sense of change, response and suffering within the divine being. Pressure for this has been considerable, notably in recent times from process theologians though it has never far from the concerns of classical theism either.[58] In fact neither has been satisfactory, as we have already had cause to see: classical theism has tended to speak of passion and change only in respect of an 'unreal' and asymmetrical relation between God and the world,[59] and process views have tended to subject God to change, suffering and passivity at the expense of his self-sufficiency and sovereignty.[60] What is being proposed here is the kind of temporality in God's being which may support the notions of change, suffering and response, but within a complete totality of the divine being where that suffering and response already lie in a relation of before-after within the whole. In this sense the perfection, self-sufficiency and sovereignty of God are secure, for it would be possible to conceive that divine suffering and response as already transfigured by the perspective of the whole—in a way that suffering and response never can be within the form of our temporality.

It also has to be said that such a conception would have to meet certain objections. It has already been noted how conceptions of God's nature and being which are based on the nature of his experience, rather than on his status as agent, may be deficient. The conception proposed here is open to just this kind of criticism: to speak of dynamic experience is not the same as speaking of action; so-called dynamic experience of the whole may all too easily reduce to the notion of static contemplation. Indeed anything else may be hard to conceive at all without smuggling some kind of tensed series of relations back into the picture. Correlatively, there may be a theological price to pay in that such a God is not easily conceived as the source of infinite novelty and creativity: if all events are complete, eternally present, is there not at best only a reworking of old themes?[61] Perhaps the analogy from aesthetic experience is misleading.

Yet the analogy may still yield more mileage in response to these criticisms. Music is performed as well as experienced. Being a God of 'before and after' is as much an action as being the musician (rather than the audience) whose concerto seems to take no time (in the tensed sense of temporality). Furthermore, the interrelation of instants suggested by the analogy of recapitulation may be conceived as infinite in 'depth' (and in some sense therefore a source of infinite novelty and creativity), rather as a recapitulated theme of music gains new meaning and 'depth' not just 'once' in relation to what is before (or after), but 'again' in the new relation set up by its new depth to that which is before and after—and so on *ad infinitum*. The point could also be made if the analogy were switched from the aesthetic to the personal realm: relations between persons may take on an ever-increasing quality of 'depth' within the same basic set of circumstances. Finally, it may not be entirely facetious to suggest that even if the analogy does err on the side of 'static completeness' this is preferable to the opposite danger of everlasting novelty— which does have something of a wearisome feel about it. We may have some reason to trust the traditional (if intuitive) representation of eternity as *rest* (as well as active love, praise and so on). And it may be that whether or not this—or any other picture—constitutes an adequate understanding of eternity will depend in the last resort on such fundamental intuitions.

The last resort, however, may not yet have been reached. There is the other option to be pursued, and one which turns the weaknesses of the first into its own strengths. Taking as fundamental the demand for novelty, creativity, and the kind of action which moves into an open future, it is possible to conceive of God faced with such an open future for himself, but for whom the world's future was still already present. That is, our time series of past, present, future, is experienced by God, as with the first option, under the before-after series of relations; but instead of being related to a tenseless divine experience it is related to a divine time series much like ours in character, though transcending it. This divine temporality might still differ from ours in so far as the past is always held perfectly in the memory, but the future (though circumscribed by divinely ordered eternal possibilities) is still future to God. The fundamental difference lies only in the fact that it transcends, or exists 'parallel' to, our time, in a different dimension (thus distinguishing it radically from process views).

But how then would we conceive the relationship between God's time ('in a different dimension') and ours? This is peculiarly difficult. Keith Ward insists that whatever else we do we must think of God as 'contemporary with every present' of our experience, running parallel with 'our' time in that sense: for 'only in that way can he hear and respond to prayer or act causally to produce new effects in the world'.[62] Presumably this cannot mean God is simultaneous with all events in the universe at a given time since the very notion of simultaneity implies a concept of absolute time (within which all events can be given a place relative to each other), which offends the very theory of relativity which previously offered some brief comfort for the notion of simultaneity. On the other hand, if that 'given time' at which God sees, and reacts with, all things worldly refers primarily to 'his' time, transcending our space-time continuum, then the strictures of a theory referring to that continuum need not dismay us. The relationship, though, remains mysterious, and a positive conception of it elusive. Perhaps the best we can do once again is to offer analogies to help: a particularly fertile picture is the relationship between the time scale of a novel and its author's time; or else between the time scale of a moment of heightened awareness (great exaltation, or a moment before death when the 'whole world' can pass before our eyes), and ordinary 'public' time; or indeed between the time scale of a dream and the dreamer.[63] Admittedly these do raise again the problem of intersection between the time scales (of which more anon), but at least they push our thought in some determinate direction.

 If we now pause to take stock of this option we can surely see some real advantages. The divine temporality is conceived, like ours, under both past-present-future and before-after series of relations, and as such is simply more easily conceivable. It avoids the problem of arguing for and ascribing priority to either one of the two series; both are included. Further, it certainly sustains the notion of divine novelty and creativity more readily, and also the analogy of divine action. And it does all this without compromising the essential transcendence of God in relation to our time. In terms of those initial demands of revelation it would quite adequately expound both the sense in which a thousand of the world's years are but as a single day of divine time, and the sense in which (from within our time) we can appear to delay or hasten his coming kingdom:[64] after all, since we cannot live in God's time we can only project onto his action the language and concepts which derive from our temporal experience where delay—and haste—is all too real.

On the other hand there are some disadvantages, notably that difficulty of conceiving the connection between the two time scales. The conception of two dimensions of time intersecting at some instant, while popular in fiction and fantasy, is not easy to sustain. J.R. Lucas subjects it to some scrutiny, and suggests that if the time of one dimension were isolated from the time of the other dimension (as in a dream, or a book, as our analogies suggest) this could be conceived—but only at the cost of its not being 'real':

> Apart from the date of the title page, or the instant of falling asleep, there must be no other connection between events inside the book or the dream and ordinary events. And this in itself is a mark of unreality.[65]

Yet I am not sure this is a decisive difficulty: it is not necessarily a crippling 'mark of unreality'. Even though there may be no temporal connection (apart from the intersecting instant) between the events of the story or dream and ordinary events, that is not to say that there is no other kind of connection. Even an instant's dream, or the moment of vision when 'one's whole life passes before one's eyes', have their effect in the course of ordinary events, and so must be accorded some significant measure of reality. Thus the world's events may be analogously conceived as the story in relation to the divine story-teller, without implying that they have no effect, no meaning, no 'reality', within the divine perspective. Further, if it is the instantaneous character of the event of creation (in relation to the divine temporality) which is taken as a mark of unreality simply because it is relatively so 'small' (an 'instant' out of 'everlastingness'), we may again ask why it is a mark of unreality. An instant which has concrete effects is not normally considered unreal. As regards the daunting tracts of everlastingness which precede that instant and its subsequent effects, these are no more of a problem in this account than they are for any non-dualistic view of God and the world. Either it is accepted as a humbling reminder of God's self-sufficiency apart from the world; or it is construed as a private experience of God which, *qua* experience, does not bear the quantitative proportions that it otherwise might have; or it does in fact take on significance in relation to the instant of creation once that instant has passed into the perfect memory alongside it. And of course these alternatives are not mutually exclusive.

So, since Lucas does at least concede the possibility (to 'speculative metaphysicians') of conceiving stories or dreams as 'injected into a basic time', this option should not be ignored. Clearly there *is* a temptation to reject any conception in which dreams spring to mind as the world's analogy (hence, perhaps, the loaded concession to 'speculative metaphysicians'), but this should be resisted. Dreams are not the only possible analogy, and even if they were one might well retort that we should *expect* God's eternity to be more real than our temporality. In any case, there is no bad pedigree to the view that 'we are such stuff as dreams are made on'!

I should repeat that these options are both highly speculative, as warned. They are intended only as signposts to some positive indications of how divine eternity might be conceived in itself, as well as in relation to our time, in order to fulfil two basic conditions, viz. to retain meaning in talk of divine personhood, and at the same time to safeguard the divine transcendence of our time which is necessary to sustain the kind of action in the world we have been envisaging. The dangers are obvious: in attempting to talk of

divine eternity as some kind of temporality there is considerable
risk of speaking of it 'alongside' our own in the wrong way.
Ramsey and Heron both warn against this; *'Deus non est in genere'*:
God cannot be subsumed under any general category; our temporality must be derived from his, and not both from some *a priori*
concept apart from God.

It should also be made plain that the transcendent relation of
God to our time is being maintained as a necessary condition of
certain theological considerations, but not as a sole and sufficient
condition of theological considerations in general. Thus other theological concerns, notably the concept of incarnation, may require
that God also experiences our time as we do (under the series of
past, present, future, where the past really does vanish, and the
future really is yet to come), and that he also experiences suffering
change and response which is *not* 'already transfigured'. There
seems no reason to suppose that this projection of the transcendent
God into our time is ruled out by either conception of that transcendence so far offered; it may be that one option is particularly suited
to a doctrine of incarnation (for instance, the second option, in
virtue of the continuity proposed between the structure of eternity
and our temporality), but since both options attempt some kind of
resolution between transcendence and active, creative, personhood,
neither is particularly unsuited (though once again I must plead
that the precise conceptuality by which the incarnation is conceived
is not the chief subject of this book).

This need to talk of some other kind of divine experience within
the total divine perspective again reminds us to be cautious: it
suggests that these speculations are not only tentative in themselves,
they are also painting only part of the picture. Yet the justification
for pursuing them has already been made clear. Some positive indication of what a personal eternity might mean lends credibility to
the bare assertion that a personal God could transcend our time.
And it has already been noted how most, if not all, discussion of
God's relationship with the world requires some resolution of this
paradox of transcendence and personhood. Any attempted resolution, here in respect of time, reaches to the heart of that problem:
it helps us stand more securely within that tradition of dialectical
theology which insists that both sides of a paradox must be affirmed,
even though the conceptual difficulties are enormous.[66] The nature
of this attempt also stands within the tradition of philosophical
theology which insists that these same conceptual difficulties
cannot be shirked, even at the price of 'speculative metaphysics'!

CHAPTER SEVEN

Theodicy

Throughout this account of divine action which has been developed the theological pressures outlined in Chapter two have been at work in relation to the various other logical, conceptual and experiential demands of contemporary thought and life. As with other accounts, no doubt there has been compromise on the way, and whether or not the 'restringing' has stayed in better tune than any other attempt must now be for others to judge. Here, for the sake of clarity, is a summary of the claim, without the clutter of all its supporting arguments.

A conception of God's activity in the world has been offered which is both universal in scope and specific in relation to particular events. All events may be conceived as caught up within the divine intention which operates in and through the causal regularities and contingencies of creaturely freedom and independence, relating each event specifically and internally to a divine end; all this is sustained by a picture of God relating transcendently to time and space, as well as immanently. As such we may conceive a *transcendent* God acting *personally, specifically,* with *initiative* and *sovereign efficacy,* and also with full regard to the meaning of *love.* Again for the sake of clarity, each of these points may now be recapitulated in relation to some of those other accounts we have been considering, to sharpen the comparison and the claims being made.

First, there is the issue of transcendence and personhood. Both Wiles and Ogden tended to offer accounts of God's action in the

world which suggested impersonal analogies. In the case of Wiles
the difficulty in talking of a fully personal God lies in the uniform
relation posited between particulars and the general will and purpose
of God (the relation of cog to machine, citizen to law). In the case
of Ogden the difficulty lies in the posited nature of divine causality
as 'condition' (which suggested the impersonal analogy of the
ground causing a bowl to deflect from its course).

In this alternative account the relation between a particular event
and God's purpose is conceived as differentiated according to
specific ends, and action-causality is conceived in terms of positive
purpose and intent (rather than the passive condition of the pastness
of God). This must sustain more recognizably personal analogies
for God himself and his relation with the creation. Yet God's transcendence is also affirmed in a number of important respects. As
with Wiles and Ogden, the transcendent nature of his action is
maintained: it is action in and through worldly events, not
alongside them as one cause amongst others. Yet, more radically
than Ogden, God's transcendence of time is expounded in a way
which is integral and crucial to the concept of divine action as
universal in scope, special in relation to particulars—and so perfect
in efficacy. Further, in response to Baelz's insistence that personal
and transcendent categories should be reconciled, not merely
affirmed paradoxically, the full personhood and thoroughgoing
transcendence of God have been considered together in relation to
the problem of time and eternity: a conception of God's being
which is both beyond our time, yet having some form of
temporality, has been offered.

Then there is the question of 'specificity', 'initiative' and 'priority'.
The problem with Wiles and Ogden concerned their God's apparent
passivity in relation to particular events, his inability (for one
reason or another) to take the initiative. In both cases God has to
'wait' on the actualization of contingencies (specifically, the 'representing' response of creation) in order to act. There is some kind of
priority in the divine action in that general and universal activity of
God which is specifically represented in a particular creaturely
response, but it is only and precisely a general activity, not specifically related to particulars—except in their response. In process
views an exception could be made in so far as specific possibilities
are set before the creature. But these possibilities are to be construed
as generally and universally set by the abstract pole of God; and, in
so far as the abstract identity of God is concretely constituted by
contingencies in the world, these possibilities themselves, however
specifically related to particulars, must still be construed as waiting
on the world's response. A stronger conception of initiating action

in relation to particulars could only be conceived at some cost to the internal coherence of the underlying metaphysic.

However, our alternative account pictures instead a God beyond time, 'already' acting to arrange all contingent events into a pattern of meaning, weaving free decisions and the contingencies of the world into an already prepared context. The extent of this initiative is to be judged not only by God's knowledge of all 'future' possibilities and the ways in which they might be redeemable (Ogden and Baelz would presumably agree with that much), but by God's capacity to so determine the context of these possibilities that they are 'already' woven into his action. This is a significantly stronger account of divine initiative, and it is integrally linked with the conception of God as acting universally in scope yet realizing specific ends in relation to different particulars.

When it comes specifically to the question of sovereignty we find the issues already determined by what has been said about initiative. In process views God depends to such an extent on creaturely response that there may be no final guarantee of success. This arises from lack of initiative and the view of divine causation which underlies it. The extent to which this vulnerability goes is considerable: it is limited only by the abstract possibilities which are set up by the divine reality as the conditions for any state of the world. On closer analysis, following Baelz's treatment of the subject, a final and general end of God might be guaranteed by God's resources to deal with any frustrating, evil, possibility; possibilities whose limits he himself has set. Yet this is achieved only by admitting that some particulars are, in themselves, irredeemable—that is, they constitute genuine frustrations and force the specific end intended into the retreat of a further, generalized (and possibly externalized) end. The frustrating event may be conceived as 'pure' means to that further end, or as 'surd'. Either way it is conceived as a necessary condition of freedom.

This alternative account, however, finds no event defeating to God's purpose in itself. By virtue of his initiative, every frustrating and evil actualization of creaturely freedom and contingency is guaranteed to be woven into a context of meaning in which it is brought into direct relation with an end of God. This conception is defined positively in the analogy of perfect creativity (e.g. of a musical symphony where each note is present 'for its own sake' as well as for the sake of others). Analogies from human relationships also help define this conception, but only when universal scope of activity is allowed. This is clearly a much stronger view of sovereignty and again clearly links integrally with the conception of God acting in every event to realize specific ends.

What is also crucial is the relationship of such initiative and sovereignty to the divine love—as it relates to creaturely freedom. Most accounts, particularly those of Williams, Vanstone and other process writers, see the relationship as a necessary compromise. The meaning of initiative and sovereignty have to be seriously qualified. Within the conception offered in this account, however, the point can be turned on its head. If divine action can secure good ends in all the world's conditions (for individuals, in particular events), in and through the world's freedom, *then it ought to*. If it cannot, its creative endeavour is suspect, no longer responsible love. The meaning of love itself demands the 'full' meaning of initiative and sovereignty, not a qualified meaning.

So much for the summary. Yet even if all this were granted, it is not enough. If we are honest we have to recall the pressure of some of those riddles of experience. We know there can be, especially in the experience of suffering, an element of horror and absurdity which still cries out against such a conception, and must provoke one more area of basic discussion. For this affirmation thbat God's love secures in everything the right conditions for creaturely responses, the further assertion that it must do so if it is to be truly love, may still seem to fall foul of a fundamental objection which has been lurking throughout the discussion, which we acknowledged from the beginning within those riddles of experience: it is simply the enormous credibility gap which opens up between this conception and the actual empirical nature of some circumstances; notably, circumstances of extreme and apparently pointless suffering. In other words, we are surely bound to offer some glimpse of *what* a good end could possibly be in such circumstances, if we are seriously going to maintain *that* it is the case. As we insisted at the outset, the primary task is the bare conceivability that God is acting, not the rationale of that action: but there comes a time when the former requires at least something of the latter; a time when form needs some content.

First we should be clear what this demand means, in what sense it has already been met, and indeed in what sense it cannot ever be met. At various points, especially when considering the nature of evil, we have insisted that a wider perspective is going to be necessary. The configuration of reality within which a particular 'evil event' of our experience is related to God's good ends will often, by definition, be beyond our grasp to perceive from within our portion of space and time. We do not inhabit that wider perspective. It will therefore remain frankly a matter of faith and mystery.

On the other hand it has also been insisted that our perspective overlaps with the wider one. There is no complete discontinuity:

God experiences our limited perspective within his total experience of a wider perspective, so we should at least expect some glimpse of that wider perspective to the extent that we form part of it. More specifically, we may expect glimpses of it in those particular events which are specially revelatory, those 'key' or 'pivotal' events of the whole drama which are special in that further sense, supremely the eschatological events of Christ (again, we should recall the pressures outlined in chapter two in this respect). This is important: if we were to relegate all rationale in God's love to some wider perspective which is wholly opaque to ours, bearing no relation to our experience, then we would justly invoke the charge that God and the world inhabit such different worlds of meaning, such a different community of values, that there could be no point or possibility in talking about God's 'good' ends at all, for we could not know what 'good' means. And whereas the more rigorous positivists might welcome such an admission, we do not: we have already rejected it in D.Z. Phillips' position,[1] and are therefore committed to offering some glimpse of what God's good ends might be, at least in general terms. In this limited sense, a theodicy *is* required.

The first step, naturally, is to take good account of the integral, dependent, relationship between suffering and evil and certain pleasures and virtues. There has been a massive effort, both theologically and philosophically, to expound this relationship and employ it in the service of theodicy. John Hick's now classic 'soul-making' theodicy is based largely on this kind of approach, and while his doctrine of divine action undergirding it may not be specific enough, his insistence on divine sovereignty in relation to evil is most helpful. We should look at it in some detail, remembering the force of the biblical phenomenology which persistently witnessed to God's sovereignty in and through the suffering of his people.[2]

Hick shares the basic assumption of this account that for God to be good and for his creative love to be truly love, the conditions of the world must be capable (at least generally speaking) of serving God's good ends, specifically that they contribute to the making of moral and rational souls;[3] indeed they are necessary conditions to that end. Hick claims this to be the case in respect of moral evil: it is a 'virtual inevitability' *en route* to a filial relationship of free agents with their creator;[4] in respect of physical pain: 'an anaesthetic existence would lack the stimuli to hunting, agriculture, building, and social organization, and to the development of the sciences and technologies, which have been essential foci of human civilization and culture';[5] and in respect of suffering in general:

. . . the capacity to love would never be developed, except in a very

> limited sense of the word, in a world in which there was no such
> thing as suffering . . . The same is true in relation to the virtues of
> compassion, unselfishness, courage, and determination—these all
> presuppose for their emergence and for their development something
> like the world in which we live.[6]

In respect of excessive suffering—the 'dysteleological' nature of
some suffering which is crushing, embittering, and counter-
productive in the business of soul-making—Hick makes two
points. He first points out that excessive suffering is a relative
concept: 'unless God eliminated all evils whatsoever there would
always be relatively outstanding ones of which it would be said
that He should have secretly prevented them'.[7] I confess that, with
others, I do not find this particularly convincing.[8] But his second
point, that the very mystery of some dysteleological suffering contributes to the soul-making process, makes a better case: if all
suffering had an *evident* rationale then no attempt would be made
to relieve it, no courage, pity, compassion, would be evoked, and
souls would not be fully made.[9] Thus Hick affirms that all kinds of
evil and suffering can, in principle, be related to good ends as
necessary conditions.

A closer analysis of this kind of relationship between good and
evil is offered by A.C. Ewing.[10] Considering such goods as
courage, unselfishness and 'the highest forms of love', he claims
that some evil is necessarily involved as a condition of their attain-
ment, not as a causal necessity but as the relation of parts affects
the value of a whole. He distinguishes between three kinds of such
a relation:[11]

1. An intrinsically good whole may contain some parts which are
bad *per se*, and yet necessary for the goodness of the whole (e.g.
pain present in loving sympathy for the suffering of others).

2. Something intrinsically good may depend for its value on
something not actually contained in it that is bad (e.g. sympathy
depends on an evil which makes it appropriate).

3. The intrinsic value (or disvalue) of an action or emotional
state will depend partly on its appropriateness to a situation which
may be past and the cognition of which must be (e.g. gratitude).
In fact all three serve to illustrate how God (in his wider perspective
and context of the whole) may relate evil to good ends in general.
The distinctions will prove to be relevant to further discussion
(below) of how a theodicy can be truly adequate for certain specific
events.

This first step thus establishes a general relationship of dependence
between certain goods and corresponding evils, and so asserts that

God is justified in creating a world in which evil and suffering occur; this world's conditions serve good ends which could not be attained in any other way. And in its general form this argument would seem to need only one further point of clarification, albeit a very important one: in what sense does it contain, in the words of John Roth's strident protest, that 'fatal flaw' of many theodicies, which is to 'legitimate' evil?[12] That is, have we here a God whose creative decision positively endorses evil as a necessary instrument to certain goods? This pushes us hard back to consider Hick's view that all this is 'virtually inevitable' in a world of free persons. For if *any* world will be inevitably marred, the decision of God to proceed, redeeming its evils into new kinds of perfection, can be more easily tolerated: suffering and (redeemed) evil is the price which has to be paid for any worthwhile creative endeavour. If on the other hand there is the logical (and actual) possibility of God bringing about some world of perfection from the beginning, then his creative decision to proceed with *this* world does indeed seem to endorse the instrumentality of evil in an unacceptable way.

I am wary about the usefulness of entering the vast, unending, speculative debate about the logical possibilities of a perfect and free creation. Instead I will simply assume a mediating position, namely that whether or not the evil exercise of a free will is, in any world, strictly inevitable, virtually inevitable, or genuinely contingent, it is an inevitability in *this* world: and God's decision to create this world in which freedom results in moral evil is justified by his capacity to create different kinds of good out of it. Whether or not there can be other worlds where no such inevitability arises (where different kinds of good are therefore created) it is not necessary to know, as long as it is granted that the existence of this kind of world is, within the totality of reality, a kind of good which could not have been created in any other way. On this assumption the criticism that evil is 'legitimated', it has to be admitted, still smarts a little, for it allows that there may be kinds of perfection wholly unrelated to evil, and that God could have stopped short of this world's 'redeemed' kind of perfection, but did not. So be it. I would then appeal to that account of the nature of this world's evil already offered, in which it has but a very temporary hold on reality, and that deriving from the creature's tenuous grasp. If it is that which is 'legitimated' then maybe we can, just, bear the smart.

However, the criticism might still be put in another and sharper way, in more practical (and existentialist) terms. For it is sometimes pointed out that this kind of doctrine could seem to make nonsense of the moral imperative to relieve suffering and fight evil, since we would be fighting a necessary means to good. Indeed it could even seem that we ought actually to inflict suffering on others to produce that good. And even if good reasons can be found why *we* are in fact under an obligation to relieve suffering rather than inflict it, the same questions may be asked about God himself: in what sense can he be said to be fighting against evil when he has created a world in which it must occur?[13]

Hick anticipates this, to some extent, first in his insistence that some suffering does appear, and must appear, dysteleological (ultimately without rationale) in order to back the moral imperative to relieve it. He also points out that it is the moral imperative itself, the relieving of suffering and fighting of evil, that helps 'make the soul'.

In fact his first point hardly answers the logical question posed for those who (like Hick himself) actually believe that even this apparently disteleological suffering does in fact have a hidden rationale—and so presumably ought not to be relieved. But we could still suggest something like this: that since *we* do not know in what way good ends are served by and depend on suffering, then bringing about that suffering is rarely, if ever, justified for us. We would be more likely to do harm than produce the good ends,[14] whereas God in his infinite and perfect wisdom *is* able to know that kind of thing: he not only knows how a person will react to certain kinds of suffering, but also what kind of consequences will follow over the whole range of interrelated events, and this unlimited knowledge does license him to act in ways we should not act.[15]

But the further consideration of Hick, that moral effort in relieving suffering and fighting evil is significant for soul-making, is perhaps more important. It is not difficult to see how this might be true for us. As far as God is concerned, his activity of relieving suffering and fighting evil may relate primarily to the making of his creatures' souls, rather than his own (in certain respects). But this still places him squarely 'on our side' in the fight. Ewing makes the same basic point:[16] evil can only be part of the good organic unity if it is fought against and conquered; thus suffering and evil serve as means to a good end only in so far as they are being relieved and overcome in some wider perspective. The moral imperative could not be stronger.

We must remember, however, that all this is only a first step: it is a general argument claiming only that there is 'soul-making' rationale to be found for all kinds of evil and suffering within the context of the whole; that generally, where souls are made through the conditions of this world, its conditions are, generally, justified. The full requirements set for a reasonable theodicy go further than this, and in the terms particularly required by a universal and special action of God they are much more rigorous: what is demanded is that the rationale is found specifically for each individual within all circumstances. It is not enough, therefore, that the suffering of one individual contributes, generally, to the soul-making of another, because some specific rationale must also be found for the sufferer. Though I may indeed need the comatose victim of brain damage to evoke a soul-making response in me, *what about the comatose?* The difficulty in this instance is heightened because in this kind of suffering there is no evident opportunity for the victim to respond, grow, etc., through his experience: the victim is 'imposed' on by suffering to such an extent that he cannot, even in principle, will or accept his condition for the sake of another (thereby finding some soul-making end for himself as well). It seems to be precisely the situation of one whom 'God sacrifices . . . on the altar of his cosmic plan.'[17] The characteristic feature of this kind of situation is thus a suffering which may indeed be conceived as having some point in the general scheme of things, but which seems to have no point specifically for the sufferer. If so, it is unacceptable, because unless we can provide some rationale for this sufferer too then we are back in a world of unfortunate side effects, 'means for external ends'. This is a picture which has already been rejected: ends must be found in all circumstances for each individual; God's sovereignty and love both demand it. In principle, only a doctrine of universal and special action can sustain it, but the task remains to show how it can also be credible in practice, alongside our actual experiences of suffering.

A similar point is made by Ewing, if not so rigorously in respect of all the circumstances of each individual, at least insistently in respect of each individual's life as a whole:

> Take a human life, of which there must have been an overwhelming number, very possibly the majority yet lived on earth, in which evil exceeded good. The evil in such lives could, if there is no survival, be justified only as a means to another's good. But this would be itself immoral; it would be making a man a mere means and not an end in himself. It can only be redeemed if it eventually is to form a part of a good organic unity, but for this to happen it seems to me essential that the good organic unity should occur in the same being who endures the suffering or commits the evil acts in question.[18]

And this makes clear why the initial distinctions between various kinds of organic unity are important. The second class is, of itself, always inadequate; as long as anything contributes only externally to the value of the whole it remains a frustration of the divine purpose and (arguably) immoral.

So our task must now be to conceive how such rigorous demands can be met for the victims, and the worst victims too. Could there always be an internal rationale, for *any* case of suffering? And note, incidentally, that we are now specially concerned with the evil of apparently dysteleological suffering, as distinct from moral evil: for it is always less of a problem to conceive some internal rationale (in principle) in moral evil, however abhorrent it is, once it is agreed that the freedom it presupposes constitutes a good end, and that its actual exercise in action (mental or physical) constitutes the possibility of self-knowledge and repentence (i.e. if there were no possibility of exercising free will in morally abhorrent ways then there would be no possibility of understanding the nature of it, which is its internal rationale).

Again we have to take two steps to tackle the problem of the sufferer. The first is to take note of the fact that victims of evil circumstances, as we have seen, can serve a good purpose for others: for although this is not enough of itself, it suggests a further possibility, namely that this external end for others might somehow be related internally to the victim as well. So, for instance, if there was some wider perspective in which the victim could see the end of his suffering for others, and be given the opportunity of assenting to it for their sake, then in that assent there is also a possible 'soul-making' end for the victim. This, after all, is the supreme pattern of soul-making in Christ: it is the willingness to be the man who suffers for the sake of others which fulfils an essential condition of salvation.

Certainly the whole point and problem of many extreme circumstances within our perspective is precisely that there does not seem to be any possibility for this assent or willingness; the victim is crushed, imposed upon by brain damage, sudden death, or insuperable and embittering suffering of some kind. But it is at this point that we find we naturally take the next step, which is simply to recall that wider perspective which is always available within Christian tradition: is there not given to us some possibility of such assent (or dissent) within the complex of eschatological and resurrection beliefs, namely, survival beyond death? To be sure, the tradition that this eschaton is an event where significant decisions can be made (assent to or dissent from that for which there was no possibility of choice in the here and now) is more controversial. It is akin to some more doubtful doctrines of purgatory, and might seem to evade the apparently Biblical challenge that there is no 'second chance' after death, and that only present choices are vested with significance. But this controversy can be defused in various ways without prejudicing the present point. At the very least we might say that significant choices made beyond this life are liable to be exceptional, rather than normative. Or, more promisingly, however many or few of us they concern, they may themselves be significantly determined by the kind of choices already made in this life, thus retaining final significance for this life alone. This would simply reinforce the point that anything which may have to occur beyond this life is integrally related to the events of this life; for only then can a theodicy claim to have the moral power of God's sovereign *redemption* of all things, rather than merely appealing to his limited capacity to create a better future.

A useful illustration of this kind of theodicy can be found in the charismatic experience of the 'healing of memories'. This is an experience which is normally described as a 'reliving' of painful past events in a new perspective 'with Christ'. Part of this experience is the realization that in fact Christ was 'always there' in past events, and in the actual business of healing that realization becomes conscious and make possible a redemption even of the apparently pointless events of the past, in so far as we can now assent to them in their new perspective. If now we rephrase the description of this experience, substituting 'end' for Christ, then the picture is of God's ends always related to each event: 'realizing' it makes possible an assent which then redeems the pointlessness of those events for us. Such a picture also usefully highlights the way this conception gains intelligibility from the doctrine of time which has been offered: where there is some kind of transcendence of the past, present and future series of this world and its events, then the past is not irredeemably vanished (it is only 'before'), and so it can be 'remade' in wider perspective. This is not simply a matter of perceiving past events in a new light, but 'remaking' or 'reliving' them by assent to the newly perceived ends which have actually been forged by the divine action in the world as well as beyond it.[19]

Thus we have made a frank appeal to a wider, eschatological perspective to resolve some of the problems of theodicy. This is not uncommon. Hick and Ewing both deem it necessary: so do others, in various ways.[20] It certainly helps meet the specific and rigorous demands of relevation on the nature of God's action, as we have conceived them. It also helps defuse the more general complaint, often levelled against Hick and others, that this allegedly soul-making world just is not doing its job very well: that is, there are as many (perhaps more) souls embittered and destroyed by the world as there are being 'made', and though some of this may be attributed to our culpable failure to appropriate the potential benefits of suffering, much of it cannot, for some suffering is simply overwhelming. Eschatology, however, asserts that this unfinished job may be completed elsewhere.

Naturally the appeal to eschatology, and this kind of theodicy, is easily misrepresented. For instance, it might seem over-optimistic, even Pelagian, about human capacity (ultimately) to make the right responses, asserting as it does that there is always some further place where we can make them. In fact it need not entail anything of the kind. For this process of soul-making may (I would say *must*) be conceived as possible only in and through the Christ event: that is, the possibility of our assent in these (or any) circumstances is constituted only by Christ's own human experience of assent to the events of his life; we have moral and spiritual capacities to assent, if we have them at all, only in virtue of Christ's assent on our behalf. This point takes us into further theological regions well beyond our brief, begging many more questions; but it should at least be clear than an eschatological soul-making process can fit perfectly well with traditional Christ-centred doctrines of justification and sanctification.

Then there is also the mistaken view that this kind of final eschatological resolution implies a gradual evolution of souls through time towards that perfect end, so that we should expect the job to be visibly on the way to completion: in other words, that it implies a reinstatement of nineteenth-century evolutionary optimism. Again, it need imply nothing of the kind, and Hick himself replies to this:

> It is another misunderstanding . . . to suppose that it [Hick's Irenaean theodicy] postulates 'a gradual spiritual evolution' such as would be contradicted by a lack of signs 'that the human race is improving morally or spiritually' . . . the hypothesis of an ascent towards God through many lives in many worlds does not entail that successive generations *in this world* should show a moral or spiritual advance. Rather, the postulated movement towards human perfection should occur in the personal histories and interactions of individuals through the successive par-eschatological worlds.[21]

In fact Hick here assumes his own particular form of eschatological belief in a succession of many worlds similar to ours. But we do not have to take all that on board to accept his chief point, which is that any eschatological event (even something more akin to the 'twinkling of an eye') may show retrospectively how this world's conditions contributed to the eschatological resolution even when they appeared to be making no contribution to progress in themselves. For instance, a morally *degenerating* world—as we see it from our historical perspective—may actually be part of the business of bringing souls to their metaphorical knees: a most crucial part in the soul-*making* process.

Finally it should already be obvious that none of this implies a theodicy which merely operates on the notion of compensation for present evils. Compensation promises only a payment of future good to outweigh present evil, whereas this theodicy demands that every present evil is made to contribute to that future good.[22] This last point reminds us how rigorously the demands of initiative and sovereignty are being met. Every event is already related to an end of God, woven into the context of the whole from the beginning, and all this (through Christ) internally related to each individual. That it stands also as a contribution to theodicy, as a justification of the love and goodness of God, follows immediately on the argument already developed, that creative love must be able to guarantee precisely this universal and specific possibility of redemption in all events in order to be truly responsible love.

Of course any theodicy succeeds only in very limited terms, and there are notable gaps in this account. Yet a theodicy of this kind, at least in general terms, is not uncommon. Indeed, it is generally considered to be the only kind which seriously attempts to meet the logical and theological demands of theism. For the omnipotence normally held to belong to the very meaning of God (i.e. the capacity to do anything except perform logical contradictions), [24] and his goodness, which together oblige worship, require precisely this view that no event is ultimately without some kind of rationale, no evil is ultimately pointless.[25] Hick still echoes a mainstream of Christian thought, therefore, when he says (process and protest theodicies notwithstanding): 'there is no room within the Christian thought-world for the idea of tragedy in any sense that includes the idea of finally *wasted* suffering'.[26] What the particular form of theodicy developed here demands, namely that the rationale must in principle be related internally to each event, is less often spelt out, but I submit that it belongs just as integrally to the logic of theism. Only thus is divine sovereignty, personal initiative, and love combined, rather than compromised.

Again I must insist that such a claim is always vulnerable, for the tuning of the theological instrument is too delicate to ever rest entirely secure. These particular demands of theism may be met, but others will at the very least have been placed at risk. How easily, as we have seen, can such a scheme as this wrongly imply that evil has no reality, or that we need not resist it as we ought, or that the world has become wholly necessary in every part and every sense. A tightrope has been stretched taut between the ancient and familiar poles of monism and dualism, the sovereignty of God and human freedom, and it would be foolish to pretend that the attempt to walk it has been without its dangers. Furthermore, even if it is deemed to have been successfully negotiated it must again be acknowledged what a limited task has been at issue: there is no claim being made that this theodicy can be empirically demonstrated, in the sense of showing what end can be specified in every event—a wider perspective is necessary for that. The claim is only to have demonstrated a possible outline of theodicy, a present glimpse of how such a thing could be, in spite of almost overwhelming *prima facie* evidence to the contrary.[27] We may well cry out for more than this, but, alas, in this life I do not believe we often get it.

Yet having said all this by way of qualification, there remains the positive statement—that the power and love of God do constrain us in this way to paint this kind of picture. There also remains the fact that alternative theodicies appear to falter more, and more blatantly, on the tightrope.[28] By way of final recapitulation, therefore, in this particular matter of theodicy, it may be helpful to consider one such alternative which does *not* insist on this complex of interrelated considerations (viz. that sovereign love of God which relates good ends to every event by universal and special action) we have clung to, and see where it leads. The theodicy is a process theodicy proposed by D.R. Griffin.[29]

Griffin begins by questioning the traditional notion of omnipotence as the capacity to bring about everything except a logical impossibility. He distinguishes between the logical possibility of a state of affairs (for instance, a state of affairs where every evil serves some good end), and the logical possibility of bring about that state of affairs (an action).[30] He further questions whether it is possible for one actual being's condition to be completely determined by another's, implying that there can be no certainty of excluding ultimate evil in any being[31] He makes the point that an omnipotence qualified by these two considerations would still belong to a perfect being, a God, in that he possessed the greatest power possible for any being to have, and that the worship of such a being is perfectly appropriate since in any case we do not worship brute power but only the greatest conceivable power (and love).[32]

Now in fact we have already suggested that a state of affairs where every event is serving some good end *can* be conceived as being brought about by a God with universal scope of action, and that the condition of any actual being may still be allowed a measure of self-determination within that conception;[33] we have further argued that creative love needs this kind of power for it to be considered as responsible love (and so command worship). However, the chief point here is to compare the theodicies resulting from such different conceptions of God's power and activity: the significant fact is that for Griffin there seems no guarantee that the suffering of an individual can be redeemed for him. The resourcefulness of God may ensure that evils are overcome in the consequent pole of God's being, transformed and used to provide new aims for 'the world',[34] but as far as the individual is concerned there may be no end for him in the evil suffered. The kind of evil which crushes him pointlessly may serve some purpose for another as it is transformed in God's experience, but not necessarily *for him*[35] In some cases, there *cannot* be an end for him, since the only possible perspective for the individual is limited to this life. Griffin makes this clear by rejecting any necessity for life after death as a constituent of theodicy; his theodicy therefore requires that we find a moral perspective in this life, or not at all.[36]

Yet this is surely intolerable. It is generally agreed that there are earthly lives in which there is no evident justice or 'soul-making' for the individual—lives for which it would be morally insane to claim that there was (what, for instance, of Ivan Karamazov's tortured children?).[37] So this restriction on God's power leaves many an individual's case hopeless in its own terms, even if there is some general justification for it within the divine perspective for the sake of another. And the fact that another may benefit by the transformation of experience in the divine perspective is of little comfort to the victim. It is also of little comfort to the victim that God may be conceived as taking the consequences of this impotence by suffering himself in the transforming process;[38] he is still a God open to the charge of moral irresponsibility in that he created with no ultimate guarantee of being able to redeem. Individuals have in effect been sacrificed for the sake of a 'greater' good, used only as means to an end external to themselves. This is the sharp end implied in the logic of alternative views where accident and frustration are real and ultimate categories to God, the final implication of such tendencies as have already been noted in Ogden, Williams, Vanstone, and even Baelz.

If we are going to be fair to the protagonists of process theodicy then we should also take note how the resourcefulness of their God is generally considered to be infinite, and the *possibility* of life after death in some form is not excluded.[39] Thus some participation in the divine perspective, where the victim's suffering can be seen transformed to serve the world, *might* be possible for the victim. All the writers mentioned seem to allow for some such possibility. But even so, there is no real attempt to show how that external end could be related back to the individual, and so no real conception that such a thing would every wholly redeem the suffering in the sense of showing its specific purpose for the individual (as distinct from its general necessity as a condition for a free world, where it can be used for some other purpose). Williams expressly admits this sense in which evil can never be wholly redeemed by talking of some events as 'always' constituting a 'loss', a tragic failure; there is only the hope that 'the best can be made of a bad job'.[40]

It is of course the process God's limited capacity for initiating action which has resulted in this morally unacceptable theodicy. It highlights once more the way in which love and the power to act are interdependent concepts in God's moral nature, not at odds with each other, and therefore reinforces the view that only a conception of universal and special divine action such as that offered here can sustain all that theism requires. For the problem of evil is theism's severest test and always will be, placing extremely stringent demands on any proposed theodicy and the concept of divine action which undergirds it. And though within the terms of our present capacity to think, feel and act I doubt whether we can ever pass that test completely, we must do our best. Hence this attempt.

CHAPTER EIGHT

The Remaining Riddles: Faith and Experience

What then of our experience? If the account of God's action in the
world which has been offered is anything like true then there is a
sense in which some of the riddles of experience with which we
began resolve into uncompromising answers. The events of this
world do not in fact arise by mere chance. There is divine meaning
at work in and through them, specifically for us. We are not merely
reacting to the conditions of this world; through them we are being
acted upon. And this may be true of every event: as true of the
experience of a routine day in Surbiton as of the day of a starving
Sudanese peasant; as true of death as of life; as true of the smallest
detail of any life as of the most momentous moments of history.
Thus our deepest intuitions about the significance of every moment
of life are neither superstition nor sentimentality: they are rather
the distilled glimpses of a divine activity which roams relentlessly
and purposively through every constituent and category and
contingency of this world.

On the other hand nothing changes the fact that they may often
be distorted glimpses as well. The same egocentricity which fortui-
tously predisposes us (rightly) to accept *that* God is acting towards
us undoubtedly clouds our understanding of *what* he is doing. This
means that we should not seriously defend every interpretation of
that activity which our adolescent dreaming throws up, even
though the dreaming itself is after all closer to reality than the so-
called toughminded and wide-awake would have had us believe.

Thus it is that we desperately need the discipline and insights of faith, the conscious relating to God and seeking after his purposes, to help correct and interpret our dreaming for us.

Furthermore, even the best insights of faith will not give us the whole picture correctly. It is part of the meaning of faith that it does not. We will often have to appeal to, and trust, the wider context and configuration of ends and events, without being able to see it. That appeal is the only way we can begin to cope with the 'sickening and cumulative force' of the contrary experiences, the other side of the riddle which is both the banality of life and its horror. And even then we may not always cope existentially: we will simply cling on to the belief in that wider perspective, and to the hope that even in our failure to cope there may yet be an end of God (for while the forsakenness of Christ on the cross may indeed have a quality unique to his atoning work, it surely has also a universal quality, to reassure precisely us when we do not cope.

Occasionally it *is* given us to see what is happening, and rejoice, for this is part of the riddle too. There are luminous moments, big or small, moments when an end of God is brought so compellingly to our attention in a particular event here and now, that we *know*. These are the eschatological moments of experience which provoke the riddle in the first place: and, *pace* Goulder, they can be as trivial as finding a lost memento after an 'arrow prayer', or as crucial as the healing of a terminal illness. They come rarely, as present signs of the kingdom which is actually being forged out of every event, including those times when the prayer seemed to no avail. They are special precisely as signs, as the present clear realization of ends which in most other events remain opaque until the future. Yes, we insist that all those other events are special too, but we have no wish to deny that some (and only some) shine with special brightness.

There remains the problem of which events shine like this, why these and not others, and why so few. I wish I could say more about this. We can indeed say they are signs—but what does it mean to be a sign? Perhaps it has to do with the business of provoking the riddle in the first place and thereby engaging with conscious faith: a sign is something for faith to feed off, yet faith must also deny itself anything more than a morsel if it is to remain faith; thus only some events are given as signs in experience, and many are not. However I must reiterate that to go any further along this path—to discern these signs in relation to particular situations—is more the work of a pastor or prophet. The main task here has been rather to suggest only a general conceptual structure for belief. The belief is that God's gracious activity is in actual fact boundless, infinite, and particular to every occasion. In that sense the riddles are resolved. But in terms of our experience on those particular occasions we still have to accept that the same grace of God appears to dance through our life with a very dappled light, and indeed leaves some lives in almost complete shadow. In that sense the riddles remain—intransigent, mocking, occasionally comforting.

What else remains? Naturally there is multitude of other issues, some of which have been raised briefly, if only to be referred elsewhere. Just one of the more obvious, which arises especially for the practical Christian believer, does deserve a final word. It is the straightforward question of what difference faith makes—for if God is conceived as working in *all* things for good, and not just for those who love God and 'are called according to his purpose', what then is the significance of faithfully loving God?

The groundwork of an answer has already been laid, but it may be as well to make it explicit. This picture that has been painted of God's universal and special activity in fact takes nothing whatsoever away from the proper significance of faith, for in so far as faith perceives something of God's purposes, and responds obediently, then there is plenty of room within this scheme for the worldly contingencies to be significantly affected, and so for God to be working a different *kind* of good. It should already be clear that in and through a contingency such as faith and response (including, no doubt, our prayers) God's ends are wrought in a different way than through the contingencies of unbelief: the configuration of ends and events is significantly different.[1] For instance, as Wiles and Ogden suggest, a perceptive and obedient response may be all the more likely to call forth other good ends and responses in other creatures. Thus the responsive act may be woven into a far wider and more complex configuration of events and ends than the unresponsive, so that it more richly and variously serves the purposes of God (even though the unresponsive act can always be made to serve *some* end). Of course, unlike Wiles and Ogden, we have insisted that just because every event may be caught up to serve God's intention in some way he is not thereby dependent on the faithful so to act; our faith has no absolute leverage on God's power to act and our lack of faith exercises no absolute veto. But to deny faith that kind of significance is no loss; faith which holds God to ransom has far exceeded its proper bounds. There is, I trust, no going back on the biblical and Reformed insistence that our faith is always and only a response to ultimate reality, not a determiner of it.

It also remains to speak once more of Christ; or rather to recall that all we have been speaking of is about Christ. I mean this quite strictly, and in two senses which will serve to sketch out and make explicit the wider theological context in which the discussion may be located.

The first is rooted in the doctrines of incarnation, atonement and salvation, and has already been alluded to more than once. We may affirm the possibility of God acting to secure good ends throughout all creation just because that possibility is constituted by his having done so in the particular life, death and resurrection of Christ. The experience of 'fulfilling all righteousness', securing good ends in and through the evil and contingencies he faced as the particular man Jesus, equips the eternal God to do it through *all* time and space. From the beginning he foreordained his own experience in Christ to be the ground and possibility of bringing the whole created order to fulfilment. Hence the picture in Colossians chapter one of all things being reconciled through the shedding of Christ's blood.[2]

I merely reaffirm this point with no pretensions as to having argued or expounded it fully, but a brief illustration of how it can (and must) be conceived within the wider theological framework will do no harm—and it is the notion of reconciliation in the Colossians passage which provides a useful clue. The question it poses is this: what is meant, and required, by universal reconciliation? More specifically, and in keeping with the synoptic thought-world as well, what is meant and required by the possibility of universal forgiveness? Dostoyevsky, who helped pose some of those initial riddles, also helps pose this question at its sharpest— through Ivan Karamazov. For having described the worst kinds of torture imaginable (to innocent children) he is made to issue this challenge:

> I want to forgive. I want to embrace . . . I do not want a mother to embrace the torturer who had her child torn to pieces by his dogs! She has no right to forgive him! If she likes, she can forgive him for herself, she can forgive the torturer for the immeasurable suffering he has inflicted upon her as a mother; but she has no right to forgive him for the sufferings of her tortured child.[3]

His point is that evil, hurt, injury and disruption have repercussions beyond the sensibilities of any one injured party, so that even if forgiveness is forthcoming from him or her, it is inadequate. If we grant that forgiveness and reconciliation involves the will to absorb the evil consequences without condoning, and to react re-creatively to turn the situation to good, then we can grant that it is possible (in principle) to forgive for ourselves, but we cannot do that for all others affected. This actually means that all human forgiving is incomplete: it is not just that, through sin and weakness of the will, we *do* not bring ourselves to forgive; it is also that, through our finitude, we *cannot*, for we cannot enter into and re-create the experience of the others involved. Such are the awesome demands of universal reconciliation.

But now let this very fact of human limitation serve to highlight the divine possibilities. The heart of the Gospel is that God has indeed constituted for himself universal possibilities of reconciliation, and this begins to make sense only and precisely when the picture of universal and special divine activity is grounded in the particular experiences of God in Christ, and conversely when that particular experience is set in the context of a universal and special activity. For if we suppose that God 'first' (logically, not temporally) equips himself in Christ with the experience of forgiving within particular human conditions—that is, absorbing hurt and re-creating the situation to a greater good—then we may suppose that he can use that experience redemptively in relation to every situation as it affects every individual. Thus it is that the universal and special activity of the God-who-was-in-Christ confers a unique capacity to forgive and reconcile for others; we may even dare to say that it confers a unique *right* to forgive, in that he alone is able to take every consequence of evil, in relation to every victim, and re-create it in relation to some good end. We might also add that it is only because of this that we too have the right to forgive (or at least to try), when as far as others are concerned the repercussions of the evil are still crying out like the blood of Abel from the ground.

Christ, then, is central because he is that event which constitutes the possibility of effective reconciling action everywhere else. As such he is the substance and point of the universal and special action.[4] So while we have insisted that *our* faith and action cannot determine ultimate reality, *his* faith and action most certainly does: his is the ontological primacy and necessity undergirding all final creation, recreation and redemption.

Christ must also be recalled in his central place in a second sense, as an epistemological, as well as an ontological, necessity. The events of Christ's living and dying and rising do not just constitute for God the possibility of being and acting in this universally effective way, they also constitute for us the possibility of knowing and believing it. For his is the supremely luminous and eschatological moment in history, the place where a complete configuration of ends and events—from beginning to end—is brought into time and 'played out' for us, that we might know and believe. This side of eternity, the opportunity to see it is given only to some, according to their particular position in history and geography, but it is publicly given nonetheless.

This is what we originally assumed about revelation. It means we are bound to start looking *there*, at these particular events of Christ, if we are going to begin to have confidence to believe this otherwise preposterous story that God works *all* things for good. The confidence does not derive from our experience, whatever glimpses we may be given, but from these particular events of his living and dying and rising. For the nature of them throughout reveals this same compelling theme with which we have been concerned: whatever happens, whatever events are thrown up at him, whether the pressing crowds he healed or the betrayal of Judas and political intrigue which nailed him up, we see an effective divine control catching it all up to serve his intention. From his cry of joy and gratitude to the Father to his cry of dereliction on the cross we see not only the dappled light and shadow of experience, but also, in the retrospect of the resurrection, the perfect power and glory of the actual divine plan of salvation. There, uniquely, we are granted the total configuration of meaning, that we may begin to see and believe it elsewhere.

Thus all experience has to pass through the hour-glass centre of Christ, if we are truly to understand it. The riddles in the sands of *our* experience must be strained out through *his* experience. We may then return to our experience and legitimately find "elsewhere" the testimonies of those who have been able to see and believe with this kind of faith. Even then, the experiences are for the most part private and inaccessible, authenticated only to those actually caught up in the events of which we try to speak. But such testimonies do abound nonetheless, and one recent public example provides an irresistible illustration and a fitting conclusion. It comes from Bishop Dehqani-Tafti, the exiled Bishop of Iran, and, even in barest summary, could not illustrate this faith better.

Early in his life he wrote a brief autobiographical account of his spiritual journey called *Design of My World*[5] which charted the providence of God in the circumstances of his upbringing and development. Some of the interpretations of God's activity he offers could easily be scorned, for he is very specific in his claims. It is not for me to say. In any case his faith and its interpretation was soon to be severely tested. The shadow of the Iranian Revolution fell, and fell darkly, across his path. His own life was again picked out for special attention by the general circumstances of the time. His son was murdered. But then comes this prayer, written by the Bishop himself, which is rightly becoming a celebrated and treasured expression of faith worldwide:

O God

We remember not only Bahram
  but also his murderers;

Not because they killed him in the prime of his youth
  and made our hearts bleed and our tears flow,

Not because with this savage act they have brought further
  disgrace on the name of our country among the civilised
  nations of the world;

But because through their crime we now follow Thy footsteps
  more closely in the way of sacrifice.

The terrible fire of this calamity burns up all
  selfishness and possessiveness in us;

Its flame reveals the depth of depravity and meanness and
  suspicion, the dimension of hatred and the measure
  of sinfulness in human nature;

It makes obvious as never before our need to trust in God's
  love as shown in the Cross of Jesus and His resurrection;

Love which makes us free from hate towards our persecutors;

Love which brings patience, forbearance, courage, loyalty,
  humility, generosity, greatness of heart;

Love which more than ever deepens our trust in God's final
  victory and His eternal designs for the Church and for
  the world;

Love which teaches us how to prepare ourselves to face
  our own day of death.

O God,

Bahram's blood has multiplied the fruit of the Spirit
  in the soil of our souls;

So when his murders stand before Thee
  on the day of judgement

Remember the fruit of the Spirit by which
  they have enriched our lives,

And forgive.

Here, surely, is a most apposite triumph of the kind of faith with which we have been dealing. Reconciliation is at the heart of the prayer, as it is at the heart of the gospel, and its possibility is sustained precisely by appeal to the wider perspective in which God's universal activity is able to take the specific occurrence of evil and weave some good end out of it for all involved (all this deriving from the particular event of Christ). And it is all uncompromisingly the activity of love. If such a faith lies beyond many of us to experience, we are nonetheless glad that someone else can express it for us, especially when we are still on the dark side of our experience. Certainly we are persuaded that this is a far nobler faith than mere self-dramatization could ever be.

I do not apologise for concluding with a vision of faith which stirs the heart as much as the mind. For though the endeavour of this book has been directed mostly to the intellect, to the business of conceiving and articulating the vision as sensibly as we can, the last word must be to acknowledge again the limitations of this sort of enquiry, which will always owe its greatest debt to deeper intuitions of faith and revelation than the intellect will ever fully grasp. It is a last word I gladly leave to the eloquence of H.H. Farmer:

> It must indeed be once and for all admitted that it is not possible for our minds to grasp how it should be possible for all events whatsoever to fall within the scope of the divine providence and be made ultimately subservient to His purpose. The mystery of it is inscrutable even to a monism which seeks to see everything as the result of the direct, unmediated activity of God, or as phases of the Absolute; but for theistic faith of the kind we are discussing, which is bound . . . to attribute to man and his world a relative independence of God, it is even more so. That events should be really the result of the interplay of intramundane causes, including the choices of beings who are free to resist God, and yet also be controlled and directed by His manifold wisdom and sovereign will; that God has a purpose which He is working out in history, so that men can have genuine co-operative fellowship with Him here and now, yet which, being God's purpose, transcends history altogether so that man cannot interpret it adequately in terms of this life; that in spite of all the confusion and heartbreak and frustration of life, the sins, follies, accidents, disasters, diseases, so undiscriminating in their incidence, so ruthless in their working out, every individual may, if he will, not in imagination but in fact, rest upon a love which numbers the very hairs of his head—that is a conception before which the intellect sinks down in complete paralysis. It is possible to maintain because in the religious awareness something deeper than intellect is involved. Such a conviction is primarily given . . . through the primordial rapport of the soul with God, and it is developed and deepened as that rapport is cleansed and enlarged into true sonship to God through the Christian experience of reconciliation.[6]

Notes

1 *The Riddles of Experience* (pages 9 - 21)

1 T.S. Eliot, *Gerontion' Selected Poems* (London, 1961) 31.
2 cf A.D. Moody, *Thomas Stearns Eliot Poet* (London, 1979) 69.
3 Augustine, *Confessions*.
4 Dr and Mrs H. Taylor, *Biography of James Hudson Taylor* (London, 1973).
5 David Wilkerson, *The Cross and the Switchblade* (New Jersey, 1964).
6 See J.P. Sartre, *Being and Nothingness: An Essay on Phenomenological Ontology* (E.T. New York, 1956).
7 Cf Anthony Flew's contribution to the famous 'University Discussion', reproduced under the title 'Theology and Falsification' in A. Flew and A. MacIntyre (eds), *New Essays in Philosophical Theology* (London, 1955) 96-98.
8 See M. Goulder and J. Hick, *Why Believe in God?* (London, 1983).
9 P.L. Berger, *A Rumour of Angels* (Harmondsworth, 1970) 72, 73.
10 F.W. Dillistone, *The Christian Understanding of the Atonement* (London, 1968) 157.
11 K. Popper, *The Open Society and its Enemies*, 2, (London, 1966) 245. Cf also Helen Oppenheimer *The Hope of Happiness* (London 1983) Ch. 9. She argues persuasively for the 'irreplaceable' value of individuals.
12 Joseph Conrad, *Lord Jim* (Harmondsworth, 1957) 236.
13 F. Dostoyevsky, *The Brothers Karamazov*, (Harmondsworth, 1958) 286.
14 Cf Arthur Koestler, *Darkness at Noon* (E.T. London, 1940). See especially the final chapter, 'The Grammatical Fiction'.
15 See B. Mitchell, *The Justification of Religious Belief* (London, 1973), especially chs. 3, 4.

2 *The Demands of Revelation* (pages 22 - 55)

1 K. Barth, *Church Dogmatics* 2/1§28 (E.T. Edinburgh, 1957) 261.
2 See B. Hebblethwaite's discussion in his *The Problems of Theology* (Cambridge, 1980); also B. Mitchell's insistence on 'common criteria' of rationality in *The Justification of Religious Belief* ch. 5.
3 See J.D.G. Dunn, 'The Authority of Scripture According to Scripture' in *Churchman* 96 (1982) 104-122, 201-225.
4 See G.E. Wright, *God Who Acts: Biblical Theology as Recital* (London, 1952). Its shortcomings are pointed out by Langdon Gilkey, 'Cosmology, Ontology and the Travail of Biblical Language' *Journal of Religion* 41 (1961) 194-205; also by B.S. Childs, *Biblical Theology in Crisis* (Philadelphia, 1970) chs. 1 and 2. See also J. Barr, 'Biblical Theology' and 'Revelation in History' in *The Interpreter's Dictionary of the Bible*, Supplementary Volume (Nashville, 1976).
5 R.H. King, *The Meaning of God* (London, 1974) 47.
6 J. Barr, *Old and New in Interpretation* (London, 1966) ch. 3.
7 Rom. 3:28; 4:1; 19; 8:1, 3, 4, 10, 11.
8 1 Cor. 15:1-8.
9 1 Sa. 8:21.
10 Dt. 11:12.
11 Gn. 3:8.

12 Ps. 2:4.
13 Is. 42:14.
14 See R.E. Clements, *Old Testament Theology* (London, 1978), 59.
15 Cf. Eichrodt, *Old Testament Theology*, 1, (E.T. London, 1961) ch. 2.
16 Ho. 11:1-9; Je. 31:20; Ho. 2:2; Je. 2:1-3.
17 Eichrodt, op. cit., I, 210ff.
18 Westermann, *What does the Old Testament say about God?* (E.T. London, 1979) 58.
19 Clements, *Old Testament Theology* 55.
20 Is. 46.
21 Lk. 11:20.
22 Acts 2:30; 7:17; 26:6; Rom. 11:29; 2 Cor. 1:20.
23 Mk. 12:27.
24 Acts 17:25; Rom. 4:17.
25 Heb. 10:31; Jn. 1:3-4.
26 Mt. 20:1-16.
27 Rom. 9:18.
28 Eph. 1:1-23.
29 Acts 17:22-31.
30 Heb. 1:1-2; 13:20.
31 Ex. 19:18; Dt. 4:32,33,36; Ezk. 1:27,28.
32 Ps. 104:2.
33 Hg. 2:5; Zc. 4:6. Geoffrey Lampe notes in his *God as Spirit* (Oxford, 1977) 5C that 'Spirit' is used in Isaiah 31:3 to denote the otherness of God: 'The Egyptians are man (*adam*) and not God (*el*), their horses are flesh (*basar*) and not spirit (*ruach*).' But even here it is not that the personhood of God is at stake, rather that his sovereign transcendence is being stressed.

34 See Eichrodt's discussion, op. cit., I, 218ff., 406ff.
35 1 Jn. 1:5.
36 1 Jn. 4:8,9.
37 Heb. 12:29; Rev. 1:14.
38 See M.F. Wiles, *Faith and the Mystery of God* (London, 1982), especially ch. 7.
39 Lampe, *God as Spirit* 50.
40 See below, ch. 4.
41 Is. 45:7,12; 51:13,15.
42 Is. 46:9-11.
43 Eichrodt, op. cit., II, 109-10.
44 See L. Scheffczyk, *Creation and Providence* (ET, London, 1970) 19.
45 Gn. 8:22; Job. 38:33; Ps. 19:1-6; Je. 5:22; 31:55ff.
46 Dt. 32:39ff.; Is. 45:12ff.
47 Scheffczyk, op. cit., 19.
48 Mk. 10:45.
49 Mt. 18:11.
50 Jn. 10:10.
51 Mt. 3:15.
52 Lk. 4:16ff.
53 Lk. 9:51.
54 Cf. E. Stauffer, *New Testament Theology* (ET, London, 1955) chapter 9 'The Priority of the Divine'.
55 Cf. J.C. O'Neill, *The Theology of Acts in its Historical Setting* (London, 1961) chapters 2,7.
56 Rom. 11:32.

57 H. Ridderbos, *Paul: An Outline of his Theology* (ET, Grand Rapids, 1975) 345ff.
58 Rom. 8:20.
59 Col. 1:15-20.
60 Jb. 38:4.
61 Is. 44:24.
62 Cf. Scheffczyk, op. cit., 12, 13 and refs.
63 J. Goldingay, *Approaches to Old Testament Interpretation* (Leicester, 1981) 68.
64 See Clements, *Old Testament Theology* 87ff.
65 Gen. 12:2 (as blessing); Ps. 72 (as bringing prosperity); Is. 2:2-4 (as the place where the nations come).
66 Especially Amos.
67 Je. 46-52; Ezk. 25-31.
68 Clements, *O.T. Theology* 69ff.
69 W. Zimmerli, *The Old Testament and the World* (ET, London, 1976) 9, 10, discussing Dt. 26:5-10a.
70 Gn. 8:22.
71 Ho. 2:8.
72 Westermann, *What does the O.T.. say about God?* 41, 42.
73 Ps. 135:7.
74 Jb. 28:26.
75 Jb. 38:8-11.
76 Jb. 39:26.
77 Ps. 104:11,21.
78 Zimmerli, *The O.T. and the World* 8,9.
79 ibid., 12.
80 Ps. 148.
81 Acts 1:8.
82 Eph. 1:10; Col. 1:15ff.
83 Scheffczyk, op. cit., 30.
84 Scheffczyk, op. cit., 31.
85 J. Gray, *The Biblical Doctrine of the Reign of God* (Edinburgh, 1979) 326.
86 Mt. 6:26ff.
87 Mt. 5:45.
88 Acts 14:17.
89 Rom. 8:19ff.
90 Rom. 8:28; Rom. chs. 1 and 2.
91 Gray, *The Biblical Doctrine of the Reign of God* 163.
92 There are various surveys of the way New Testament theologies have been attempted. See for instance the Introduction to G.E. Ladd, *A Theology of the New Testament* (Grand Rapids, 1974) 13-33.
93 See C.E.B. Cranfield, *The Gospel According to St Mark* (Cambridge, 1959), especially his comments on Mark 1:15. (62-68)
94 See J. Jervell, *Luke and the people of God* (Minneapolis, 1972) for detailed treatment.
95 Jn. 1:14; 12:32.
96 Eph. 1:10; cf. Col. 1:15ff.; 1 Cor. 15:20ff.
97 Heb. 9:26ff.
98 Gn. 12:2.
99 Ps. 72.
100 Is. 2:2-4.

101 Is. 42ff.
102 C.F.D. Moule, *The Interpreters Dictionary of the Bible*, op. cit., (on 'God: N.T.').
103 Ho. 2:23; Mal. 1:2,3.
104 e.g. Ps. 22:10.
105 Mt. 10:30 (Lk. 12:7).
106 Mt. 18:10.
107 See Col. 1:20; Rom. 9-11; 1 Cor. 15:3-11; Acts 22:1-21.
108 Eichrodt, op. cit., I, 231.
109 Is. 46:10.
110 G. von Rad, *Genesis: A Commentary* (ET, London, 1961) 43-44. Cf. also Barth, *Church Dogmatics*, 3/1§41.
111 For example, Enuma Elish, Babylonian Creation Epic.
112 Zimmerli, *The O.T. and the World* 23.
113 Ps. 89:10; 74:14; cf. 51:9f.
114 Ps. 74:13.
115 Is. 27:1.
116 Ps. 104:26; Jb. 40:15ff.
117 Ex. 15:21.
118 Jdg. 5:20f.
119 Is. 45:1.
·120 Je. 1:6ff.
·121 Gray, op. cit., Gray argues this on the basis of the Ras Shamra texts, against von Rad and Eichrodt.
122 Gray, op. cit., 273.
123 2 Cor. 12:9.
124 See especially the context of 'glory' in the fourth gospel.
125 Rom. 9; Rev. 1:8; Mk. 10:27; Lk. 1:37.
126 Acts 1:24; Lk. 16:15; Rom. 2:16; 1 Cor. 4:5.
127 Mk. 11:25ff.
128 Acts 4:24.
129 Cf. W.G. Kümmel, *The Theology of the New Testament* (London, 1974) 39.
130 Mt. 5:34; 23:22.
131 Lk. 12:8f.
132 1 Cor. 15:24ff.
133 Rom. 8:31ff.; 2 Cor. 12:7ff.
134 Cf. Ridderbos, op. cit., 92.
135 Jn. 1:10,11.
136 Jn. 12:32.
137 Rev. 2:10; 13:5.
138 Col. 1:20;; Eph. 1:7ff.
139 1 Cor. 15:22f.; Rom. 5:12ff.
140 Heb. 9:26.
141 Cf. Eichrodt, *Theology of the O.T.* II, 111, 103, 104.
142 Clements, op. cit., 42, 43; God gives himself by 'name and glory', not by being summoned. Cf. Dt. 12:5; Ex. 40:34f.; 1 Ki. 8:27; Ps. 139.7.
143 Is. 41:4.
144 Am. 1, 2; Is. 13-23; Je. 46-52; Ezk. 28-32.
145 Zimmerli, op. cit., 29,30.
146 Ex. 10:1ff; Is. 45:1-7.
147 Kümmel, *Theology of the N.T.* 48. Mt. 24:44,50; Mk. 13:22; 4:26ff.
148 Mk. 4:3-8; 26-29. Cf. Gray, *Reign of God* 328.
149 Gray, op. cit., 369.

150 Acts 2:23; (cf. 4:28).
151 Eph. 1:4, 10.
152 Rom. 5:6ff.
153 Gal. 1:15ff.
154 Rom. 9-11.
155 Stauffer, *N.T. Theology* 1.
156 Is. 48:12; Rev. 1:8; 21:6.
157 Cf. O. Plöger's discussion in *Theocracy and Eschatology* (ET, Oxford, 1968).
158 Gen. 6:6; Ex. 32:14; 2 Sa. 24:16; 1 Ch. 21:15; Je. 26:19.
159 Ho. 11:8,9.
160 Gray, *Reign of God* 53.
161 Mt. 13:58.
162 2 Pet. 3:12.
163 *Faith and the Mystery of God*, ch. 4.
164 Mk. 8:22ff.
165 e.g. Mk. 5:34,36; 9:23.
166 Rom. 11:32.
167 Col. 2:14.
168 *Church Dogmatics*, 212, 458-506, part of the larger section 'The Determination of the Rejected'.
169 e.g. Jn. 9:1ff.
170 Jn. 14:30.
171 1 Cor. 15:28.
172 1 Cor. 15:36,42ff.
173 Gn. 2:16f.
174 Is. 1:18; 55:6f.
175 Ex. 7:13; 9:12; 10:1ff.
176 Je. 1:4,5.
177 Jb. 39:5.
178 Rom. 8:21.
179 Rom. 7:19.
180 Rom. chs. 1 and 2.
181 1 Cor. 11:32; Heb. 12:5ff.
182 Rom. 9-11.
183 Eph. 1:4; Rom. 8:29.
184 Stauffer, op. cit., 61-64.
185 e.g. Je. 2:2; Hos. 1-3; 5:1-2; Ps. 103:13.
186 D.D. Williams, *The Spirit and the Forms of Love* (Welwyn, 1968), 22.
187 Mk. 1:11; 9:7.
188 Jn. 17:20-26.
189 Rom. 5-8.
190 Rom. 8:31-39.
191 Eph. 3:18-21
192 Ho. 11:8.
193 Is. 42ff.
194 D.D. Williams, op. cit., 37.
195 Ibid. (emphasis mine).
196 Thus what is true for Christ (Heb. 2:10) is derivatively true for his followers: e.g. 1 Pet. 1:6,7. Cf. Rom. 11:32-36.
197 Cf. D. Bonhoeffer, *Letters and Papers from Prison* Enlarged Edition ed. Eberhard Bethge (London, 1971) 299f. See also D.F. Ford, *Prayer and Righteous Action* paper presented to the Conference of the Society for the Study of Theology. Conference 1985: ". . . there is here no easily understood

powerlessness . . . it is still a God "who wins power and space in the world by his weakness." What sort of power? It is one that has been through the crucifixion . . . that is identified by that suffering and death, but yet still is power beyond our categories and possibilities." (p. 5).
198 2 Pet. 3, especially verses 9 and 12.
199 1 Cor. 13; Rom. 8:38,39.
200 Scheffczyk, op. cit., 13.
201 Mk. 1:15; Lk. 17:21.
202 Cf. Kümmel, op. cit., 339.
203 Mk 11:25. See E. Schillebeeckx, *Jesus: An Experiment in Christology*, Collins, (ET, London, 1979), 206-213.
204 Rom. 8:22ff.; 2 Cor. 5:4f.
205 Heb. 9:26; 7:25; 4:11.
206 Schillebeeckx, op. cit., 172.

3 The Compromises of Theology (pages 56 - 95)

1 See G.W.H. Lampe, 'Christian Theology in the Patristic Period' ch. 2, in H. Cunliffe-Jones and B. Drewery (eds), *A History of Christian Doctrine* (Edinburgh, 1978).
2 Thomas Aquinas, *Summa Theologiae* (ET, London, 1964) Ia. 13,7.
3 S. Ogden, *The Reality of God* (London, 1967) 51.
4 Cf. E.H. Gilson, 'St. Thomas Aquinas', *Proceedings of the British Academy*, 21 (1935), cited by M.J. Langford, *Providence*, (London, 1981), p.47.
5 *De Potentia Dei* III, 7c.
6 *Commentary on Aristotle's Physics*, transl. R.J. Blackwell, R.J. Bath, W.E. Thirkell, (Yale, 1963) II, 185 and 250.
7 *Summa Theologiae*, Ia. 105aa, 6-7.
8 Ibid., a5.
9 See I.G. Barbour, *Issues in Science and Religion* (London, 1966) 40-43.
10 Langdon Gilkey, 'Cosmology, Ontology and the Travail of Biblical Language' 195.
11 *Church Dogmatics*, 3/3, 133ff., 154ff.
12 Calvin, *Institutes of the Christian Religion*, 1.16.5 Beveridge translation 177
13 Gilkey, art. cit. 203.
14 Scheffczyk, op. cit.
15 ibid., 18.
16 ibid., chs 2, 3, 4 respectively.
17 See, for example, E. Brunner, *The Christian Doctrine of Creation and Redemption* (London, 1952) ch. 1.
18 Scheffczyk, op. cit., 84.
19 ibid., 102, 103.
20 ibid., 148 referring to Aquinas, *Summa Theologiae* Ia. 103.2.
21 Scheffczyk, op. cit., 176-77.
22 Brunner, *Creation and Redemption* 149-151.
23 A.R. Peacocke, *Creation and the World of Science* (Oxford, 1979) 79, 80.
24 *Issues in Science and Religion*, 417.
25 See, for example, J. Macquarrie, *Principles of Christian Theology* (London, 1977) chapter 10.
26 ibid., 239.
27 ibid.
28 'Does Christology rest on a mistake?' in S.W. Sykes and J.P. Clayton (eds), *Christ, Faith and History* (Cambridge, 1972), 7,8.

29 'On Revelation' in J. Deschner, L.T. Howe, K. Penzel (eds), *Our Common History as Christians: Essays in Honour of Albert C. Outler*, (New York, 1975). Ogden there distinguishes his view both from Kierkegaard's particularism and the Socratic view of timeless truth.

30 M.F. Wiles, *The Remaking of Christian Doctrine* (London, 1974) 33ff.

31 ibid., 34.

32 Reference is now being made to the essay 'Religious Authority and Divine Action' in M.F. Wiles *Working Papers in Doctrine* (London, 1976) ch. 11.

33 ibid., 134.

34 R. Bultmann, 'Bultmann replies to his Critics' in H.W. Bartsch (ed), *Kerygma and Myth*, 1. (EET, London, 1953), 197-199; quoted in Wiles, *Working Papers* 135.

35 *Remaking*, 37-38.

36 'Religious Authority and Divine Action', 137ff; see also *Remaking*, 38.

37 'Religious Authority and Divine Action' 140.

38 ibid. 141.

39 *Faith and the Mystery of God* (London, 1982), especially chapter 2.

40 ibid., 28.

41 ibid., 29.

42 ibid., 29.

43 ibid., especially ch. 4.

44 'Does Christology rest on a Mistake?', 3-7.

45 This is the charge brought against Bultmann by Ogden; cf. S. Ogden *Christ Without Myth* (London, 1962); cf. also Wiles, 'Religious Authority and Divine Action' 135 and 139.

46 *Remaking* 37-38. Quoted above p. 66.

47 'Religious Authority and Divine Action' 141.

48 ibid., 140-141.

49 Cf. J.A. Pike, *A Time for Christian Candour*, (London, 1965) 102ff.

50 Cf. P.R. Baelz's answer to Wiles' 'Does Christology rest on a Mistake?': 'A Deliberate Mistake?' in *Christ, Faith and History* ch. 2, especially page 19. Baelz makes just this point; he also raises the question treated above, as to whether uniform activity is properly personal activity.

51 *Faith and the Mystery of God* 26.

52 'Farrer's Concept of Double Agency' *Theology* 84 (1981) 245.

53 'Continuing the Discussion' *Theology* 85 (1982) 13 (emphasis mine).

54 S.M. Ogden, *The Reality of God and Other Essays* (London, 1967) ch. 6.

55 ibid., 166.

56 ibid., 168.

57 Cf. Wiles, *The Remaking of Christian Doctrine*, 30-31.

58 Ogden, op. cit., 171.

59 He notes the exception Bultmann makes of the 'Christ-event': 'Bultmann falls back into the very mythology he wants to overcome. By saying that God acts to redeem mankind *only* in the history of Jesus Christ, he subjects God's action as the Redeemer to the objectifying categories of space and time and thus mythologizes it'. Ogden, op. cit., 173. See also *Christ Without Myth* (London, 1962) 111-26.

60 Ogden refers to Charles Hartshorne, *The Logic of Perfection and Other Essays in Neoclassical Metaphysics* (La Salle, 111., 1962) 133-147; also *Man's Vision of God and the Logic of Theism*, (New York, 1941) 174-205.

61 S.M. Ogden *Faith and Freedom: Toward a Theology of Liberation*, (Belfast, 1979) 74.

62 Hartshorne expounds and justifies this 'Law of Polarity' in C. Hartshorne and W.L. Reese (eds), *Philosophers Speak of God* (Chicago, 1953) 1-15.

63 See especially *The Reality of God*, 49ff.

64 ibid., 177.

65 ibid., 179.

66 ibid., 180.

67 ibid., 180ff.

68 ibid., 184 (emphasis mine).

69 ibid., 186.

70 *Faith and Freedom* 76.

71 ibid., 77.

72 ibid., 91.

73 ibid., 83.

74 ibid., 83.

75 R.A. Evans, T.D. Parker (eds), *I Believe In: Christian Theology, A Case Method Approach*, (New York, 1976) 43.

76 ibid., 43.

77 Hartshorne, *Man's Vision of God* 109-111; also 238-9.

78 cf. D.D. Williams, 'How Does God Act?' in W.L. Reese and E. Freeman (eds), *Process and Divinity: The Hartshorne Festschrift* (La Salle, Ill. 1964), 171 (Here it is specifically Whitehead's process thought which is being expounded.)

79 Cf. John Cobb's account of 'Process' causation, based on our own subjective experience of 'making things happen': 'if God acts or functions as an efficient cause, it is . . . by constituting himself in such a way that other events, such as human experiences, take account of him. By constituting himself in a particular way God affects the way in which he is taken account of by others.' 'Natural Causality and Divine Action' in *Idealistic Studies* 3 (1973) 207-22. Reprinted in O.C. Thomas (ed), *God's Activity in the World* (Chico, 1983) 112.

80 C. Hartshorne, *Anselm's Discovery: A Re-examination of the Ontological Proof for God's Existence* (La Salle, Ill., 1965) 185.

81 Langdon Gilkey, *Vox Theologica* 43 (1973).

82 A criticism made equally of Gordon Kaufman's *God the Problem* (Cambridge, Mass., 1972): it has been made by James McClendon, 'Can There Be Talk about God-and-the-World?', *Harvard Theological Review* 62 (1969) 4-46, p.45, note 12; also by David Kelsey, 'Can God Be Agent Without Body?', *Interpretation* 27 (1973) 358-62.

83 Cf. H.P. Owen, *Concepts of Deity* (London, 1971), arguing from the viewpoint of classical theism; also C. Gunton, *Becoming and Being: The Doctrine of God in Charles Hartshorne and Karl Barth* (Oxford, 1978).

84 *Faith and Freedom* 74.

85 See *Man's Vision of God* 265 (though this is qualified in *Philosophers Speak of God* 284).

86 See *The Divine Relativity* 139.

87 'Effective Causality in Aristotle and St Thomas: A Review Article' *Journal of Religion* 25 (1945) 29.

88 See also *Creative Synthesis and Philosophic Method* (La Salle, Ill., 1970) 277.

89 Cf. Gunton, op. cit., 34, 44; Hartshorne, *Man's Vision of God* 109, 110.

90 Gunton, op. cit., 45ff; Ogden, 'Christian Theology and Neoclassical Theism' *Journal of Religion* 60 (1980), 205-209.

91 Hartshorne, *Creative Synthesis and Philosophic Method* 277.

92 The title essay 'The Reality of God', op. cit., could be read as a sustained attempt to conceive of God as personal; see especially 57ff.

93 See his essay 'What does it mean to affirm "Jesus Christ is Lord"?' op. cit., 188-205, especially 203-204.

94 See especially 'What sense does it make to say, "God acts in history"?' op. cit., 178.

95 P.R. Baelz, *Prayer and Providence* (London, 1968).

96 My addition. Cf. Baelz, ibid., 81.

97 ibid., 82.

98 ibid., 51ff., 81.

99 ibid., 121.

100 ibid., 122f.

101 ibid., 125. These limits of possibility are akin to Hartshorne's abstract possibilities.

102 ibid., 126.

103 ibid., 127.

104 ibid., 128-132.

105 ibid., 132.

106 ibid., 134.

107 ibid. See D.Z. Phillips, *The Concept of Prayer* (London, 1965).

108 ibid., p. 136. See D.M. Baillie, *Faith in God and its Christian Consummation* (Edinburgh, 1927).

109 *Prayer and Providence* 137.

110 Baelz, ibid., 125.

111 Cf. C.S. Lewis, *Prayer: Letters to Malcolm* (London, 1966) 59.

112 *Prayer and Providence* 141.

113 D.D. Williams, *The Spirit and the Forms of Love* (Welwyn, 1968).

114 op. cit., 116.

115 ibid., 119.

116 ibid., 128.

117 W.H. Vanstone, *Love's Endeavour, Love's Expense* (London, 1977).

118 ibid., 46.

119 ibid., 45.

120 N. Pittenger, 'Trinity and Process: Some Comments in Reply' in *Theological Studies* 32 (1971) 296.

121 Cf. Hebblethwaite, 'Some reflections on predestination, providence and divine foreknowledge', *Rel. Stud.* 15 (1979) 448.

122 P.L. Berger, *A Rumour of Angels* ch. 3. (See above, p. 7).

123 ibid., 73-74.

124 See for instance J.A.T. Robinson, *In the End God* (London, 1950).

125 See *Tragedy and Christian Eschatology*, lecture delivered at the Christian Theological Seminary, 1962.

126 *Love's Endeavour, Love's Expense* 62, 63.

127 ibid., 65.

128 ibid.

129 ibid.

130 See *The Spirit and the Forms of Love* ch. 6. (Williams acknowledges a debt to Heidegger and Whitehead in this respect.)

131 Cf. I.M. Crombie 'The possibility of theological statements' in B. Mitchell (ed), *Faith and Logic* (London, 1957) 58.

132 See below, pp. 114ff., 132.

133 John Hick and Michael Goulder, *Why Believe in God?*, 73-79.

134 Goulder, ibid., 87-89.

135 David Brown. *The Divine Trinity* (London, 1985) 21. He develops a careful case for the 'interventionist' God of theism, with special reference to the experience of prayer and the *personal* nature of divine activity.

4 Another Attempt: a Structure for Divine Action *(pp. 95 - 121)*

1 *Pace* F.B. Dilley, who wants to present a stark choice between a God who acts by miracle or a God who acts in a uniform way through natural and historical causes. This seems to me a false alternative, see 'Does the "God Who Acts" Really Act?', *The Anglican Theological Review* 47 (1965), 66-80. Reprinted in O.C. Thomas (ed), *God's Activity in the World*, (Chico, 1983) 45-60.

2 R.H. King, *The Meaning of God* 42-48. See also A.R. Peacocke, *Creation and the World of Science*, especially page 133; he likewise affirms the suitability of the model of agency to express God's transcendence (and immanence)—albeit with some qualifications; see pages 137ff., 208ff. See also W.J. Abraham, *Divine Action and History* (unpublished doctoral thesis, submitted to the University of Oxford, 1977) chapter 1; Abraham affirms the centrality of the model as integral to theism, crucial in devotion, doctrine and revelation. Barth is also insistent on talking of God as agent, *Church Dogmatics* 2/1 257ff. Cf. also I.G. Barbour, *Myths, Models and Paradigms* 158-161; Barbour is quite sympathetic with the model of agency, but points to the problem of identification: how can we identify God when he has no body? This is further discussed below, 100f., cf. also Christoph Schwöbel, 'Divine Agency and Providence', paper presented to the Conference of the Society for the Study of Theology, 1985.

3 T.F. Tracy, *God, Action and Embodiment* (Grand Rapids, 1984). See also a recent essay by F.G. Kirkpatrick, 'Understanding an Act of God' in O.C. Thomas (ed) *God's Activity in the World* 163-180.

4 King, op. cit., 47, 48.

5 See especially I.T. Ramsey *Religious Language. An Empirical Placing of Theological Phrases* (London, 1957) 38f.

6 Cf. J.L. Austin, 'A Plea for Excuses' in his *Philosophical Papers* (Oxford 1979³) 178ff.

7 This 'introvert' tradition of the will may be traced in Descartes, Hume, William James. Cf. A. Kenny, *Will, Freedom and Power* (Oxford, 1975), chapter 2. The will in this tradition is 'a phenomenon, an episode in one's mental history, an item of introspective consciousness. Volition is a mental event whose occurrence makes the difference between voluntary and involuntary actions. For an overt action to be voluntary is for it to be preceded and caused by a characteristic internal impression or conscious thought', ibid., 13.

8 This may be traced in Wittgenstein, Austin, and especially Gilbert Ryle. See Kenny, op. cit., 12-14.

9 See especially G. Ryle, *The Concept of Mind* (London, 1949), chapter 3, especially 68.

10 Ryle has been criticized for doing just this, in spite of protestations to the contrary (op. cit., 25f.). Cogent criticism of Ryle's treatment of the mind in general and of his reductionist tendencies, is offered by C.A. Campbell, 'Ryle on the Intellect', chapter 13 of his *In Defence of Free Will* (London, 1967). Also H.D. Lewis, *The Elusive Mind* (London, 1969), especially chapters 1-3, 15-96.

11 The distinction between action and event has been well charted by such as Richard Taylor, *Action and Purpose* (London, 1966); also John Macmurray, *The Self as Agent* (London, 1957), especially 152ff.

12 Kenny, op. cit., 26. He anticipates criticism, and guards against it, by claiming that a volition does not have to be a voluntary state (which would again beg the question of infinite regress) for the action proceeding from it to be voluntary.

13 Cf. Abraham, op. cit., chapter 2, especially 33ff., where he argues that speech acts are necessary to interpret the divine intention which may not be entirely self-evident in the action.

14 See especially P.F. Strawson's discussion in *Individuals: an Essay in Descriptive Metaphysics* (London, 1959) and Tracy's reply, op. cit., chapter 4.

15 G.M. Jantzen, *God's World, God's Body* (London, 1984). See also W.D. Hudson, 'Some Philosophical Problems Concerning Providential Agency', paper presented at the Conference of the Society for the Study of Theology, 1985.

16 ibid., chapter 6.

17 Charles Hartshorne tries to deal with this with his distinction between 'sub-individuals' and 'super-individuals', *Man's Vision of God* chapter 5. Tracy is not convinced: see his discussion, op. cit., 115.

18 ibid. See also King, op. cit., 86-87.

19 Jantzen, op. cit., 88f., 107.

20 Miss Jantzen is happy to pay this price, ibid., chapter 7, especially 143ff., on the familiar grounds that God must always be a creative God. My equally familiar response is to appeal to the doctrine of the Trinity to account for the eternal and necessary element of creativity.

21 King, op. cit., 87ff.

22 See for example K. Nielsen, *Contemporary Critiques of Religion* (London 1971), chapter 6.

23 I.M. Crombie, 'The Possibility of Theological Statements', chapter 2 of B. Mitchell (ed), *Faith and Logic* (London, 1957).

24 ibid., 58.

25 Tracy op. cit., 59f.

26 P.J. Donovan, *A Philosophical Analysis of the Doctrine of Providence, with reference to Theology of H.H. Farmer* (unpublished Doctoral thesis, University of Oxford, 1971) 211-212.

27 See Kirkpatrick, art. cit. 171-174.

28 G.E.M. Anscombe, *Intention* (Oxford, 1957).

29 I.G. Barbour, *Myths, Models and Paradigms* (London, 1974), 158.

30 See Goldman's view that neurological and mental events can be conceived as simultaneous, not causally related, *A Theory of Human Action* (Englewood Cliffs, N.J., 1970) 161-5, which could be developed in a non-determinist way. See also A. Farrer, *The Freedom of the Will* (London, 1958), chapters 2 and 5.

31 See H.L.A. Hart, 'The Ascription of Responsibility and Rights' in A. Flew (ed), *Logic and Language*, (Oxford, 1955).

32 King, op. cit., 62. Cf. H.H. Farmer, *The World and God* (London, 1935), 164: 'It is of the very essence of such awareness [of ourselves as "will"], that we are conscious of . . . shaping the course of events in the world'.

33 King, op. cit., 61.

34 Cf. Donovan, op. cit., 212ff. and A.C. Danto, 'Basic Actions' in A.R. White (ed), *The Philosophy of Action* (Oxford, 1968) 43-58.

35 Cf. E.L. Mascall, *Christian Theology and Natural Science* (London, 1956), especially chapter 5:3.

36 W.G. Pollard, *Chance and Providence* (New York, 1958). A recent critique of Pollard is provided by D.J. Bartholomew, *God of Chance* (London, 1984) especially pages 125ff.

37 See A.R. Peacocke, *Creation and the World of Science* 125.

38 Cf. Kirkpatrick, art. cit., 164ff. Also Bartholomew, *God of Chance*, 142f.

39 See I.G. Barbour, *Issues in Science and Religion* 419-420. See also Chapter 3 above, pages 57-59.

40 G.D. Kaufman, 'On the Meaning of "Act of God" ' *Harvard Theological Review*, 61 (1968) 175-201 reprinted in O.C. Thomas *God's Activity in the World*, 139-40.

41 Barbour, *Myths, Models and Paradigms* 158.

42 It has affinities with the overall picture of the Thomist and neo-Thomist scheme of primary and secondary causes (though not depending in the same way on a particular set of metaphysical categories and assumptions). A brief but useful summary is offered by I.G. Barbour, *Issues in Science and Religion* 425ff.

   A more modern treatment of this kind of relationship between God and the world, depending more on a panpsychist metaphysic, is H.H. Farmer's work, *The World and God*. Cf. also Karl Barth, *Church Dogmatics*, 33, 133; A.F. Peacocke, *Creation and the World of Science*, 33-35, 203ff. Peacocke makes the same general point that the model of agency allows God to 'express his intentions within a law-like physical network'—though he does not press the point as to how this many be conceived as relating to specific events. Cf. also Kirkpatrick, art. cit. 173. Using the analogy of human action he insists that just as we initiate specific events without violating causal laws, so we can conceive God doing the same: 'The interference of the agent with the causal region of nature is not, therefore, a violation of causal law but its employment by a dimension of reality which "goes beyond" causal law'. See also G.H. Von Wright, *Causality and Determination* (New York, 1974).

43 A. Farrer, *Faith and Speculation* (London, 1967); *A Science of God?* (London, 1966).

44 B.L. Hebblethwaite, 'Providence and Divine Action' *Religious Studies* (1978) 223-236. Hebblethwaite's charge occurs on 223. But see also Wiles' response, 'Farrer's Concept of Double Agency', *Theology* 84 (1981) 243-249.

45 Farrer, *Faith and Speculation* 62.

46 Hebblethwaite, art. cit., 226.

47 ibid.

48 Farrer, *Faith and Speculation*, chapter 4.

49 ibid., chapter 5.

50 ibid., 62.

51 ibid., 66.

52 'Farrer's Concept of Double Agency' 245.

53 See D. Galilee and B. Hebblethwaite, 'Farrer's Concept of Double Agency: A Reply' *Theology* 85 (1982) 7-10.

54 Kaufman, art. cit.

55 ibid., 54-55.

56 ibid., 55.

57 For example, *A Science of God?* 76-80.

58 *Faith and Speculation* 104.

59 ibid., 159.

60 King, op. cit., 87ff.

61 See above, pp. 100f.

62 King, op. cit., 90.

63   ibid., 90ff.

64   ibid., 94-96.

65   Cf. T.F. Tracy, op. cit., 125ff.: as long as God's aseity is taken dynamically, not statically, then the starker problems of the classical doctrine can be eased.

66   Farrer, *A Science of God?* 76ff.; also, 'The Prior Actuality of God' in *Reflective Faith* (London, 1972) 179.

67   D.L. Sayers, *The Mind of the Maker* (London, 1941).

68   Sayers, op. cit.; see especially chapter 9. The point is denied by Jean-Paul Sartre, *What is Literature?* (ET, London, 1950) 29. He rejects the notion that created characters can, in any strict sense, have a 'life of their own': 'Thus the writer meets everywhere only his knowledge, his will, his plans, in short, himself. He touches only his own subjectivity'.
Other literary critics would tend to disgree and side with Miss Sayers. A brief but useful discussion of the subject, from the literary critic's point of view, can be found in G. Steiner, *Tolstoy or Dostoevsky* (Harmondsworth 1967) 165ff.

69   Hebblethwaite, 'Providence and Divine Action' 230-231.

70   *A Science of God?* 78.

71   Barth, *Church Dogmatics*, 3/3, 133, 167.

72   Cf. Barth, *Church Dogmatics*, 3/3, 152-154: 'God accompanies the activity the creature as its Creator and Lord. And this means that even the effects of this activity . . . are still subject to His disposing and control . . . God outruns the creature, and His activity follows the activity of the creature, in the sense that He acts as the Lord even of the effects of creaturely activity . . . *As an event . . . the effect of the creature is in the hands of God . . . It is wholly subordinated to the context of His wider purpose.*' (emphasis mine).

73   Cf. Barth's treatment of Judas in *Church Dogmatics*, 2/2, 458-506.

74   See *Faith and Speculation* 62; *A Science of God?* 78. For this conception of divine 'arranging', depending on God's intimate relationship with every level of activity, yet invisible to strictly empirical tools of analysis, compare H.H. Farmer, *The World and God* 178:
If we must form a picture, it might be along (these) lines . . . that God so uses His all-inclusive rapport with the ultimate entities which constitute the inner, creative, present reality of the natural order, that their various routine activities are not overriden, but used by redirecting them in relation to one another. Just as man brings about effects in nature which would not otherwise happen by redirecting its routines in relation with one another, so does God, except that God acts from the inside, so to say, by inner rapport and not by external manipulation in the gross. Such rearranging and bringing together of different series of routine events would in the nature of the case not be observable by science.

75   Cf. 'Transposition' in C.S. Lewis, *Screwtape Proposes a Toast* (London, 1965)

5 *Taking it to Extremes* (pages 122 - 142)

1   Cf. P.T. Geach, *God and the Soul* (London, 1969) 71-72.

2   Cf. A. Farrer, *Faith and Speculation* especially 82, 154.

3   Kaufman, *art. cit.*, 55.

4   ibid.

5   Donovan, op. cit., 239ff.

6   ibid., 243, 242.

7   ibid., 244.

8   ibid.

9   Knowledge of the event is of course a prior and necessary (though not sufficient) condition of action-with-intention: 'Intentional actions appear to be a sub-class of voluntary, conscious actions', (Kenny, *Will, Freedom and Power* 53). Kenny also cites Aquinas (19) which I quote from the Gilby translation: Perfect knowledge of an end 'consists not only in apprehending a thing which in fact is an end, but also in recognizing its character as an end', (*Summa Theologiae* Ia, IIae 6.2).

10 Donovan, op. cit., 240, 246-248.

11 A task, nevertheless which was popularly undertaken in the nineteenth century; cf. William Paley's attempt in his classic exposition of the argument from design: *Evidences of Christianity* (1794); see also *Natural Theology of Evidences of the Existence and Attributes of Deity collected from the Appearances of Nature* (1802).

12 Kaufman, art. cit., 156-157.

13 Donovan, op. cit., 243.

14 Cf. P.T. Geach, *Providence and Evil*, (Cambridge, 1977) p.32.

15 ibid 34, 35: 'the very notion of means and ends is difficult to apply to God. The ordinary notion of means and ends involves that the agent choose the means because he wills the end. But God cannot be said to will or choose anything on account of some cause'. He refers us to Aquinas: *'Non propter hoc vult hoc'*, *Summa Theologiae* 1 19 a.5. The reason, of course, within Aquinas' whole metaphysical and theological framework, is that God must be conceived as first cause of everything.

16 Kenny distinguishes carefully between them, *Will, Freedom and Power* 56ff.

17 P.T. Geach, *Providence and Evil*, 34.

18 There must be a multiplicity of means available, one of which is chosen having a certain side-effect. If that is the reason for choosing this means rather than another then it is 'intended', Kenny, op. cit., 58.

19 Kenny, op. cit., 57.

20 ibid., 54. Cf. the 'Accordion' effect, discussed first by J. Feinberg, 'Action and Responsibility' in M. Black (ed) *Philosophy in America* (New York, 1965); referred to in 'Agency' by D. Davidson in R. Binkley *et al* (eds), *Agent, Action and Reason* (Oxford, 1971), especially 16-18.

21 Kenny, op. cit., 59ff.

22 *Pace* Farrer, *Love Almighty and Ills Unlimited*, (London 1962). He cannot bring himself to abandon the category of accident, even from the divine perspective: 'Accidentality is inseparable from the character of our universe', op. cit., 76. An accident, says Farrer, may be 'foreseen, provided against, discounted, or profited by', but 'it cannot be intended or arranged', 164. If it could, as argued above, it would of course cease to be an accident.

23 C.S. Lewis, *Prayer: Letters to Malcolm* 57-59. cf. S. Hampshire, *Public and Private Morality* (Cambridge, 1978) 52. On justifying what has to be done in public, political morality, he defines responsibility as: 'first, accountability to one's followers, second, policies that are to be justified principally by their eventual consequences, and, thirdly, a withholding of some of the scruples that in private life would prohibit one from using people as a means to an end, and also from using force and deceit'. Whatever the validity of this sort of position for the human business of managing affairs, it is precisely what one *cannot* attribute to the divine creativity.

24 Farrer, *Love Almighty and Ills Unlimited* 76, 164.

25 Cf. P.T. Geach, 'Good and Evil' in P. Foot (ed), *Theories of Ethics* (Oxford 1967), chapter 4: 'we cannot sensibly speak of a good or bad event, a good or bad thing to happen. "Event", like "thing", is too empty a word to convey

either a criterion of identity or a standard of goodness; to ask "Is this a good or bad thing (to happen)?" is as useless as to ask "Is this the same thing that I saw yesterday?" ', 71-72.

26 See J. Hick, *Evil and the God of Love* (London, 1966) 186.

27 ibid., 395.

28 G.F. Woods, *Theological Explanation* (London, 1958), especially chapter 8.

29 Cf. Farrer, *A Science of God?* 33.

30 K. Ward, *The Concept of God* (Oxford, 1974), chapter 8, especially sections 5 and 6. See also some revised discussion in *Rational Theology and the Creativity of God* (Oxford, 1982), chapter 2, and R. Swinburne's *The Existence of God* (Oxford, 1979). Note that our notion of 'limited explanation' is not to be confused with Swinburne's distinction between complete explanation (ultimate brute fact) and absolute explanation (logically necessary or self-explanatory), which refers primarily to the way in which we conceive the being of God, not to the status of events in the world. Naturally the former will bear implication for the latter: for instance, it may be that we cannot conceive any sense of contingency in the world as arising from a wholly and logically necessary God; there must be some contingency in God as well as necessity. Ward sets out to show that this is indeed the case. We will touch on it in relation to time and eternity, though must plead that the business of conceiving the being of God 'in himself' is not the primary concern here.

31 *Concept of God* 149.

32 Ibid. 149-150. Cf. also Bartholomew, *God of Chance:* Bartholomew argues for a God of chance; that is, a God who has created a world in which there is real randomness at most levels, and who is able to use such a structure for furthering certain good ends: ' . . . chance is seen as grist for the providential mill rather than as an obstacle to providential action' (143). In general terms this could adequately fit our understanding: 'chance' events would have the same status as events of the human will which may always be integrated into a pattern in which they serve divine intentions. However, Bartholomew allows this only for the large-scale aggregate of such events: 'We can agree that everything which happens is ultimately God's responsibility while denying that every single happening has a meaning in terms of God's intentions. His purpose is rather to be seen in aggregate effects of such happenings' (118). And he takes issue with Geach, for whom 'each individual event is divinely directed to some identifiable end, rather than merely playing a contributory role in producing the aggregate effects of a large number of such happenings' (133). Like many others, Bartholomew adopts his position partly through fear of an unacceptable determinism if divine ends are found in every events. But he is driven to this only because he rejects the possibilities afforded him by a God outside time, for whom, every event ('chance' or otherwise) is foreknown and 'contextualized' in the way that we will have envisaged. (God's transcendental relationship to time is briefly, but suspiciously, considered on 148. Cf. also 153).

33 E.g. Peter Baelz, 76ff.

34 In fact Ward is familiar with Wood's notion of explanation, above, but seems ambivalent in his use of it. In some respects he finds it too weak, in other respects he seems to have found it helpful. Compare *The Concept of God*, 142-143, 150-151.

35 See S. Ogden, *On Revelation.*

36 A category mistake noted, amongst others, by R.M. Hare; see his *Freedom and Reason* (Oxford 1963) 37-40.

37 See 96f., above.

38 H.R. Niebuhr, *The Meaning of Revelation* (New york, 1941) 110, 129f.

39 See Ogden, *Christ Without Myth* chapter 3 and *the Reality of God* 173. Cf. also Langdon Gilkey's comment in 'Process Theology' in *Vox Theologica* 43 (1973) 5ff.: 'To be sure, Process Theology better than most understands how God can relate individually and so novelly to each particular occasion. But nonetheless, in understanding these unique or particular actions metaphysically it understands them always under an identical category, necessarily applicable to all such events alike and thus special to none. *God's redeeming activity is thus understood categorically as a part of His general creative activity*' (emphasis mine).

6 Time and Eternity *(pages 143 - 160)*

1 P.S. Laplace, *A Philosophical Essay on Probabilities* (ET, New York, 1961), especially p. 4. The claim is: 'Given for one instant an intelligence which could comprehend all the forces by which nature is animated. . . for it nothing would be uncertain, and the future, as the past, would be present to its eyes'.

2 Cf. D.M. MacKay, *Science, Chance and Providence* (Oxford, 1978), chapter 2. He points out that the notion of 'chance' in Heisenberg's uncertainty principle, which seems to rule out the possibility of sure prediction, may not in fact exclude the 'chance' events being determined by some other causation (e.g. direct divine causation), and so after all being predictable in principle—for God. For more detailed discussion see Bartholomew, *God of Chance*, especially chapters 2 and 4.

3 Cf. B.L. Hebblethwaite, 'Some reflections on predestination, providence and divine foreknowledge' *Religious Studies* 15 (1979) 433-448.

4 Geach offers the analogy of a Grand Master in a chess game who can foresee every possibility and act accordingly, but cannot tell which possibility will be actualized, see *Providence and Evil* 58. Cf. also Hebblethwaite, art. cit.

5 Process theologians tend to be ambivalent on this point. See for example, D.D. Williams, *Tragedy and Christian Eschatology*. See further 174-176.

6 Cf. D. Basinger, 'Human freedom and divine providence: some new thoughts on an old problem', *Religious Studies* (1979) 15 491-510. He points out precisely that the chess-player analogy, and the view of God's relationship with the world it represents, secures only very general ends for God—and this is incompatible with 'a number of popular Christian tenets'.

7 See W.C. Kneale, 'Time and Eternity in Theology' *Proceedings of the Aristotelian Society* (1960-1961) 87-108.

8 *Philosophiae Consolationis* V.6; quoted by Kneale, art. cit., 95.

9 *Summa Theologiae* Ia 10.1, quoted by Kneale, art. cit., 96.

10 *Institutes* III. 21. 5.

11 *The Christian Faith* para. 52-53.

12 A distinction insisted on by W.L. Craig in terms of 'before and after creation' in 'God, Time and Eternity' *Religious Studies* 14 (1978) 497-503.

13 See Hebblethwaite, 'Reflections on Predestination . . .' 434-435.

14 P.T. Geach, 'Some Problems about Time' in *Logic Matters* (Oxford, 1972) 305; also *God and the Soul*, chapter 7 'Praying for things to happen', 93.

15 *God and the Soul*, 92.

16 N. Pike, *God and Timelessness* (London, 1970) 101ff.

17 ibid., 110ff.

18 R. Coburn, 'Professor Malcolm on God' *Australasian Journal of Philosophy* (1963) cited by Pike, op. cit., 88ff.

19 Pike, op. cit., 53ff.

20 ibid., 121ff.

21 Quoting W.C. Kneale, art. cit., 99.

22 This is Craig's advice, art. cit. 502.

23 Craig traces the various options available, depending on whether a Newtonian or relational view of time is taken, but concludes that either way some sort of sense could be made of it: 'On a Newtonian view of time, God would exist changelessly in an undifferentiated time prior to creation. On a relational view of time, God would exist changelessly and timelessly prior to . . . creation', art. cit., 501-502.

24 J.M.E. McTaggart: see *The Nature of Existence*, (Cambridge 1927) vol. II, book V, chapter 33.

25 For more detailed discussion on the relation and status of these two series see R.M. Gale (ed), *The Philosophy of Time* (London 1968), especially sections 1 and 2. Though Gale's own comments favour the priority of the past-present-future series, A. Grünbaum's article, 'The Status of Temporal Becoming' is especially cogent in argument for the priority of the before-after series.

26 A.C. Ewing, *Value and Reality* (London, 1973), 279ff.

27 ibid., 281.

28 N.B. The notion of an 'extended specious present' is hardly new: interpreters of Boethius have found it an appropriate expression to describe *his* view: e.g. I.T. Ramsey, 'The Concept of the Eternal' in *The Christian Hope*, S.P.C.K. Theological Collections Number 13 (London, 1970) 41.

29 Ewing, op. cit., 283.

30 Jantzen, *God's World, God's Body*, chapter 4, especially 60ff.

31 Ewing, op. cit. 284.

32 D.L. Sayers, *Unpopular Opinions*, (London 1946) 53-56.

33 Another analogy is suggested by Keith Ward to support the view that it is possible to talk of God as timeless and have temporal things originate from him: 'Rather as my bodily actions can be caused by my anger, which is not in any spatial relation to my body, so temporal events may be caused by a reality, God, which is not in any temporal relation to them', *The Concept of God* 154.

34 R.L. Sturch, 'The Problem of Divine Eternity' *Religious Studies* 10 (1974) 487-493.

35 He justifies this with the help of an elaborate analogy, Pike op. cit., 89ff.

36 *Philosophiae Consolationis* V.6 lines 75-80, quoted by Pike, op. cit., 75.

37 See Pike, op. cit., 63ff. Human foreknowledge does not 'impose necessity', but divine foreknowing does, for God's foreknowledge is true not as an additional contingent fact, but as a necessary fact deriving from his essential omniscience. (Though see n. 39 below).

38 *Value and Reality* 285.

39 However, some discussion in 'Religious Studies' suggests that even foreknowledge could be conceived in such a way as not to infringe on human freedom. Thus R.W.K. Patterson observes that it is an 'erroneous supposition that if God has foreknowledge of what someone will do, this must be because he in some sense *causes* that person to do it', 'Evil, Omniscience and Omnipotence' *Religious Studies* 15 (1979) 1-23 quoting from 6. He justifies this by distinguishing between inferential and intuitive certainty, a point also made by S.T. Davis in the same cause, 'Divine Omniscience and Human Freedom' *Religious Studies* 15, (1979) 303-316.

D.M. Ahern more cautiously suggests that no solution to the problem is possible - in principle, 'Foreknowledge: Nelson Pike and Newcomb's Problem' *Religious Studies* (1979) 15 475-490.

40   The suggestion is Pike's *God and Timelessness* 124. But he immediately goes on to make plain that since he cannot conceive of a timeless God *acting*, the sense in which he can allow that God knows (as a mental act) is seriously qualified.

41   Sturch, 'The Problem of Divine Eternity' 490-491.

42   *God and Timelessness* 12ff. especially 14.

43   ibid., 12.

44   See especially the 'Epilogue' to C Hartshorne and W L Reese (eds) *Philosophers Speak of God* entitled 'The Logic of Panentheism'; cf. C. Gunton, *Becoming and Being* chapter 1: 'The Rejection of Classical Theism'.

45   See, for example, O. Cullmann, *Christ and Time* (ET, London, 1951), especially Part 1 chapter 3 'Time and Eternity'; cf. J. Barr's critique of Cullmann in *Biblical Words for Time* (London, 1969²), especially chapter 3. Barth also departs from strict classical views—though Cullmann (63) takes him to task nonetheless for still being unduly influenced by 'that Platonic conception of timeless eternity', see *Church Dogmatics* 2/1; Chapter 6 § 31.3. 31.3.

46   I.T. Ramsey, 'The Concept of the Eternal', *loc. cit.*

47   ibid., 43-44.

48   ibid., 47.

49   ibid., 45.

50   A. Heron, 'The Time of God', a paper presented at the conference of the Society for the Study of Theology, 1979.

51   *Timaeus* 37. Though it is interesting to note that Pike, taking a different passage from the *Timaeus*, traces Boethius' doctrine of sheer timelessness from it. Pike, op. cit., 15. See Heron, art. cit., 16.

52   There are further theological grounds for this in the incarnation; the *aeon* cannot be parallel to but must intersect the *chronos*, Heron, art. cit., 19-20.

53   ibid., 18.

54   ibid., 19.

55   See for example C. Hartshorne, *The Divine Relativity* 69; cf. also J.R. Lucas, *A Treatise on Time and Space* (London, 1973) 306-307.

56   See further below, 157-159.

57   Cf. Lucas, op. cit., 1:8, who argues for directionality as a defining characteristic of time.

58   See Ogden's formulation of the problem in *The Reality of God* especially 17f.

59   ibid.

60   This occurs in the concrete, consequent, pole of God's being-in-process. He is actually, in time, being constituted by the world, responding to it, and so becoming. While there is also a changeless, timeless abstract pole of God, it has already been suggested that the logical and ontological priority belongs to the former (see above, 75, 78 (note 89)).

61   Cf. D.D. Williams, *The Spirit and the Forms of Love* 138: 'Much conventional religiousness . . . makes the goal the peace of completion rather than the peace of openness to new experience'. 'Love does not put everything at rest; it puts everything in motion . . . Love does not resolve every conflict; it accepts conflict as the arena in which the work of love is to be done.' The demand for novelty is also strong in Jantzen's chapter on time, *God's World, God's Body* 53.

62   Ward, *Rational Theology and the Creativity of God* 163-164.

63 Cf. Lucas, *A Treatise on Time and Space* 38-40.
64 See 52 above.
65 Lucas, op. cit., 40.
66 cf. John Macquarrie, *In Search of Deity: An Essay in Dialectical Theism* (London, 1984), especially chapter 13. His conclusion about time and eternity (182) is particularly apposite: 'There is a sense in which everything is already fulfilled in him [God], and it is the vision of all things subjected to God, *sub specie aeternitatis*, that has acted as a powerful source of hope and confidence among human beings . . . Yet, if the struggle is real, it must be real for God, too'.

7 Theodicy *(pages 161 - 176)*

1 As in his *The Concept of Prayer*, see 83 above and the ensuing discussion.
2 See Chapter 2 above, especially 40ff.
3 Hick, *Evil and the God of Love.* Also summarized in his contribution to S.T. Davis (ed) *Encountering Evil* (Edinburgh, 1981).
4 *Evil and the God of Love* chapter 14:6. This is obviously a controversial point: see further below, 167.
5 ibid., 359-360; also chapter 15 'Pain'.
6 ibid., 361-362.
7 ibid., 363.
8 See, for instance, Frederick Sontag's critique in *Encountering Evil*, op. cit., 55f.
9 *Evil and the God of Love* 370.
10 *Value and Reality*, chapter 9.
11 ibid. 217-219.
12 J.K. Roth, 'A Theodicy of Protest' in *Encountering Evil, op. cit.,* 7-22.
13 Cf. T. Penelhum, *Religion and Rationality* (New York, 1971) 240. Cf. also H.J. McCloskey, 'God and Evil' in N. Pike (ed) *God and Evil* (New Jersey, 1964) 61-84.
14 Some justification could be found, for example, for inflicting reformative punishment on a child. Even in this case, however, limited human knowledge make the undertaking a risky one and means that strict limits should be set on the kind of suffering inflicted. The morality of the action is also determined according to the appropriateness of the relationship between the sufferer and the one who inflicts suffering. Thus a father may indeed have a proper obligation to discipline a child for whom he is responsible, without thereby being licensed to discipline all and sundry. God's responsibility, like his knowledge, is obviously without limits.
15 Cf. C. Dore, 'Do Theodicists Mean What They Say?' *Philosophy* 49 (1974) 357-374: Dore makes a similar point, but contrasts God's *knowledge* that good ends are served through suffering to our *faith* that this is the case. Our contrast is between God's perfect and unlimited knowledge of how this may occur and our imperfect and limited knowledge.
16 Ewing op. cit., 221.
17 P.R. Baelz, *Prayer and Providence* 125.
18 Ewing op. cit., 233-234.
19 Cf. 'On Undoing the Past', a paper delivered at the Conference for the Society for the Study of Theology, 1979, by Elizabeth Templeton. She claims that some kind of 'unmaking' or remaking of the past is necessary to theodicy (and relates the notion to Irenaeus' doctrine of recapitulation).

20 See for instance S.T. Davis' defence of his essay 'Free will and evil' in *Encountering Evil* op. cit. 95.

21 Hick, *Encountering Evil*, 66.

22 Cf. Hick, *Evil and the God of Love*, 375-377. Also *Encountering Evil* 65.

23 Animal pain is one such gap. It is indeed hard to see any internal rationale for an animal's suffering since the animal does not need any process of soul-making. This is a familiar problem for such theodicies; cf. Hick, *Evil and the God of Love* 346ff. If pressed one would simply have to plead that precisely because animals are not ensouled persons in the same way as humanity, different criteria as to what could be of value for them would have to be employed—and these are criteria we cannot know from within our (personal) perspective. It also requires a sufficiently coherent conception of the nature of life after death to sustain all that hangs on it - a task I will not begin to attempt here, but leave to others who have laboured long and hard over it: see for instance Hick's own attempt in *Death and Eternal Life* (London, 1976); also Paul Badham, *Christian Beliefs about Life after Death* (London, 1976).

24 Though see further 174ff. below for an alternative view of omnipotence. Cf. also Geach, 'An Irrelevance of Omnipotence' in *Providence and Evil*.

25 Cf. T. Penelhum, 'Divine Goodness and the Problem of Evil' *Religious Studies* 2 (1966) 95-107: 'It is logically inconsistent for a theist to admit the existence of a pointless evil' (107). Cf. also C.A. Campbell, *On Selfhood and Godhood* (London, 1957) 301; J.L. Mackie, 'Evil and Omnipotence' in Pike (ed.) *God and Evil* 47; J.N. Findlay, 'Can God's Existence be Disproved?' A. Flew and A. MacIntyre (eds.) *New Essays in Philosophical Theology* (London, 1955) 51ff.

26 Hick, *Evil and the God of Love* 280.

27 Cf. D.R. Griffin, *God, Power and Evil: A Process theodicy* (Philadelphia 1976) 254: 'Those who do not affirm the reality of genuine evil [Griffin here means pointless evil] do not reject the view that reasoning on the basis of experience would lead one to affirm the probability that genuine evil exists. They only maintain that it is *possible* that justifying reasons for all *prima facie* evils exist'. He quotes M.B. Ahern, *The Problem of Evil* (London, 1971) 50: to know that there is some unjustified evil, 'it would be necessary to have an exhaustive knowledge of possible good and its logical connection, if any, with actual evil. We lack this knowledge'.

28 This has already been implied in a number of places; see especially 69 (on Wiles' position); 81ff (on Baelz's position); 86ff (on Vanstone Williams' position); see also 129ff.

29 *God, Power, and Evil* especially Part 3.

30 ibid. 262ff.

31 ibid. 268f.

32 ibid., 272-274.

33 See above, especially 115ff.

34 Griffin, *God, Power, and Evil* 303-304.

35 ibid. The argument is notable for what it does *not* say about the individual.

36 ibid., appendix 'Theodicy and Hope for a Future Life' 311-313. See also his contribution to *Encountering Evil*, op. cit., 131.

37 F. Dostoyevsky, *The Brothers Karamazov* Book 5, chapter 4.

38 Cf. Griffin, *God, Power, and Evil* 303.

39 Even Griffin notes the possibility; see *Encountering Evil* 132, 135.

40 D.D. Williams, *Tragedy and Christian Eschatology*, loc. cit.

Faith and experience: the remaining riddles (pages 177 - 184)

1 See above, 133-135, 138.
2 Col. 1:15ff.
3 *The Brothers Karamazov*, 287.
4 Cf. King, *The Meaning of God* 138-151.
5 H.B. Deqhani-Tafti, *Design of My World* (Guildford, 1982).
6 Farmer, *The World and God* 100-101.

General Index

Index of Authors